# THE ASSEMBLY OF LISTENERS: JAINS IN SOCIETY

Although the Jains have exerted an influence on Indian society and religion out of proportion to their relatively small numbers, they have received very little attention from scholars until the last few years. *The Assembly of Listeners* is the first book to analyse the sociology of the Jains, and to discuss the notion of the 'community' based on religious affiliation in India. The contributors include sociologists, anthropologists, and scholars of Indian classical religions and languages, each addressing, as a central organising principle, the conception of the Jains as a community. *The Assembly of Listeners* represents an important theoretical addition to existing studies, which have hitherto focussed mainly on caste and class politics as the fundamental units of Indian society, and provides unique ethnographic information on the Jains, derived from recent fieldwork.

# THE ASSEMBLY OF LISTENERS
## JAINS IN SOCIETY

Edited by

MICHAEL CARRITHERS

Reader in Anthropology
University of Durham

CAROLINE HUMPHREY

Department of Social Anthropology
University of Cambridge and
Fellow of King's College Cambridge

*The right of the University of Cambridge to print and sell all manner of books was granted by Henry VIII in 1534. The University has printed and published continuously since 1584.*

CAMBRIDGE UNIVERSITY PRESS

Cambridge
New York Port Chester
Melbourne Sydney

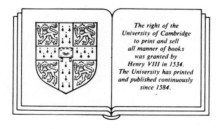

Published by the Press Syndicate of the University of Cambridge
The Pitt Building, Trumpington Street, Cambridge CB2 1RP
40 West 20th Street, New York, NY 10011, USA
10 Stamford Road, Oakleigh, Melbourne 3166, Australia



First published 1991

Printed in Great Britain at the University Press, Cambridge

*British Library cataloguing in publication data*
The assembly of listeners : Jains in society.
1. Jainism
I. Carrithers, Michael II. Humphrey, Caroline *1943–*
294.4

*Library of Congress cataloguing in publication data applied for*

ISBN 0 521 36505 8 hardback

SE

# Contents

# Illustrations

# Contributors

Marcus Banks *Demonstrator, Institute of Social Anthropology, University of Oxford*

Michael Carrithers *Reader in Anthropology, University of Durham*

Christine Cottam Ellis *Visiting Professor in Social Sciences, Quaid-i-Azam University, Islamabad, Pakistan*

Paul Dundas *Lecturer, Department of Sanskrit, University of Edinburgh*

Caroline Humphrey *Lecturer, Department of Social Anthropology, University of Cambridge and Fellow of King's College, Cambridge*

Padmanabh S. Jaini *Professor, University of California, Berkeley*

J. Howard M. Jones *Lecturer, Agricultural Extension and Rural Development Centre, University of Reading*

Mukund Lath *Department of History, University of Rajasthan, Jaipur, India*

K. R. Norman *Professor, Faculty of Oriental Studies, University of Cambridge*

Josephine Reynell *Now working for an organisation concerned with relief for refugees, Oxford*

Vilas Sangave *Director of the Shahu Chhatrapati Research Institute, Shivaji University, Kolhapur, India*

N. K. Singhi *Professor, Department of Sociology, University of Rajasthan, Jaipur, India*

# Acknowledgements

This book consists of the papers given at an international colloquium on 'The Jain Community' held in the Centre for South Asian Studies in Cambridge in June 1985. We believe that this was the first occasion on which Jainism was discussed by an international gathering of anthropologists, Indianists and sociologists, and we are grateful for the inspiration given to our efforts by the work of Vilas Sangave and P. S. Jaini, both of whom have published books concerned with the social aspects of Jainism.

We would like to acknowledge the great help given to the colloquium by Gordon Johnson and Lionel Carter of the Centre for South Asian Studies, Cambridge. Financial backing for the colloquium was generously given by the Nuffield Foundation, and King's College, Cambridge, provided accommodation.

M.C. and C.H.

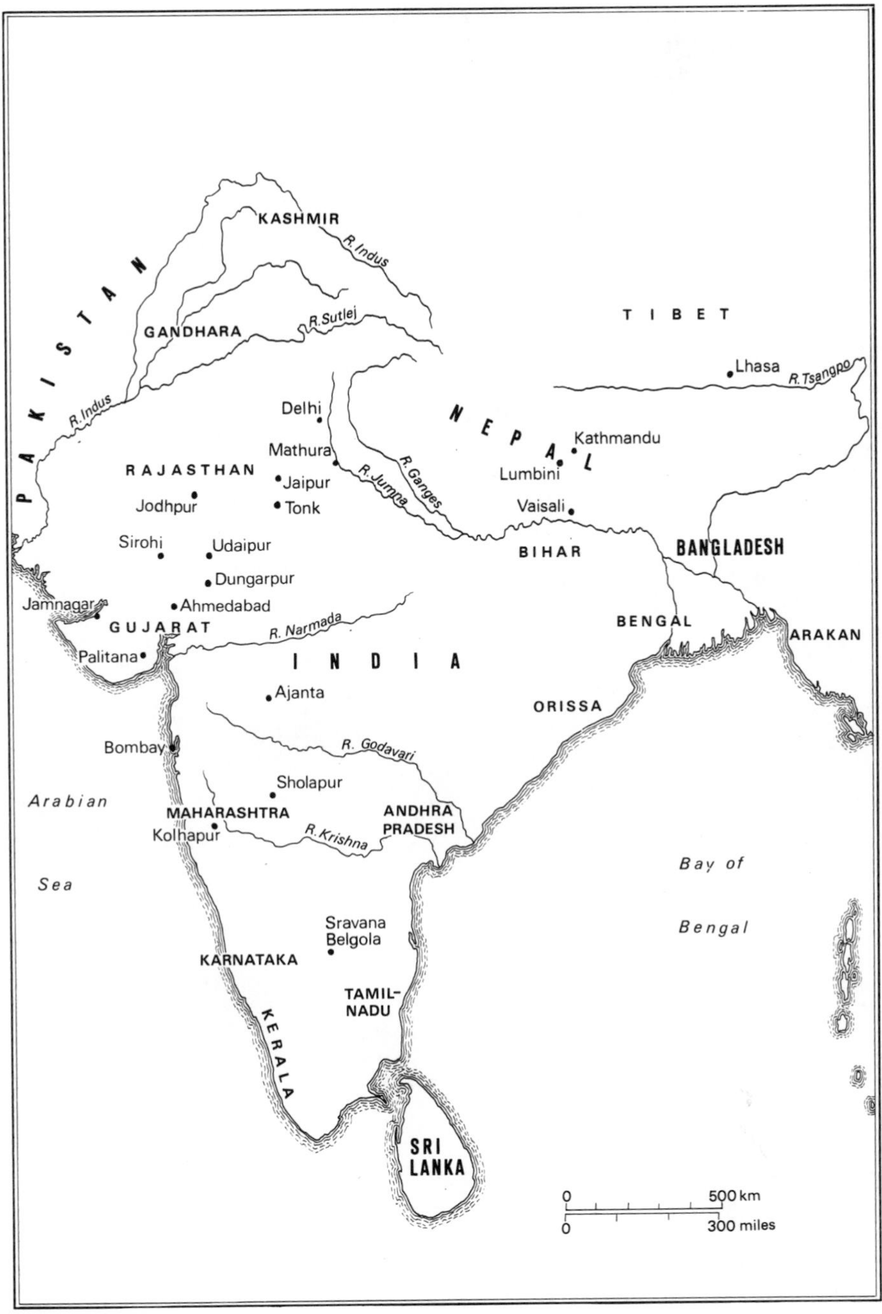
KASHMIR
R. Indus
PAKISTAN
GANDHARA
R. Sutlej
TIBET
Lhasa
R. Tsangpo
R. Indus
Delhi
NEPAL
Kathmandu
Mathura
Lumbini
RAJASTHAN
Jaipur
R. Jumna
R. Ganges
Jodhpur
Tonk
Vaisali
Sirohi
Udaipur
BIHAR
BANGLADESH
Dungarpur
Jamnagar
Ahmedabad
GUJARAT
R. Narmada
BENGAL
ARAKAN
Palitana
INDIA
Ajanta
ORISSA
Bombay
R. Godavari
Sholapur
Arabian
MAHARASHTRA
ANDHRA
PRADESH
Kolhapur
R. Krishna
Bay of
Sea
Bengal
Sravana
Belgola
KARNATAKA
TAMIL-
NADU
KERALA
SRI
LANKA
0
500 km
0
300 miles

South Asia

# Introduction

Michael Carrithers and Caroline Humphrey

The Jains of India are a relatively small section, about one-half of 1 per cent, of the Indian population. Yet they have exerted a significant influence on India's, and the world's, history. In ancient India, Buddhism and Brahmanism took up the characteristic Jain doctrines of *ahiṃsā*, non-violence and vegetarianism, and made them primary principles of Indian culture. In the medieval period, Jain practices and doctrines significantly affected major Hindu sects as well as quasi-Hindu ones, such as the Lingayats. In early modern and modern India, Jains have played a role in commercial and political life out of all proportion to their numbers. And through its indirect formative effect on Gandhi, Jainism has given the principle of non-violence to world culture.

For scholars, as for Jains themselves, the imaginative force of Jainism springs from two fundamental facts. First, Jain doctrine espouses an extraordinarily uncompromising and single-minded pursuit of individual asceticism. Jains are to avoid harm to even the smallest living thing, to purify themselves strenuously through self-mortification, and to conduct lives of strictest moral rectitude. These principles are embodied in those exemplary individuals, the ascetics, *muni*s. Some go naked, while others wear face masks to avoid inhaling and killing the least insect. Many Jain laymen follow the ascetics' example by undertaking rigorous fasts. Both ascetics and laymen occasionally take a vow of self-starvation and die. Whatever complications and complexities are found to accompany Jain life, this individual asceticism remains a fundamental ideal and makes Jainism unusual, even in India.

But if Jainism seems to be in this respect a radically individual religion, it nevertheless possesses a powerful sense of the Jains as a community. This sense is embodied in the image of the *samavasaraṇa*, the 'assembly of all'. The reference is to the occasion on which the founder of Jainism, the Jina, had achieved liberation from suffering through his austerities. He emanated a divine sound and all living beings in the universe, represented as being assembled in concentric circles below him, turn to listen. Hence Jains call themselves *śrāvaka*s, 'listeners'. This scene is represented with tremendous colour and detail in Jain sculpture, painting, and scripture throughout India. Probably no other traditional Indian religion possesses such a vivid symbolic expression of community. Whether this expression is realised in fact, as many Jains and other observers believe it is, remains a difficult question to which much of this volume is devoted. But Jains certainly possess extraordinary poetic imagery in which to conceive community.

The intrinsic interest and importance of the 'assembly of listeners' has not until recently found any collective response from the assembly of scholars. The conference, Jains in the Community, held at Cambridge in June 1985, which gave rise to this volume, was the first occasion on which studies of Jainism had matured sufficiently to support a truly international seminar attended by Indians and Westerners, Jains and non-Jains. Moreover, Indian studies have matured towards an increasing rapprochement between the speakers of very different scholarly languages, Indology and sociology. Indologists and social scientists were represented about equally at the conference, and found they had a great deal to say to each other. We hope that this volume helps us to achieve a profounder collective understanding of Jainism, an understanding equally available to Indologists, sociologists, anthropologists, and historians.

The form of this book derives to a great extent from the experience of the conference. In order to focus the papers and the discussion on common concerns, the editors wrote the position paper, 'Jains as a community', chapter 1 below. This was circulated to the participants before they wrote their papers. The position paper proposed a checklist of the characteristics of community which seemed to us to be important among Jains. This checklist was intended to emphasise the empirical differences between local Jain groups, or between periods of Jain history, or between Jain sects that we felt sure would emerge from the papers. We hoped, on other words, that the rich diversity of the Jain world would be made clear as well as its fundamental unity. The position paper was also intended as a challenge for the participants to produce a better checklist, a better way of conceiving community among Jains in general.

The consequences were partly a pleasant surprise. The wide variation among Jains emerged very clearly from the papers, and even more clearly from the discussion. Moreover the variation was along lines that our limited imaginations could not have conceived beforehand. Jains in one part of, say, Rajasthan were different from Jains in other parts of Rajasthan in quite unexpected ways. Jains in the South differed from Jains in the North quite spectacularly and intriguingly. It therefore seemed appropriate to reflect the diversity, especially that which arose in discussion, in brief prefaces to the papers.

The consequences were also a discomfiting surprise. It turned out that there was variation not only between Jains, but also between participants. There were different opinions about what counted as constituting community, about whether this group or that could be called a community, and about how to approach the question altogether. The participants brought very different experiences and very different viewpoints to the conference. But these amiable disagreements were fruitful as well, for they forced us to see that our checklist had to be amended and expanded. Indeed they forced us to question the very idea of community. We have not rewritten the position paper nor rejected it, but have instead written a conclusion that reflects the richer and more complex picture which emerged through the conference. Therefore, we hope there is some dynamic development through the book.

Perhaps the most gratifying consequence of the conference was that we learned, all of us, how much more there is to learn. The Jain world, let alone the larger Indian world of which it is part, has been quite unimaginably prolific in symbolic forms, in social arrangements, in responses to the vicissitudes of history. We hope that this book, which is primarily documentary and ethnographic rather than theoretical in nature, will provide a basis for future work. This is an invitation to more research, to a yet deeper understanding of this fascinating version of human experience.

Readers should note that there are different styles of rendering Indian-language terms into English among Sanskritists, South Asian scholars and anthropologists. Since we felt it unlikely that our contributors would agree to a unified rendering we have kept the transliterations provided by the authors. The glossary gives the variants for particular terms as they appear in this book.

I

# Jains as a community: a position paper

Michael Carrithers and Caroline Humphrey

Although Jains have exerted an influence on Indian society and religion out of proportion to their relatively small numbers, they have received very little attention from scholars until the last few years. The purpose of this volume is to represent the current state of Jain studies, from both a sociological and an Indological point of view, and to lay the groundwork for further studies. The theme which we have chosen, that of Jains as a community, concerns what we feel to be the central problem in our understanding of Jainism. If this can be solved, then we will be better able not only to comprehend Jains, but also to contribute to the wider sociology of Indian religion and society.

It should first be remarked that the sense in which Jains are a community has not always seemed problematical. V. A. Sangave, in effect the pioneer of sociological studies of Jainism, did not so regard it. In his seminal monograph, *Jaina Community: a Social Survey*, he assumed from the outset that Jains do constitute a community in a significant sense, and he proceeded to lay out for us the anatomy of that community on an all-Indian scale. The value of this assumption has been plain to any scholar who has used Sangave's work.

We feel, however, that the way ahead for the sociology of Jainism is to build on his work by questioning this assumption and, by questioning, to refine it. Such a course seems to be demanded by our own research, which has focussed more narrowly upon local groups of Jains and upon the fine grain of Jain life. We have found that, though it seems convenient to describe Jains as a community, the sense of this usage remains puzzling and demands elucidation. Such an elucidation would test the worthiness of the idea of community to take its place alongside such categories as caste, village, class, and region in the sociology of India.

It should first be remarked that the word 'community' itself, in our and Sangave's usage, is not limited to sociology. It is now used commonly in Indian English, and some equivalent is used in the Indian vernaculars known to us, to refer to Jains and indeed to the collectivity of members of any caste or religion: for example, 'the Maratha community', 'the Sikh community', 'the Harijan community'. Carrithers has noted that such a usage, in English and the vernacular, goes back in Indian journalism and public speech at least to the last decades of the nineteenth century, and it is certainly considerably older. In this respect the usage is equivalent to such English usages as 'the Jewish community' or 'the Italian community of New York', and as such seems to represent simply the recognition in common speech of the social reality of ethnic, religious, or other divisions in a complex society.

Sociologists and other scholars are entitled, however, to ask more of a term than that it be in common usage. It seems to us that there are five criteria inherent in 'community' which would justify its use as an autonomous analytic term for describing Jains. First, the Jains must share, in some significant sense (1) *a common culture, belief, and practice, as well as some common interests.* Moreover, they must be (2) *significantly different from the surrounding society in their culture, beliefs, practices, and interests.* This much is inherent in the ordinary application of the term in public speech, and subsumes what Jain spokesmen would probably insist upon, namely the specifically religious characteristics of Jainism.

But for Jains to fulfil these criteria alone would not justify speaking of them other than as a discriminable category in Indian society. They must also (3) *be conscious of an identity as Jains.* This is relevant because we have observed that there are many individuals and groups in India who are Jains, at least by birth, but who have little or no consciousness of such an ascription differentiating them from the surrounding society. Indeed, the campaigns by Jain leaders in this century to have Jains register as Jains and not Hindus on the census reflect just this.

Moreover, we are in essence asking of the term 'community' that it designate a distinct and real social entity with its own logic and irreducible explanatory power. This means that the community must, as such, be a distinct causal agent. It must be (4) *effective as a collectivity in social, political, and/or economic life.* 'Effective' here has two senses. First, it means that membership in the collectivity is an attribute which not only distinguishes the members from others, but also significantly affects their place in social life. There seem, in contrast, to be discriminable collectivities, such as the worshippers of a particular deity who gather annually at a pilgrimage centre, who fulfil the first three criteria but who are not thus placed differently from the pilgrims to another similar god. Second, the community must be effective in that it urges its beliefs, or presses its interests, upon its own members and upon the circumambient society, whether through informal pressure or through formal organisations. In this latter respect the effectiveness of community admits of degrees. It is not necessary that such efforts always, or even frequently, be fully successful.

Finally, it appears to us that a community, to deserve the term fully, must be (5) *able to reproduce itself.* The sense of this criterion is that whatever we designate as a community must have some enduring existence, and not just be a temporary constellation, such as an interest group, whose existence is contingent upon temporary historical circumstances. Moreover, to specify how Jains reproduce themselves from generation to generation would be to show just how their specific culture and interests are preserved in the face of the so effectively assimilative Hindu society around them.

It seems unlikely that any local Jain group, still less the Jain population of India, always or completely conforms to all of these criteria. Rather, the criteria are meant as a checklist of significant features which may be compared against the material gathered by individual scholars. There might be historical variation within local Jain groups. We have observed, for example, that the Digambar Jain population of southern Maharashtra and northern Karnataka may very well have exhibited few of the relevant features at the end of the nineteenth century, but that by 1982 a combination of long-term efforts by local Jain leaders and political pressures had created a community where none existed before. Or there might be variations between groups. Jain farmers in the Deccan, for example, seem less effective or conscious as a community than the urban Jain businessmen there, whereas in Rajasthan it is the rural Jain traders who seem more effective and conscious than the urban businessmen. We regard these criteria as an invitation to produce a detailed and coherent anatomy of Jainism and local Jain communities.

Indeed the criteria give rise to a number of specific questions. First, are Jains that different from the Hindus around them? Many Jains, for example, observe Hindu festivals. Moreover, the basic form of Jain worship, *pūjā*, uses much of the same materials and idioms as Hindu *pūjā*. In the south the Jain *bhaṭṭārak*s seem to play the role of caste gurus played by similar figures in Hinduism. Hindu terms, forms of thought, and indeed ideas of caste and *varṇa* seem to have permeated much of Jain literature. The attitudes of Jain laymen to Jain *muni*s seem in many respects to be no different from Hindu attitudes to their own renunciants. And, in the south, there is a caste of temple priests which has been designated, perhaps justly, as 'Jain Brahmans', while in the north Brahmans proper sometimes act as priests to local Jain societies. These and many other pieces of evidence might make the sceptic query whether Jains are in fact different from Hindus, whatever the Jain consciousness of the matter might be.

Similarly, many Jains are businessmen; but are they significantly different, or do they organise themselves separately, from other businessmen? Various Weberian hypotheses have been proposed to suggest that they are in fact culturally distinct as businessmen, or that they organise themselves better as an interest group within business. Others have argued that such divisions do not play a significant part in the Indian commercial world, or that there is a 'business community' which transcends caste and religious barriers.

Moreover, it is notable that Jains in nineteenth- and twentieth-century India have been very prolific in founding specifically Jain social and religious associations. It might be asked, however, whether such organisations are really at all effective – as many such Indian organisations are not – in achieving their objectives, and therefore whether such organisations in fact conform to criterion (4) above by making the community an effective collectivity in social, political, or economic life. Some such organisations, for example, seem more an arena for status display, a way of turning financial capital into social capital, than a method of furthering the ends of the community. And in the same vein it might be asked whether the very size and internal variation in some very large Jain populations, as in the southern Deccan or Gujarat, do not prohibit their acting effectively for ends to which they commonly subscribe. Members of the same local group frequently belong to different political parties or factions, and may represent different economic classes and opposed interests.

There are also powerful sectarian divisions among Jains, especially in Gujarat and Rajasthan. In Jaipur, for example, many organisations and *ad hoc* committees designate themselves 'All Jain', while systematically excluding all Digambars from participation. In the same regions different sects compete for membership among the same nominally Jain population. Under these circumstances the effectiveness of community among Jains must be radically modified by these sometimes bitter internal divisions.

Finally, it might be asked whether we do not already have a perfectly good analytic term for describing Jains, namely caste. After all, Jains form castes just as Hindus do, and the rules and attitudes governing those castes lead to much the same consequences as among Hindus. They are endogamous or, at best, hypergamous, and in many places Jain castes have the same sort of consciousness of themselves that we have postulated for Jains as a religious group. Conflict has occurred on the basis of caste within Jain local societies just as it has within Hindu society. Moreover, each Jain caste interacts with the Hindu castes around it, as part of a hierarchy of interaction and attribution.

On all these grounds it might therefore be argued that Jains are not a separate community, and that they can be adequately explained by ideas of Hinduism and caste already available to us. Just such a view is taken in India by Hindus and by some sociologists who are not Jains.

We feel, however, that to take such a view would be radically to miscomprehend Jains and Jainism. Thus, though Hindu terms, ideas, and practices have exerted a tremendous influence upon Jainism, Jains have usually interpreted and applied such offerings from Hinduism according to the peculiar genius of Jain culture. It is true, for example, that some Jains have adopted the sacred thread, but their use of it is quite contrary to its use among Hindus. Jains, like Hindus, take vows and fast, but their way of doing so is unmistakably Jain. The Jain religious calendar, though sharing many dates and festival periods with Hindus, has its own peculiar observances and logic.

Similarly, while it is true that much Jain literature, particularly in the early medieval and medieval periods, has taken over Hindu terms

1 The division of labour in the reproduction of Digambar Jainism in action at the consecration of a new image in the village temple at Halondi, near Kolhapur. A village priest (*upadhye*) in the foreground makes the requisite offerings while Laxmisen *bhaṭṭārak* (at 11 o'clock from the priest) presides with the ritual text. The *munis* are present as charismatic observers – one of them recommended that the temple be expanded with the new image – but have no part in the ceremony.

and ideas, these are set in a doctrinal context which is peculiar to Jains. In fact it seems most appropriate to regard Jain literature as a quite distinct sphere of discourse in which Jains address other Jains, and argue against Hindu writers. And to do so they have developed their own original philosophical methods.

Moreover, Jain literature and its associated practices subsist upon a base of peculiarly Jain institutions. The order of Jain *munis*, whether Digambar or Svetambar, observe rules which clearly distinguish them from Hindu ascetics. The organisation of Jain temples, even in the south where Hindu influence has arguably been greatest, is quite different from the organisation of Hindu temples. And even those most Hindu figures, the *bhaṭṭāraks*, 'caste gurus', participate in a distinctly Jain way in the life of the community. Indeed, if we take the

Jain laity into account, there are grounds for arguing that the Jains are not just distinct in their religious organisations, but are actually better at being a community, better at organising themselves and bringing different sections of the community together for common religious and cultural purposes.

Finally, the proposal that Jains are explicable solely with reference to caste is vulnerable to the objection that it does not explain all that needs to be explained. It is true that Jains are organised in local caste groups or in wider marriage circles, and that such groups are communities in the narrow sense, not used here, that they are groups of kin or caste mates known to each other in a village, neighbourhood, or marriage circle. But this is not an interesting use of the term 'community', nor does it exhaust the integrative resources of Jain society. Jain castes do interdine with each other. Jain temples, at least within the larger sect divisions, are commonly open to any Jain caste. Many castes, such as Aggarwals and Oswals, include both Jains and Hindus, and the Jain members of such castes clearly have an interest in a Jain community not shared by their Hindu caste mates. The traditional communal Jain ceremonies, as well as the modern Jain organisations, usually accept as wide a participation as possible from the Jain society of a particular sect or region. Indeed, the very existence of such communal institutions, ranging from the traditional *pañcakalyān* ceremony to the educational and religious trusts, certifies a larger sense of community than one limited to a village, neighbourhood, or even regional endogamous group.

There do appear to be natural limits, however, to the extent to which Jains can effectively form communities. In the first place, the division between Digambars and Svetambars, as well as between sects within those categories, means that an inevitable constraint is placed upon the participation in community practised by any populace of Jains. It is true that Jains have sometimes cooperated across these barriers, and it could even be argued that the very conflict that arises between them, as over pilgrimage sites, reveals a deeper shared culture. Nevertheless, effective communities, in the sense of organisations or informal groups which represent coherent aims to Jains or to the wider society, seem to be confined within particular sects and particular regions.

Moreover, communities which are effective in this sense are probably not to be thought of as being continually effective or active.

In northern Karnataka and southern Maharashtra, for example, the public expression of the effective community is vested to a large extent in the Dakṣin Bhārat Jain Sabhā, with its community newspaper and its educational institutions. Though the Sabhā has carried on its affairs in a well-organised manner since the turn of the century, there have been many periods in which it was hardly visible, and hardly important, to the vast majority of Digambar Jains in the area. Jains continued to marry endogamously and attend the local temple without its intervention. It has, however, evinced the potential to react, or to help organise a reaction, against perceived threats or to take advantage of perceived opportunities. Here we had best speak perhaps of potential communities which rise only occasionally to the surface of social life.

These potential communities are also imagined communities, to adapt the phrase which Benedict Anderson (1983) applied to nation states. That is, a sense of common culture and shared interests is created and kept alive, through the terms of public discourse and journalism, although the participants in that common sensibility may in daily intercourse, or in the extension of marriage circles, have nothing to do with each other. In this respect the creation of an effective and active community is continually desiderated by the elite of Jain society, as if the community always already existed but merely needed to be awakened to its nature.

But even if Jain communities are potential and imagined, they are by no means unreal. They are distinguishable social entities, effective in the social and political life of India. And in this sense Jains are a test case, close to, but not part of, the Hindu mainstream. On the one hand we have every reason to believe that groups as far or farther from the mainstream – Christians, Muslims, Sikhs – will evince the importance of community at least as much as Jains do. On the other hand, there are many movements and organisations, similar to the Jain ones, which are closer to or within the mainstream. Though scholars have been in the habit of referring to these as castes and their organisations as caste associations, in the present perspective it seems more useful to refer to them as communities – effective, potential, or imagined. Ideas and practices of caste may provide the foundation upon which a community's identity and separateness are erected, but do not in themselves create a community. In this respect, we argue, India is not just a society of castes or of classes, but also a society of communities.

# Part I

# Jain ideals and Jain identity

## 2

# Jain ideals and Jain indentity

Michael Carrithers

The doctrines of Jainism recommend an extreme of self-mortification which made Mahavira and his followers a benchmark for ascetics in ancient India. Many, such as the Buddha, rejected such extreme practices, but few failed to recognise the sincerity with which Jain renouncers adhered to their harsh discipline. The question is: how could such a creed, so designedly opposed in all matters to everyday life, become a religion of ordinary people?

The short answer is that Jainism developed a code of lay practice – *śrāvakācāra*, literally 'listener's deportment'. This was conceived as a diluted version of the ascetic's code, as lower steps on the ladder to true asceticism. The lay life was recognised as inferior to the ascetic's life, but at the same time a distinctly Jain identity for laymen was created. Jains were not only those who supported Jain ascetics, but also those who behaved in a particular way. In medieval India the genre of Jain *śrāvakācāra* literature grew to rival the Hindu *dharma-śāstra* literature in complexity and meticulousness, far outstripping the Buddhists' exiguous efforts in that direction. Jains may have been fierce in prescribing for their monks, but they were also expansive in prescribing for their laity.

This much is already clear from R. Williams' pioneering study *Jaina Yoga* (Williams 1963), which lays out in detail the precepts of the *śrāvakācāra* literature. What is not so clear is how these ideals related to actual life, to the historical people who professed or now profess them. Each of the following three chapters addresses that issue.

In chapter 3 Mukund Lath, an Indologist, discusses a key text of the lay deportment literature, the *Upāsakādhyayana* of Somadeva Suri, a text of the tenth century AD. This work is remarkable partly for its setting in a longer work of mixed prose and poetry, the *Yaśastilaka-campū*, the Embellished Epic of Yaśastilaka. Lath argues that 'the story is an important prologue to understanding the spirit' of the code of behaviour.

At first glance this seems unlikely. The plot of the story, recounted by Lath, appears quite surrealistically complex, a lush tangle of nested stories, of plot and sub-plot, set in ornate and vivid language. Characters, mostly royal, often manifesting the earthiest drives, are reborn in life after life, changing their names, their relations – mother and son become brother and sister, for example – and even their species, from human to animal and back. The story is clearly fit for a sophisticated and probably well-to-do readership. What is not so clear is whether it is fit to support the stern and dry ethical prescriptions which it precedes.

But in fact the very lushness of the story grows from uncompromisingly ascetic roots. If humans die and are reborn in an animal or less favoured human state, then that is the consequence of evil and unconsidered acts, *karma*, in the previous life. This is illustrated again and again. And if even kings are repeatedly moved to leave their estates and become homeless monks devoted to self-mortification, that is because they experience *vairāgya*, the disgust and world-weariness which are the only reasonable responses to fleshly life. So if Somadeva's readership was first drawn to his story by its elaborate sensuality, it remained to find the fundamental values of Jainism confirmed and reconfirmed by the fate of his characters.

Such stories are more than merely icing on the cake of Jain philosophy and practice, though Jains themselves sometimes speak in this vein. For such stories are now frequently read, or retold in sermons, and this must always have been true. In this respect homiletic stories are more the vehicle than the passengers of Jain philosophy, for they allow generation after generation of Jains to grasp the dry prescriptions of asceticism as living, as having consequences in the lives of characters, of persons, even though those characters are fictional. Josephine Reynell writes in chapter 5 of the reproduction of Jain values; certainly such stories are a powerful force in that reproduction.

In the second part of his chapter Lath considers how Jains rationalised their acquiescence to the institutions of caste, and ends by remarking that Jains even came to prescribe the expensive and ostentatious 'glorification' (*prabhāvanā*) of their religion. The second chapter, by Roy Norman, takes up that theme and explains how the role of the Jain laity may have come into being and how that role is conceived. He argues that the vows laid on the laity were always less strenuous, and the stricter prescriptions less frequently observed, than the *śrāvakācāra* literature implies. He shows that the actual demands on laity were conceived pragmatically to allow them to amass wealth in order to support ascetics and to glorify Jainism publicly.

There was a lively discussion at the conference on the issue of ostentation and asceticism. In an early paper (Reynell 1985b) echoed briefly in her chapter here, Reynell had argued that Jains in Jaipur today can be sharply critical of ostentatious giving. Norman's paper argued that this was to misunderstand the rapprochement which Jains had early achieved between ascetic ideals and lay necessities. Some participants reported criticism of ostentation similar to that in Jaipur in other parts of the Jain world. Since both are evidently true – that Jains criticise ostentatious giving and that Jains have a clear rationale for such giving – then it was speculated that Jainism must have room, as other religions do, for some inherent contradictions. Jonathan Parry remarked, however, that there is a natural affinity between ostentatious wealth and the ostentatious renunciation undertaken by Jain ascetics. And Carrithers remarked that the wealthier the renouncer, the better his or her worldly prospects might be, then the more heroic and therefore more valued the renunciation. Gordon Johnson further pointed out that the expensive public festivals and street processions of Jainism themselves serve to establish and reconfirm Jain identity in the complex and turbulent urban world in which many Jains live.

It is implicit in the texts considered by Lath and Norman that Jain laymen are just that – men. In her chapter Reynell reveals that in fact Jain lay asceticism in Jaipur today, and the consequent preservation and reproduction of Jain values and the Jain community, lie not so much in the hands of men, but of women. It is women who fast, and women who largely carry the local institutions of Jain sects and sub-sects through their participation. This insight is repeated for other communities in other papers, and suggests that our picture of Jain history through male-oriented texts must be corrected by attending to the importance of women in bringing Jain values alive in Jain society.

3

# Somadeva Suri and the question of Jain identity

Mukund Lath

Somadeva Suri, a south Indian Jain monk of the tenth century AD, was the author of a work called the *Upāsakādhyayana*. It is a central text of Digambara *śrāvakācāra* literature. The aim of this literature is to lay down ideals, norms, and rules of proper conduct for *śrāvaka*s, Jain lay followers. There is a large corpus of *śrāvakācāra* literature among both the Digambaras and the Svetambaras, the two major sects into which Jains are divided. The *śrāvakācāra* literature as a genre begins only in medieval times, though it has ancient roots. It continues down to modern times, much of the modern writing being in the vernacular.

Somadeva Suri's *Upāsakādhyayana* – literally, 'the chapter on *upāsaka*s', that is, lay followers – is one of the earliest texts of the *śrāvakācāra* genre. Its influence on all subsequent texts of its kind is deep.[1] It is a crucial text, I think, in trying to understand how medieval Jains articulated their own identity in relation to Jain ideals and to the larger society around them. What I have to say here will be based mainly on this text.

The *Upāsakādhyayana* is the last part of a much larger work, an epilogue to a religious novel called the *Yaśastilakacampū*, which uses prose and verse with equal artistic care. The influence of Bana on its prose and of the sophisticated *mahākāvya* (roughly, 'epic poem') on its long and varied metric passages is obvious. The story itself, which moves through an elaborate display of linguistic and poetic virtuosity, is simple and yet a carefully constructed setting for the didactic discourse that follows. This discourse is the *Upāsakādhyāyana*. It can be detached from the story and is now printed separately. The two

[1] See pp. 21–3 of the Hindi introduction to the *Upāsakādhyāyana* edited with a Hindi translation by Kailāsh Candra Śāstrī, Bhāratīya Jñānapīṭha (Varanasi and New Delhi, 1964).

recent and more readily available editions of the work[2] that I know of do not contain the story at all. But the story is an important prologue to understanding the spirit of the work and I will briefly relate it here.

The story is of the *kathā* or narrative genre, what would be classed as a *dharmakathā*, homiletic narrative, a very popular genre among the Jains. As is not unusual in *kathā* literature, the narrative structure consists of one tale boxed into another. It begins by introducing us to Māridatta, a young and impetuous king, fond of warlike sports and the good things of life. Under the instruction of a Saiva *kulācārya* (a word meaning both 'family priest' and *kaula* or esoteric magician/mystic) named Vīrabhairava, Māridatta decides to sacrifice a young man and woman to the fierce goddess, Caṇḍamāri, the family deity. The object is to gain a magic sword capable of subduing the *vidyādhara*s, a class of powerful, semi-divine beings. The king's men go looking for suitable victims and fetch for him a young boy named Yaśastilaka and his young sister, both Jain monks, disciples of a Jain ascetic teacher named Sudatta who was spending a night near Rājapura, the city where Māridatta rules.

Māridatta is captivated by the beauty and composure of the young Jain monks who greet him with well-worded laudatory verses and songs. He asks them who they are. With this begins the main story in which Yaśastilaka recounts his autobiography, covering many lifetimes.

In a previous life, he says, he was a prince of Avanti named Yaśodhara. His father was king Yaśorgha and his mother Candramati, a daughter of an ancestor of Māridatta himself, to whom the story was being told. Yaśodhara became king when his father grew old and retired to the forest in order to practise strenuous austerities.

Late one night Yaśodhara suddenly woke up from his sleep after a long bout of love-making with his wife Amṛtamati, whom he loved dearly. She was not in his bed. He looked for her and discovered her in the arms of an ugly hunchback, a *kubja*. His first impulse was to kill the adulterous couple, but he controlled his anger. He said nothing about the incident to anyone but became full of disgust and *vairāgya*, world-

[2] One edition I have already mentioned in the previous note. The other is contained in the *Śrāvakācāra Saṅgraha*, a multi-volume collection of *śrāvakācāra*s of the Digambaras from medieval to modern times. The *Upāsakādhyayana* is the fifth text in volume I, printed with a Hindi translation, edited and translated by Hīrālāl Siddhāntālaṅkāra, Sholapur, 1976.

weariness. Wanting to retire to the forest as a monk, he called his ministers in the morning and said to them that he had seen a dream which he must now fulfil. He told them that in his dream he had handed his throne to his young son and left his kingdom for the forest.

Yaśodhara's mother Candramati guessed the real reason for his son's *vairāgya:* She knew he had spent the night with Amṛtamati; she was told by a palace maid about how Amṛtamati was always casting glances of longing and desire at the *kubja*. 'What else can come of allowing freedom to women?' she wisely concluded to herself. To her son she spoke of the utter meaninglessness of dreams. Dreams, she said, were just a product of the body's humours, or they merely reproduced past experience. She cited a palace maid who had told her of a dream in which the poor girl turned into a cup of porridge and was eaten by Brahmins invited for a ritual feast. However, she proposed to have a propitiatory *pūjā* performed before the family deity in order to destroy the ill effects of the dream.

Here the story takes a peculiarly Jain turn. It becomes a kind of ancient novel of ideas or of polemic and debate where the Jain *ahiṃsā* (non-violence) religion is defended and pitted against the orthodox Brahminical scriptures which permit *hiṃsā*, harm to living beings.

Yaśodhara's mother proposed to sacrifice 'animals of every kind' before the family deity. Yaśodhara was appalled at this. He had, it now turns out, recently become a staunch believer in *ahiṃsā*. A long debate follows between mother and son in which Candramati argues on the basis of Brahmanical law books that *hiṃsā* can be a part of *dharma*, true religion. Yaśodhara vehemently opposes this view by quoting, from the same species of law book, passages enjoining *ahiṃsā*. Candramati is taken aback at finding her son talking like a Jain. Palace officials inform her that Yaśodhara had been conversing with a Jain monk despite efforts by the family priest's son to stop him and that he had greatly changed after the event. Angrily she abuses the palace officials as 'demons, public enemies, destroyers of her kingdom and her son'.[3]

Then she addresses her son as a Cārvāka, an irreligious person, and rebukes him for his faith in the Digambara *dharma*, which is outside

[3] 're, mama putrasya ca tantrasya sarvasvakhādinaḥ, prajāṇāṃ ca lañcāluñcāḥ, niśācarāḥ . . .' *Yaśastilakacāmpakāvyam*, edited by Mahāmahopādhyauya Paṇḍita Śivadatta, Kāvyamālā series, no. 70, vol. II (Nirṇayasāgara Press, Bombay, 1903), p. 104.

the pale of Brahmanical orthodoxy. She calls it an upstart religion which originated in the false and evil Kali age. It could never be the valid source for right conduct, the only valid source for which, she says, are the Vedas. And if, she adds, her son was bent on doing *bhakti*, devotion, he should turn to eternal gods like Siva, Visnu, or the Sun, not to a man and a Kali Yuga man at that.

Yaśodhara argues at length in defence of Jainism. He says that it is as ancient – or rather as eternal – as the most ancient religions and the six philosophies.[4] All these, he asserts, are part of the fabric of the world itself, they are of the very nature of things, being as eternal as the seas and the seasons. Somadeva, through his mouthpiece Yaśodhara, quotes a large number of authorities to establish the antiquity of Jainism.[5]

After much argument, mother and son reach a compromise. Yaśodhara agrees to sacrifice a cock made of dough in place of the real one. Meanwhile Amṛtamati, Yaśodhara's unfaithful wife, also comes to realise that her husband knows of her escapade the previous night. She invites him and his mother to her palace and poisons them.

Next follows a series of rebirths in which Yaśodhara and his mother Candramati are born as various animals. Their quarrel continues only now it becomes more serious: the one seeks to kill the other. Ultimately, they are born as cock and hen and they are present when the Jain monk Sudatta argues for Jainism and *ahiṃsā* against a group of four people: one a Brahmin, a hedonist who believed that man is imperfect by nature and will remain so; another a *vāmamārgī śaiva*, a mystical magician; the third a Buddhist who, strangely enough, believed both in the Buddhist doctrine of the illusory nature of the self and in hedonism; and the fourth an agnostic who argues against other philosophies but is also a spiritual seeker. Sudatta speaks to him of *ahiṃsā* as the true path. He points at Yaśodhara and Candramati, the cock and the hen, as illustrations of what happens to those who believe in *hiṃsā* as *dharma*, telling the story of their previous lives. Yaśodhara

[4] Ibid. p. 114. The commentator, Śrutadeva Sūri, names the four 'eternal' *samaya*s or 'faiths' here as Jain, Jaimini (Mīmāṃsā), Buddhism and the doctrine of Śaṃkara. The six philosophies are Sāṃkhya, Lokāyata, plus the above four faiths. Somadeva Sūri himself does not specify which four faiths and six philosophies he means.

[5] Modern Jains too argue for the antiquity of Jain *dharma*, but their aim is to show that it is historical. In India, history is now in and eternity out in the defence of religion.

and Candramati achieve true understanding, their *karma* is destroyed like seeds in fire and they attain real *vairāgya*.[6]

Killed once again, this time by Yaśomati, Yaśodhara's son, they are born as his progeny. Yaśodhara is born as a boy and named Yaśastilaka and Candramati is born a girl and named Madanamati. Yaśomati becomes a disciple of Sudatta whom he meets on a hunting expedition. Sudatta tells him the story of his children's previous life. Yaśomati takes a vow of celibate asceticism, but before he does so he tells his two children the stories of their previous lives. Though they were very young, only eight years old, they became monks, disciples of the Jain teacher Sudatta.

With this Yaśastilaka ends his story. Māridatta is moved. He gives up all thoughts of *hiṃsā* and becomes a seeker for true knowledge. He meets Sudatta and asks him the age-old question: 'What is *dharma*, true religion?' The *Upāsakādhyayana* follows as an answer to this question. The story leads up to the answer in many ways, at different levels. It seeks to use the enchantment of literary style (*rasa* and *alankāra*) for didactic ends. It vindicates Jainism by arguing against its detractors, both polemically and through the power of story-telling. It clothes the ideals of Jainism vividly in action and characters, however fabulous. Readers, most of whom must have been Jains – for the tale is obviously meant for them – feel their roots in their faith strengthen and are now in a more receptive frame of mind for the message that follows: if they cannot renounce the world completely, they can at least set foot on the path to liberation. Such, at least, seems to have been the intention.

## *II*

Sudatta (that is, Somadeva) begins by defining *dharma* as the path to *mokṣa*, liberation.[7] The only true path to liberation, he argues, is the Jain path, which he also calls the Jain *samaya*. *Dharma*, or true religion, is in his usage synonymous with Jain *samaya*. By the word

[6] He quotes a philosopher called Nīlapaṭa (a *śaiva*?) who believed in sex as the ultimate bliss. *Yaśastilakacampūkāvyām*, vol. II, p. 252.

[7] yasmādabhyudayaḥ puṃsāṃ niḥśreyasaphalāśrayaḥ|
vadanti viditāmnāyāstāṃ dharmaṃ dharmasūrayaḥ||
*Yaśastilakacampūkavyām*, vol. II, p. 268

*samaya* Somadeva means 'faith' as used in a phrase like 'the Christian faith', implying a specific set of beliefs, doctrines, practices, rituals, duties, norms of conduct. The total body of those who follow the Jain *samaya* are the Jain *samayi*s. They consist of both monks, or *muni*s, and *śrāvaka*s, or lay followers who are householders. The *Upāsakādhyayana* describes the Jain *samaya* for *śrāvaka*s.

There is a difference between the *muni*'s path and the *śrāvaka*'s. The *muni*'s path is the path of *nivṛtti*, of withdrawal from the world, of giving it up. He is directly on the path to liberation. This path is pre-eminent, as Yasastilaka's story so richly attests. The story is not chiefly about virtuous lay people, but about lay people who experience *vairāgya* and renounce the householder's life altogether. There the real heroism lies.

Yet there is a place for the virtuous *śrāvaka*, even if his path is more circuitous. He follows the *dharma* of *pravṛtti*, of 'doing' or 'action', engaged in the affairs of the world. His path, too, if he follows the Jain *samaya* faithfully, would ultimately lead him to liberation.

This definition of *pravṛtti* fits in well with the Jain notion of *aṇuvrata*s, or 'lesser vows', the milder version of the monk's *mahāvrata*s or 'great vows'. For example, if the *mahāvrata*s prescribe complete celibacy for the monk, the *aṇuvrata*s prescribe intercourse only with one's own wife for the layman. The monk must own nothing – not even clothes among Digambaras – but the *śrāvaka* is allowed a deliberately restrained amount of property to gain his livelihood. Though the *śrāvaka* is on a lower stage of the path to liberation, his precepts are made of the same stuff as the monk's.

One could expect therefore that a description of the *aṇuvrata*s would suffice to define the Jain *dharma* or *samaya* for householders. But the *śrāvaka*'s *samaya*, at least in the *Upāsakādhyayana*, encompasses much more. For Somadeva it has to if it aims at covering not only personal, individual, rules of behaviour, as for the monk who looks only to his own liberation, but also rules of social conduct for laymen who remain tied to the world.

To take one rule, a central one in the Indian context: the Jain *śrāvaka* must come to terms with the question of *varṇa* and *jāti*, that is, of social category and caste. The entire society in which the Jains lived, of which they were a part, was divided into castes, *jāti*s, each affiliated to one of the four hierarchically arranged *varṇa*s. What should be the Jain attitude to *jāti*?

In medieval times, the concept of *jāti* became the centre of an important debate between the Mīmāṃsakas on the one side and Buddhists and Jains on the other. The Buddhists and the Jains vehemently opposed the notion of *jāti*: they accepted *varṇa* but understood it on a purely functional basis, having nothing to do with the birth or parentage of a person, namely, his *jāti*.[8] Kumārila, the great medieval Mīmāṃsaka, argued strongly in favour of *jāti* by birth, especially the *brāhmaṇa jāti*. Kumārila wrote:

na ca tapa ādīnam samudāyo brāhmaṇyam. na tajjanitah saṃskāraḥ, na tadabhivyaṅgyā jātiḥ. kiṃ tarhi? mātāpitṛjātijñābhivyangyā pratyakṣa-samadhigamyā.

(From the *Tantravārtika*)

(Brahminhood does not consist in a set of qualities such as asceticism, nor in a set of tendencies or propensities caused by these qualities [meaning traditions of conduct or behaviour handed down in families]: *jāti* is not indicated by such things. What is it then? It is something directly perceivable in a person given the knowledge of who his, or her, parents are.)

To this the Buddhist and Jain reply was:

na ca kṣatriyādibhyo vyāvṛtto brāhmaneṣvanuvṛtah kaścidākāraviśeṣo mātā-pitṛsambandhajñenāpi pratīyate. tasmād brāhmaṇadiśabdavyapadeśyamātā-pitṛsantānajanmatvopādhiko brāhmaṇādisabdo na jātivacanaḥ.

(From *Nyāyasudha*)

(One can discern no distinct physical characteristics which occur in Brahmins and not in Ksatriyas or others, even if one knew their parentage. Therefore, words like 'Brahmin' do not denote a really distinct *jāti* or class of things but only an apparent or imaginary one [an *upādhi*], indicated by a specific birth and parentage.)

Prabhācandra, a Jain philosopher, comments in his *Nyāyakumudacandra*:

[8] The Jain *Ādipurāṇa* has the following verse:

manuṣyajātirekaiva jātināmodayodbhavā|
vṛttibhedādāhitādbhedāccāturvidhyamihāsnute||

(Mankind is one single *jāti* and the name *jāti* applies to it as a whole [distinguishing it from other *jatis* such as 'cows', 'horses', etc.]. But because different men follow different *vṛttis* [conduct, means of livelihood], this imposes a four-fold division among men [implying that the division is not natural or given in any sense].

na khalu yathā mahiṣyādisaṅghe gavāṃ gojātiḥ vailakṣaṇyena pratibhāsate . . . tathā brāhmaṇyamapi.

(Among a herd including both buffaloes and cattle, cattle can be identified as a separate *jāti* or species. Brahmins cannot be thus distinguished from other men.)

'Nor,' he adds, 'can purity of lineage be proof of *jāti*, because purity of lineage can never be established with any certainty.'[9]

Though this was the rational view propounded by their philosophers, the Jains in practice did not repudiate *jāti*. Those who devised codes of social conduct for Jains, the *śrāvakācāra* writers, had to make room for it, justify it somehow and yet make it acceptable as part of the specifically Jain *samaya*.

The early Digambara *śrāvakācāra*s thus speak of a distinct Jain *cāturvarṇya*, a Jain set of four *varna*s. The *Mahāpurāṇa*, a pre-Somadeva text, which like the Hindu *purāṇa*s contains legislative material besides myths and legends, tells the following story to justify *cāturvarṇya* among the Jains.[10] It traces its creation to the ancient King Bharata, son of the first Jain founder, Ṛśabhadeva, the primal monarch, the culture hero who established the institutions, skills, arts and sciences of civilisation. Ṛśabhadeva was also the great Jain ascetic who established the Jain order consisting of the complementary groups of monks and lay followers.

The son Bharata, however, discovered that not all *śrāvaka*s were alike and he devised a plan to grade them. He put them to a test which involved the *vrata* concerning the observance of *ahiṃsā*. This helped him to grade them from the best to the worst. In this way *śrāvaka*s became *brāhmaṇa*, *kṣatriya*, *vaiśya*, or *śudra*.

Clearly, what the *Mahāpurāṇa* is attempting to do is to justify an existent social phenomenon, which was not only too big for a codifier to fight, but which he perhaps – in this case – thought to be right and just and in the very nature of things. But being a Jain he wanted to identify with it as something which was also essentially Jain.

Somadeva also attempts to justify the acceptance of the *varṇa* scheme by the Jains – which in practice meant the acceptance of *jāti*, because this is how *varṇa* actually operated. But his justification was

9 The above report of Jain and Buddhist views is based on G. C. Pande's *The Śramaṇa Tradition*, L. D. series no. 66 (Ahmedabad, 1978), pp. 53–63. The translation is mine.

10 *Mahāpurāṇa*, parva 83, verses 7–23. See *Śrāvakācāra Saṇgraha*, vol. 1, pp. 29–30.

not mythic. It was a more rational and conceptual justification. Unlike the author of the *Mahāpurāṇa*, Somadeva does not seem to have found the *jāti* scheme 'natural' or somehow desirable in itself. He was learned in philosophy and perhaps knew of the Jain philosophers' arguments against *jāti*, though he does not speak of them. Yet in adopting a position in which he accepts *jāti*, he does seem to have been aware that he was justifying something which he did not really consider to be just.

The *dharma* for the householder, he says, is of two basically different kinds: *laukika*, 'worldly', and *pāralaukika*, 'otherworldly'. *Pāralaukika dharma* is the true path to liberation, the Jain *samaya*, which every Jain – indeed, every man – should follow in order to attain Ultimate Knowledge. But there is also a *laukika dharma*, consisting of social norms, customs, laws, rules, institutions, upheld by the people among whom the Jains live. No harm is done, says Somadeva, if a Jain follows the *laukika dharma*, provided this does not undermine or distort the performance of *pāralaukika dharma*. To quote him:

> dvau hi dharmau gṛhasthāṇām, laukikaḥ, pāralaukikaḥ|
> lokāśrayo bhavedādyaḥ paraḥ syādāgamāśrayaḥ.||[11]

(For the [Jain] householder there are two *dharmas*, *laukika* and *pāralaukika*. The basis of *laukika dharma* is *loka*, the social world as it is. The basis of *pāralaukika dharma* is the Jain canon.)

We have here a remarkable division (for its time and place, *deśa* and *kāla*) of human affairs into two categories, similar somewhat to the Western categories of 'secular' and 'religious'. This is a categorisation of *dharma* quite alien to the Hindu law books. The Hindu law books do speak of many *dharmas* – in fact *dharma* is the sphere of the many rather than the one, hence its conflicts and dilemmas. There are separate *dharmas* for the student, the teacher, the householder, the ascetic, the king, the judge, and so forth. Some of these *dharmas* are more concerned with the affairs of the world and some more with a happier after-life (*svarga*) or with liberation. But there is no clear divide within the realm of *dharma* into the two opposing categories of *laukika* and *pāralaukika*.

[11] *Upāsakādhyayana*, kalpa 34, verse 476.

For Somadeva Suri, *pāralaukika dharma* is the real *dharma*, the necessary *dharma*. The *laukika* is contingent, though it must be followed because of the exigencies of the social world in which the Jain lives.

Through this categorisation, Somadeva offers a justification for letting *jāti* prevail among Jains. In the very next verses following the above, he says:

> jātayo'nādayah sarvāstatkriyāpi tathāvidhāḥ|
> śrutiḥ śāstrāntaram vāstu pramāṇaṃ kātra naḥ kṣatiḥ||
>
> svajātyaiva viśuddhānāṃ varṇānāmiha ratnavat|
> tatkriyāviniyogāya jaināgamavidhiḥ param||
>
> yadbhavabhrintinirmuktihetudhastatra durlabha|
> saṃsāravyavahāre tu svataḥsiddhe vṛthāgamaḥ||
>
> sarva eva hi jaināṇāṃ pramāṇaṃ laukiko vidhiḥ|
> yatra samyaktvahānirna yatra na vratadūṣaṇam||

(Let the *jāti*s and all their various practices be something that has come down from the beginning of time or let their basis be *śruti* [Veda] or some other *śāstra*: what harm can this do to us [Jains]? We are like precious stones, naturally pure in '*jāti*' [of a gem, the mine from which it comes] and '*varṇa*' [the hue or lustre of a gem]. The only valid basis for what we should do are the ordinances laid down in the Jain canons. The affairs of the world are *svataḥ-siddha* [they are their own basis and do not need any other], but they cannot teach a man the true way out of the delusion of the world. All *laukika* norms [*vidhis*] are valid for us Jains provided they are not in contradiction with our *samyaktva* and our *vrata*s [our doctrines and our religious practices].)

Having thus justified *jāti* for a Jain, Somadeva lays down the following marriage code for a *śrāvaka*, as part of his *brahmacarya aṇuvrata*, his lesser vow of celibacy: a Jain householder should marry within his own *jāti* – but of course keeping courtesans (*vittastrī*, women you can buy) does not hamper the *vrata*.[12]

This points to the kind of difficulty in which Somadeva finds

[12] *Yaśastilakacampūkāvyam*, vol. II, p. 359.

himself. For the intention of the *aṇuvrata* is surely to prescribe a milder version of the monk's celibacy, which other Jain writers take to mean that the layman must be faithful to his wife. Here, however, Somadeva seems to adapt his argument to some *laukika* custom, some practice of taking courtesans common perhaps in the well-to-do Jain society he knew. Similarly, in making his apologies for *jāti*, Somadeva assumed that *jāti* was a contingent, *laukika dharma* and that its acceptance was consistent with Jain doctrine. His arguments seem to be aimed at Jain philosophers who opposed the validity of the idea and practice of *jāti* altogether. But there is no reason to believe that belonging to a *jāti* and being a Jain could be so easily distinguished as Somadeva assumes.

Yet what else could a medieval writer of codes for Jains have done? One way of escaping the problem of caste versus *samaya* found in texts like the *Mahāpurāṇa* and the *Upāsakādhyayana* is to speak of a specific Jain *cāturvarṇya* with its *jāti*s as though it were a body separated from the rest of Hindu society. Yet this could not be very helpful. Were the Jains actually separate, they could have dealt directly with *jāti* by removing it, since they were at base quite opposed to it.

But *jāti* was obviously too deep-rooted among Jain *śrāvaka*s to deal with so directly. The fact seems to have been, as it is in Rajasthan today, that the Jains had dual identity: a *jāti* identity and a Jain identity. Both pulled in different directions. Somadeva realised that it was impossible for Jains to sever their *jāti* identity. So he exhorted them to take their Jain identity as their real, *pāralaukika* identity, even if they retained the other contingent one. He could still maintain that Jains, as Jains, are still set apart, like precious stones from the best of mines: they are purer, they have more lustre.

A sense of identity demands a sense of solidarity, prestige, respect, power, glory. Somadeva exhorts the Jain *śrāvaka*s to seek all these for the Jain *samaya*. Thus he says:

> *Vatsalatā* [affection] is proper behaviour towards other Jains [*sadharmasu*]. How can a man be a *samayī* who does not joyfully show proper *vatsalatā* towards the Jain *saṅgha* [collectivity] consisting of the four *varṇa*s?[13]

And also:

[13] *Yaśastilakacampūkāvyam*, vol. II, p. 315–16.

One should seek to increase the glory of the [Jain] path by [constructing] small and large temples, arranging for *pūjā*s and ceremonies as well as through *jñāna* and *tapas* [wisdom and asceticism].[14]

These are what a *śrāvaka* was expected to do, not as part of his *laukika dharma*, but as part of his *vrata*s, as part of his *pāralaukika dharma*.

[14] caityaiścaityālayairjñānaistapobhirvividhātmakaiḥ|
pūjāmahādhvajādyaśca kuryānmārgaprabhāvanam||
*Yaśastilakacampūkāvyam*, vol. II, p. 309

# 4

# The role of the layman according to the Jain canon

K. R. Norman

Josephine Reynell (1985b) has considered the practice of Jain laymen in modern Rajasthan, and has pointed out that there is therein a paradox between renunciation and ostentation, between the strictly ascetic renunciatory spirit of Jain doctrine and the opulence and wealth which is emphasised in its practice.

She points out that detachment from worldly phenomena is an essential step towards enlightenment. Such detachment is encapsulated in the principle of *aparigraha*, which is one of the five vows taken by laymen. She explains that this means non-possession, and it is taken as referring to the non-possession of both internal and external attachments, the former including pride, deceit, etc. Laymen have to follow fourteen principles of renunciation of external things, which she lists (1985b: 21), abstaining from or limiting themselves within various aspects of daily life, for example, food, clothing, adornments, etc. This code of behaviour is intended to lead to a situation where laymen would eventually wish to renounce the world and become ascetics.

The paradox which strikes her lies in the contrast between the goal of non-possession of wealth and goods, and the luxurious dress and life style of many lay Jains, especially on festival days. The same luxurious state of temples and shrines contrasts sharply with the emphasis on austerity and renunciation preached in those temples. Nor can it be said that wealthy Jains put all their wealth into their

Texts referred to:
Prakrit: *Uvāsaga-dasāo*, edited and translated by A. F. R. Hoernle, vol. I, 1890, vol. II, 1888, Calcutta.
Pāli: *Dīgha-nikāya*, vol. III, edited by J. Estlin Carpenter, London 1911.
*Majjhima-nikāya*, vol. I, edited by V. Trenckner, London 1888.
*Viinaya-piṭaka*, vol. I, edited by H. Oldenberg, London 1879.

religion, for much is spent on luxury goods for the home. Wealth permeates religious practices, for often people cannot participate fully in the religious life of the community unless they are wealthy and can make generous gifts (*dāna*). In this sense *aparigraha* is interpreted as the layman donating his excess wealth. Although this should be done in secret, it is in fact a matter of ostentation.

As is well known, there is an extensive medieval Jain literature devoted entirely to the role of the layman. Williams, in what has been described by Elisabeth Strandberg as 'the only existing detailed study of Jain lay discipline' (1981: 181), states (1981: xvi) that

> initially the lay estate was admitted by the Jina only in deference to human frailty, and was regarded in theory as a stage of preparation for the ascetic life. In the early period of Jainism the *Śrāvakācāra* was therefore of minimal importance, and as it has grown progressively in significance various expedients have had to be adopted to make up for the silence of the canonical texts on the subject. The corpus of the lay doctrine is in fact a creation of the medieval period.

As Strandberg points out (1981: 18), it is not entirely correct to say that the canonical texts are silent on this matter. It is not clear why Williams wrote in the way he did, for he himself states (1963: xvi) that the *Upāsaka-daśāḥ* (better perhaps known by its Prakrit name of *Uvāsaga-dasāo*) supplied the framework for the *vratas* (vows), each with its five typical *aticāras* (infractions), and the *pratimās* (the stages of spiritual progress). An unwary reader might assume from this that the *Uvāsaga-dasāo* was a medieval text, instead of being the seventh *aṅga* of the Śvetāmbara Jain canon. Even if it is one of the later books of that canon, nevertheless it belongs firmly to what Williams calls the early period (1963: xii) – the dark age covering the first millennium – of Jain history. We should perhaps take a charitable view, and assume that he meant the 'partial' or 'relative' silence of the canonical texts.

A hint towards a solution to Reynell's paradox lies in the historic background to Jainism, and in this chapter I wish to examine some of the information about laymen which is to be found in the Jain canon. The story which is told of the first layman mentioned in the *Uvāsaga-dasāo* makes clear what the layman's vows meant to a very wealthy man. Ānanda's estate is described in detail (§ 4): he had four krores of gold on deposit, four krores of gold out at interest, a well-stocked estate to the value of four krores of gold, and four herds, each consisting of 10,000 head of cattle.

Having heard Mahāvīra preach, Ānanda declared that he accepted the Jain doctrine. He stated, however, that although many other wealthy, famous, and important people had, following their declaration of belief in the Jain doctrine, become ascetics, he could not do the same, but he was willing to take upon himself the twelve-fold law of the layman. When he came to recite the *aparigraha* vow he stated (§ 18): 'Excepting my treasure of four krores of gold on deposit, four krores of gold out at interest, and my estate of four krores, I renounce the possession of other gold, and excepting my four herds, each of 10,000 head of cattle, I renounce the possession of other animals.' He went on to limit his other possessions: 500 ploughs, 1,000 carts, 8 boats, and then a long list of domestic possessions, bath-towels, tooth-sticks, etc., for each of which he set limits. The precise reduction in his proposed use of these is not specified, but it is clear that as far as his money, estates, and herds were concerned, he was merely limiting himself to his present holdings, and undertaking not to increase them.

Having taken these vows, Ānanda states (§ 58) that he will, as far as possible, have nothing to do with the members or the gods of any heterodox (i.e. non-Jain) communities. He makes a formal promise to provide Jain ascetics with all their necessities.

It is noticeable that when Ānanda states that he will take upon himself the layman's vows, he does not have to ask what they are. Whereas there is a reference in the Jain canon to Mahāvīra preaching a sermon in which he tells the monks about the rules which they must follow, there is no corresponding sermon for laymen. This suggests that the rules in the *Uvāsaga-dasāo* form a stereotyped list, which has been inserted at a later date, possibly being taken from an early *upāsaka* text. Such texts date from the fifth century (which is the time of the closing of the Jain canon) and later, although Jaini (1979: 80) refers to a text of this category dating from the second century.

We might guess that at an earlier date the Jain rules for laymen were not so stereotyped. That was certainly the case for Buddhist laymen. The Pāli canon tells of the first two persons to become laymen, namely Tapussa and Bhalluka. They became laymen by the two-word formula, that is, they took refuge in the Buddha and the Dhamma, and asked the Buddha to take them as laymen (*Vinaya-piṭaka*, I, 4, 21 ff). By the time that Yasa's father asked to be taken as a layman, there was a Saṅgha (order of monks) in existence, so he was the first to be taken by the three-word formula, whereby he took refuge in the Buddha, the

Dhamma, and the Saṅgha (*Vinaya-piṭaka*, I, 16,35 ff). There is no mention of vows being taken, and even in the *Sigālovāda-suttanta* (*Dīgha-nikāya*, III, 180–93) which Childers called 'the whole duty of the Buddhist layman' (Rhys Davids 1921: 168), when the Buddha explained to Sigāla that the four vices to be avoided are the four points which form the content of the first four vows, Sigāla merely asks the Buddha to take him as a layman, and does not undertake the five vows (*pañca-sīla*). Clearly the practice which Gombrich mentions (1971: 65), whereby a layman takes the three refuges and the five precepts, had not yet come into existence. It is noteworthy that at an early date, as I. B. Horner points out (1951: ix), ordination into the Buddhist order was also by the three refuges, and only later did a more elaborate and formal method come into existence.

Jacobi long ago noted (1884: xxiii) that the Buddhists and Jains agree closely in four of their (first) five vows, although they are in a different order. He was of the opinion that the close resemblance between these two sets of rules was not because one had borrowed from the other, but because both had borrowed from the Brahmanical ascetics (*sannyāsins*), whose fifth rule was liberality. The other two religions had to have a different fifth rule, because as Jacobi remarked (1884: xxiv) liberality could not be enjoined upon wandering ascetics such as the Buddhists and Jains, who were themselves totally dependent upon the liberality of others. When the rules for monks were adapted for laymen, the Buddhists took the first five of the monks' ten rules, so that the Buddhist layman, like the monk, has to avoid intoxicating drink. The Jain layman has the same rules as the monk, but the fifth is interpreted differently.

'Renunciation' is a reasonable interpretation of the word *aparigraha* for a monk, who has no possessions at all, but it is not appropriate when used in connection with a layman. It is clear that if we are to take the account of Ānanda given in the *Uvāsaga-dasāo* at its face value, for him *aparigraha* did not mean 'renunciation', but 'limiting'. Jaini notes (1979: 177–8) that the texts accept this interpretation, and lists the ways in which the *aparigraha* vow could be circumvented by devious and subtle means whereby the limits could be exceeded, while seeming to be retained. Williams (1963: 98–9) deals with the same excesses.

Jaini also quotes the interpretation of *parigraha* as the delusion (*mūrcchā*) 'that this is mine' or 'I made this', which leads to the view that one can hold on for ever to what one now possesses (1979: 177). Williams too makes the same point (1963: 99). By this interpretation, the negative form *aparigraha* would mean not clinging to something, in the sense of not believing that it was one's permanent possession. The word *aparigraha* occurs in Pāli, and its usage there seems to support this Jain sense. The word is not common in the Pāli canon, but when it occurs it is in conjunction with the word *amama*, 'not regarding as mine'.

If I am correct in believing that the complexity of the rules which Ānanda adopts indicates a later extension to earlier rules for laymen, then it is possible that at one time one became a Jain layman simply by saying that one was so, just as a convert to Buddhism merely asked the Buddha to accept him as a layman. If this is so, then the most important part of Ānanda's statement was not his acceptance of the vows, but his promise to avoid other religions and support only the Jains. In origin the word *upāsaka* (layman) means one who sits at the feet of a teacher, someone who was attracted enough by the teacher's doctrine to want to listen to it, but not to take the vows of mendicancy. He was willing to give generously to mendicants, because this gained merit for him, and he might well have been willing to give to members of more than one religion. With growing competition for food between sects and religions, however, it became useful to have a donor restrict his giving to one group. So the term *upāsaka* came to mean one who was tied to a particular religion.

Both the Buddhists and the Jains correctly realised that no religious institution can survive without the laity being involved in an active way. If there is no laity, or if the laity renounce all their wealth, then the institution cannot survive. The essential concomitant of a begging wanderer is a non-wandering donor, whose generosity (*dāna*) enables the ascetic to live and gain release (*mokṣa*). Williams states (1963: xvi) that the lay estate was admitted by the Jina only in deference to human frailty, and this might be deduced from Ānanda's statement (§ 12) that he could not enter the monastic state. Similarly Gombrich (1971: 326) implies that the lay estate was instituted for those who could not make total renunciation, but this is to believe that both the Jina and the Buddha were so lacking in worldly wisdom that they could not see that if all laymen renounced the world and gave away their possessions, both Jainism and Buddhism would have found it difficult to survive, even at the 'primitive' level of the early non-property-owning religions. Without *dāna* there could be no ascetics, and therefore no transmission of the doctrines of Jainism and Buddhism. As for insisting on kings abandoning their kingdoms, this would have been tantamount to throwing away rich and powerful patrons, who might have been expected to protect them against the ever-present threat of Brahmanical revival.

As Williams points out (1963: xx), from implying merely the feeding of religious mendicants, the duty of *dāna* came to mean the provision of rich ecclesiatical endowments, and the *dāna-vrata* (1963: 149) became the single most important element in the practice of Jainism. The same development can be observed in Buddhism from a very early date. At the beginning of his reign Aśoka fed daily 60,000 brahmans. They were replaced by 60,000 Buddhists, and then Aśoka endowed *vihāras*, built *stūpas*, erected pillars, etc.

The importance of giving was emphasised by a whole genre of literature which came into being. Texts such as the Buddhist *Dasavatthuppakaraṇa* and the Jain *Dānāṣṭakakathā* were written to encourage the faithful to give generously by telling them of the rewards which had been gained by others who had been generous donors. Why should one be a donor? To gain merit, to amass good *karma*, to gain a better *gati* (state of rebirth) in one's next existence. For a layman, rebirth in a good *gati* is as important as destroying *karma* is for the ascetic. Each of the ten stories about laymen in the *Uvāsaga-dasāo* ends, as Strandberg reminds us (1981: 184), with a statement about the heaven in which he will be reborn as a god (*deva*) as a result of his meritorious deeds. The *dāna* literature is all part of the threats and promises which had to be employed in both Buddhism and Jainism to cajole the faithful (and not so faithful) into following good practices and avoiding bad. So there emerges a genre of 'rewards and punishments' literature: the *Vimānavatthu* and *Petavatthu* in Pāli, and the *Vivāga-sutta* in Prakrit. Williams (1963: 252) quotes the Jain author Vasunandin as expressly stating that the masses must be coerced by the fear of punishment and the hope of material reward rather than being led into a religious life by the ideal of *mokṣa*.

But there is more to it than this. We began this chapter without defining terms. What is a layman? We have mentioned the vows which a layman undertakes, but if someone is a Jain, and is not an ascetic, then he must be a layman, whether or not he has taken the layman's vows. Both Stevenson (1915: 187, 205) and Jaini (1979: 160) make it clear that a Jain layman only takes the layman's vows when he has progressed along the path of the *guṇasthānas* (they seem not to agree on whether it is the fourth or fifth *guṇasthāna* he must have reached). Having taken the vows, a layman would ideally progress along the stages of the ladder of the eleven *pratimās*, the stages of spiritual progress prescribed for a layman which Jaini lists (1979: 186), until he reached the ninth stage. In this 'stage of abandonment of acquisitiveness' (*parigrahatyāga-pratimā*) he would formally dispose of his property (Stevenson 1915: 223) and be ready to become a monk and gain enlightenment.

The partial vows and *pratimās*, while in theory set down for all laymen to observe, tend to constitute an ideal path followed only by a highly select few, and Jaini (1979: 188) notes that it is a rare individual who actually vows to accept the restraints or perform the holy activities which his religion calls upon him to do. Even the widespread practice of the *namaskāra* and the *mūla-guṇas* which Jaini lists (1979: 187) is due more to the weight of social convention than to that of spiritual obligations formally undertaken. For most Jains, the practice of the faith centres upon a diverse group of daily rituals and periodic ceremonies. Many of these may be equivalent in substance to aspects of the 'ideal' lay life, but they differ significantly in that there is no compulsion attached to them. Since he is not bound by any vow, the layman practises such activities as and when he wishes.

We may now return to the point where we started. We can see that when Reynell (1985b) expressed surprise that Jain laymen showed such ostentation despite the fact that renunciation is the expressed means to the end of enlightenment, this was to misunderstand the relationship between the mendicants' vows and those of laymen. As Williams comments (1963: 93), there is no correspondence between the fifth *mahāvrata* of the Jain mendicant and the fifth *aṇuvrata* of the layman, although both are called *aparigraha-vrata*. Since the whole structure of the begging community would be undermined if they were the same, the interpretation of the vow for laymen has, necessarily, to differ from that adopted for monks. That interpretation follows either the line of non-possession of attachment to possessions, or the idea of limitation of possessions, or a mixture of the two.

There is a further misunderstanding with regard to the aim of the

Jain layman. Reynell writes of the goal of enlightenment, but this applies only to the mendicant, although there is, of course, always the chance that a layman will progress through the *pratimās*, become more and more austere in his attitude to the world, and then undertake the vows of the monk and seek to gain enlightenment. Unless that happens, a layman's sights are set on a far lower target. As Jaini states (1979: 160), the layman's vows are a modified or weakened version of the real Jain vows. They may curb evil behaviour to some extent, but a layman's vows cannot bring him to liberation. Whether or not a layman undertakes the vows of a layman, he is hoping that the merit he acquires by giving generously to his religion will ensure that, by the working of *karma*, he will gain a better *gati* in his next existence, from which he may be able to gain enlightenment; or if not in the next existence, then the one after that, or the one after that.

Although Reynell states that donating should in theory be done in secret, it seems that this view is based solely upon the belief, held by the women whom she questioned, that public donation leads to attachment to the idea of donating itself. Men are not of the same opinion. There is no canonical injunction against giving openly, and the *dāna* type of literature is based upon the concept of giving openly as a means of encouraging others to be even more generous. It would appear that *dāna* is regarded not only as a means of acquiring merit which will lead to a better rebirth, for this will be gained whether the *dāna* is secret or open, but also as a way of emphasising the part which the individual is playing in the community, whereby the religious and economic standing of the community is strengthened. From this point of view, the more ostentatious the giving, the more community-minded the giver. It might also be suggested that the greater the ostentation of a layman's life, the greater the religious merit gained if he subsequently decides to renounce it.

As we might expect, Buddhism provides a parallel to the desire for a better rebirth. Gombrich (1971: 325–6) quotes the details about the Sinhalese layman recorded by Obeyesekere. That layman's aim, through the good *karma* he had acquired, was rebirth in heaven, where the charms of the female inhabitants appealed to him much more than the bliss of *nirvāṇa*. His view was not as uncanonical as might be thought. The Buddha himself stated (*Majjhima-nikāya*, I 142,3–8) that those who strove for the Dhamma would gain enlightenment, while those who had faith in and affection for him would be reborn in heaven. The same, second-best future also awaits those who love the Jain monks.

Probably in all religions there is, to some extent, a gulf between precept and practice. In the case of the Jain layman and his attitude to wealth, the gulf is perhaps not as great as it might appear.

5

# Women and the reproduction of the Jain community

Josephine Reynell

One of the more interesting differences between the two major sects of the Jains, the Svetambars and Digambars, lies in their attitude to women. Unlike the Digambars, who view women as spiritually inferior to men, the Svetambars avow that women are the spiritual equals of men. Whilst to the best of my knowledge scholars have not yet uncovered the reasons why the two sects should differ on this matter it seems that the Svetambar stance may have in part been influenced by a rather perspicacious and clear-sighted recognition of the importance of female support to a minority religious sect and the very crucial role that women play, not only in physically reproducing new Jain members, but also in the social reproduction of the community and its constituent institutions.

An examination of all the various ways in which the Jain community reproduces itself is beyond the scope of this chapter. Instead, I confine the discussion to ways in which women contribute to the reproductive process, a sphere in which, certainly in the Jain case, they play a particularly significant part.

Before looking at this question it is essential to consider the nature of the community which is reproduced. One of the major problems facing the investigator is that the Jains do not form a homogeneous entity but are broken up into a plethora of both secular and religious divisions. The first half of this chapter therefore investigates at what level of division the Jains can be said to form a community and in what way the various smaller sub-groups are linked within the community. From this basis I proceed to examine women and reproduction.

The hypotheses which follow draw on data collected during fieldwork in the city of Jaipur, Rajasthan. That this data was collected from a group of Jains living in a large urban centre is significant, for I suspect that the way in which the various Jain divisions (namely the *gacch*, sub-sects, sects, and castes) seem to constitute a community in Jaipur is closely influenced by, and indeed peculiar to, the urban environment: an environment which allows for linkages between the various secular and religious divisions in a way not possible in the rural areas where often the small towns and villages may only contain representatives from one sub-sect or caste.

Using the definitional framework laid out in the position paper by M. Carrithers and C. Humphrey (see chapter 1) I see the Jains as constituting two types of community. First, there is the Pan-Indian community incorporating all Jains where the members share an identity of themselves as Jains, an identity based on shared religious beliefs and practices rather than shared activity. Due to the sheer size of the community at this level interaction between members is obviously limited. Second, there is the local, small-scale community which is not only a community in terms of shared beliefs, practices, and identity, but also in terms of shared social and economic activity, and where the size of the community allows for a dense network of interactive ties between members. It is at this level that the community is most effective as a collectivity, both in terms of its own members and the circumambient society.

I suggest that what constitutes the active community may differ in degree between the small rural towns and villages and the larger urban concentrations such as Jaipur. I hope that data gathered from a variety of different areas will throw more light on whether this hypothesis is correct and, if so, on the nature of the difference between the rural and urban communities. Moreover, whilst I see economic interaction as a crucial factor linking the various groups within the community, I can only guess at the nature of this interaction as I have little data on this particular topic. Again I hope that those who have worked on Jain economic organisation will be able to add more detailed information to my general hypothesis.

## *The city of Jaipur and its Jain population*

In 1949 Jaipur was made the capital of the desert state of Rajasthan. Prior to this Rajasthan was divided into a number of states ruled over by local rulers or maharajas. Jaipur was the capital of Jaipur state and was founded in 1727 by Maharaja Jai Singh. As it lay on an important trade route between Agra and Pakistan it quickly attracted both Hindu and Jain merchants. In addition, the residence of government officials and the presence of the royal court made Jaipur an important consumer centre especially for luxury items. Thus Jaipur rapidly expanded, becoming an important centre for banking, the cloth trade, and gem cutting, particularly emeralds. In 1940 the first modern industries were established but on the whole industrialisation has remained limited in Jaipur.

By 1760 there was a large Jain community in Jaipur (Roy 1978: 56) and today it encompasses both the major Jain sects, the Digambars and the Svetambars. These two sects are further sub-divided into sub-sects. In addition to this the population is divided into endogamous caste groups which do not cross-cut sect divisions. Thus the Svetambars and the Digambars constitute discrete caste and sect groups.

In Jaipur the Digambar sect is dominant and its members are involved in both business and government administration. The Svetambar sect is the most prominent in the south and west of Rajasthan particularly in the towns of Jodhpur, Bikaner, and Udaipur. Nevertheless, the Svetambars also form a sizeable community in Jaipur. On the whole they dominate the jewellery business and a smaller proportion are involved in the cloth trade.

My fieldwork concentrated on the Murti Puja sub-sect of the Svetambar Jain sect and was confined to the orthodox group of Murti Pujas living within the old walled city of Jaipur. Their homes are clustered around a group of five Murti Puja temples in an area known as the Jauhri Bazaar or jewel market.

In the process of my work on this one sub-sect I gained an idea as to the links existing between this group and other Svetambar sub-sects, together with the links between the two major sects.

## *The Jains as a religious community*

On one level the Jains as a whole can be said to constitute a community in the religious sense in that, despite their division into a variety of sects and sub-sects, all Jains share a religious doctrine whose basic tenets do not differ greatly between the sects but which differs sufficiently from the encompassing Hindu religion to warrant being identified as separate.

Certainly many of the concepts found in Jain religious doctrine are also common to Hinduism, but significantly the Jains invest these concepts with their own particular emphasis and meaning, thereby creating a distinction between the two religious groups. A few examples suffice to illustrate this.

One such example concerns the concept of *ahiṃsā* or non-violence, a principle common to both the Hindu and Jain religions. The Jains, however, have placed particular emphasis on this principle, as they see it as another facet of worldly non-attachment, the central principle underlying their religious doctrine. In accordance with this it is believed that violence creates within the perpetrator intense emotions and passions towards worldly objects which serve to further attach the individual to this world. The significance accorded to *ahiṃsā* has repercussions on both religious and secular practice which are particular to the Jains. It has led, for example, to the peculiarly Jain concern with insects and microscopic life forms. So as not to harm these creatures Jains use strained water and many Jains will not eat after sunset, for it is believed that otherwise small insects will be attracted into the house by the artificial light and may either fall into the food and be eaten or else killed in the cooking flames. Similarly, during religious ceremonies the laity wear masks over their mouths to prevent the hot air of the breath harming creatures in the surrounding atmosphere. In the Svetambar Terapanthi and Sthanakavasi sub-sects the Jain ascetics wear these masks all the time – a feature which strikingly distinguishes them as Jain.

So Jains differ from Hindus in terms of their particular beliefs and practices. They have their own temples, preaching halls, and meditation halls which are separate from those of the Hindus and, apart from certain famous pilgrimage sites (see Humphrey, chapter 13), are specifically for Jain use. The Jain religious practices which take place in these halls and temples are highly organised, drawing the Jains together at regular intervals. So in terms of actual worship the Jains are spatially separated from the Hindus. Consequently, the Jains see themselves as a religious group distinct from the Hindus and this self-perception and sense of Jain identity are of crucial significance in establishing the Jains as a distinct religious community.

Indeed, not only do the Jains see themselves as distinct from the Hindus, but, according to my respondents, they see themselves as superior to the Hindus in terms of purity, explaining that the emphasis on non-violence in their religion makes them particularly meticulous with regard to food habits and cleanliness. The greater spiritual purity of the Jains was often emphasised by my respondents, who characterised Jains in terms of *tyag*, or sacrifice of worldly pleasures, as opposed to the Hindus, whom they characterised in terms of *bhog*, or pleasure and therefore, worldly attachment.

We can say, therefore, that the Jains at this very broad level form a community in the sense of sharing a common identity based on shared religious beliefs and practices which differ significantly from the Hindu. They do not, however, constitute an active community in the sense of a group within which there is a high degree of religious, social, and economic interaction between members. The two main Jain sects are linked by certain social and economic ties, but these ties are loose and, at best, localised, so that one cannot categorise the wide religious community of those who adhere to the Jain religion as a tightly integrated and effective social and economic unit.

In Jaipur it is at the level of the local sect that one finds a group of Jains more tightly integrated in terms of religious, social, and economic activities and, as far as the urban context is concerned, it is at this level of division that I designate the Jains to be an active religious, social, and economic community. Of course, the local sect community itself is not homogeneous but is divided into smaller religious and caste groupings. In the urban context these groups combine to function as larger groups in certain situations, and in other situations function separately as smaller groups. In Jaipur, therefore, the local sect community is made up of a series of small groups linked by cross-cutting social, economic, and religious ties. In terms of social reproduction women play a role at all the constituent and various levels.

## *The divisions which constitute the Jaipur Svetambar community*

The Svetambar sect is divided into two basic categories: the religious and the non-religious.

The sect itself is sub-divided into the sub-sects of the Murti Pujas, the Sthanakavasis, the Terapanthis, and the Naya Terapanthis. The Svetambar Murti Pujas are further sub-divided into groups called *gacch*. Each *gacch* possesses its own religious buildings and is headed by its own ascetic community. It appears that the *gacch* originated as a result of rivalries between different ascetic leaders. The two Murti Puja *gacch* in Jaipur are the Tapagacch and the Kharataragacch.

Caste constitutes the most important non-religious division. Whilst Jain doctrine denies the existence of caste the Jains are in fact divided into caste groups. In Jaipur the majority of the Svetambar Jains belong to the Oswal and Srimal castes, and I write of them unless otherwise noted. There are a few representatives from two other castes, the Porwals and the Paliwals, but in general these two castes are more numerous in the south and west of Rajasthan respectively. The castes are ranked in terms of status with the Oswals and Srimals at the top and the Porwals and Paliwals at the bottom (from the first two groups points of view). The castes are further sub-divided into sub-castes, the higher status sub-caste called *bisa* (meaning twenty) and the lower status sub-caste called *dasa* (meaning ten). At the lowest level the sub-castes are divided into *gotra* or lineage groups.

For the sake of clarity I shall first explain the economic and social significance of caste, as in Jaipur the various religious groups and sub-groups within the sect are united through intra- and inter-caste marriages. Against this background it is easier to see how the various religious categories form sub-groups within the caste group.

Amongst the Jaipur Svetambars, while caste endogamy seems to be the most common pattern of marriage, intermarriage between the two major castes is quite frequent, with girls being given in both directions, indicating an equality of status between the two. However, the Srimals claim that they were originally higher in status than the Oswals and that prior to the 1950s would only take girls from the Oswals but would not give girls, in accordance with the North Indian hypergamous rule that wife-givers are inferior to wife-receivers. Subsequently, they claim, the small size of their caste has led to a flexibility in the marriage rules. Conversely, the Oswals, who are by far the largest Svetambar caste group in Jaipur, claim that it is they who used to hold highest status.

For both these castes intermarriage with other Jain castes or with non-Jain castes receives strong disapproval. As far as sub-caste is concerned virtually all of my respondents were Srimal or Oswal *bisas* and seemed to have married with other *bisas*. It is worth noting though that within the urban context of Jaipur people did seem less concerned with the sub-caste divisions of *bisa* and *dasa* than in the villages or small rural towns where such divisions are as important as the major caste divisions (see e.g. Banks 1985: chapters 3 and 5, on Jain sub-caste divisions in a small town in Gujarat). To illustrate my point, in Jaipur one wealthy *dasa* family had taken a *bisa* girl in marriage and people explained that this was acceptable, as sub-caste divisions are no longer important. Another example concerned the marriage of a rural *dasa* girl from south Rajasthan into a *bisa* family who had not even enquired about sub-caste status prior to the marriage. Admittedly these are isolated examples but they are indicative of a change of emphasis in the importance of sub-caste in the urban areas.

While many Jain castes are exclusive solely to the Jains, some contain both Hindus and Jains. The Oswals are one such caste, made up of Svetambar Jains and Vaisnava Hindus. In Jaipur, marriages between Jain and Hindu Oswals were rare, indicating a clear preference for marriage within the same religious group. However, there were a few cases where Oswal Jain men had married Oswal Vaisnava women and this was considered acceptable for several reasons. First, as the Jains consider themselves to be of higher status than Hindus, the practice of Jain men taking Hindu women conforms with their hypergamous marriage rules.[1] Secondly, the woman is expected to convert to her husband's religion and thus the Jains do not actually lose a member of their group through the marriage. Thirdly, as Vaisnavas tend to be vegetarian they are considered by the Jains to be reasonably similar in terms of customs and practices. Lastly, and probably more significantly, many of the Vaisnava Hindus, like the Jains, also belong to trading groups in Rajasthan, so marriages with Vaisnava women serve to give the Jains an entry into a parallel business resource group.

[1] The two exceptions I found to this pattern were where Jain women had married Vaisnava men. Both these cases concerned very poor families. What seems to have occurred is that poverty made finding suitable Jain spouses for these women difficult as the number of poor Jain families are few, certainly in Jaipur. Secondly, poverty brings low status within the wealthy Jain business community, so poor families are less concerned with status considerations in marriage. Hence, the hypogamous situation of Jain women being married to Vaisnava men.

As far as the *gotras* are concerned, the Jains follow the four-*gotra* rule whereby marriage is forbidden with individuals from a person's father's, mother's, father's mother's and mother's mother's *gotras*, thus precluding marriages with close relatives and increasing the internal cohesion of the community as a whole. The *gotras* themselves do not appear to be ranked and there is no custom, certainly in Jaipur, to marry with only certain *gotras* and not others.

Within the parameters set by caste and *gotra* it is considered essential to marry one's son or daughter into a family of suitable wealth and status. Although marriages are set within a hypergamous idiom it is common in practice for marriages to take place between a couple from families of equal wealth or status or else for the girl to marry a boy from a family of slightly higher wealth and status. This latter type of marriage is important as a means of reaffirming and building upon a newly acquired level of wealth and status in the bride's family. Marriages between the offspring of families of vastly different social and economic standing are not encouraged. While marriages take place within a hypergamous idiom they have not led to the emergence of strongly defined groups who are recognised as collectively superior to other groups and therefore unable to give women to these groups. Finally, a significant practice in that it contributes to the internal cohesion of the Jaipur community is that many Jain families marry their children into other families within Jaipur rather than outside. This makes for an even denser network of internal ties within the community and is a practice in contrast to that of rural areas, where daughters are married into families outside their natal town or village.

In terms of caste-based religious organisation the de-emphasis on caste boundaries is also apparent. Amongst the Murti Puja Jains in Jaipur the Oswals and Srimals own separate temples, *upasrays*, and preaching-halls which are managed by separate caste-based committees. Nowadays, however, the two castes rarely worship separately. Oswals and Srimals will visit each other's temples, and for religious ceremonies and preachings the Srimals join the Oswals in the Oswal preaching hall and worship together. This is in part due to the urban situation and in part encouraged by the apparent lack of Srimal ascetics. During the *caturmās* periods of 1982, 1983, and 1984 only Oswal ascetics visited Jaipur. The only occasion on which caste divisions became obvious was during Paryusan, when separate preaching sessions would be held for the two castes. As only Oswal ascetics were present they would preach to the Oswals in the morning and to the Srimals in the afternoon. Families with links to both castes would often attend both ceremonies.

Although my data on economic organisation is limited, it appears that the two castes also form one economic group; amongst the jewellers, for example, both Oswals and Srimals cooperated. In addition, through intermarriage dowry wealth is exchanged between the two castes and the affinal links thus established develop into economic links in the next generation, down which business information, support, and credit can flow.

It is likely that in Jaipur the two castes constitute not only one social group but also one economic group, or, to use Timberg's phrase, a business 'resource group' (Timberg 1978: 15), a group which has begun to override caste boundaries and which, as I show in the following section, is bounded along religious lines.

## *Sect*

The doctrinal differences between the two major sects are surprisingly few despite the fact that the Digambars refuse to accept the Svetambar canonical literature. However, each sect has its own religious buildings and ascetic leaders and often the festivals of the two sects differ – in cases where they share the same festival the dates on which the festival falls differs slightly between the two sects. The religious division between the sects is most graphically expressed in the acrimonious and frequently publicised disputes as to which of them own certain important pilgrimage sites.

The two sects are also distinct social entities in that they are made up of separate caste groups, intermarriage between which is strongly disapproved, certainly in Jaipur. Consequently, members of the two sects rarely meet either for religious occasions or for social ceremonies.

However, it appears that in Jaipur the sects are not totally separate economically. Whilst each sect in Jaipur appears to constitute a distinct economic resource group, helping its own members, business links do exist between the Svetambar and Digambar jewellers, for example. This was revealed by one of the few Svetambar families belonging to the Paliwal caste. This particular family had been involved in a long dispute with the Digambars over the ownership of the pilgrimage place, Mahāvīr-ji (see chapter 13). Whilst it is now owned by Digambars the Paliwal family claimed that it was originally a Svetambar site which the Digambars had stolen, overcoming Svetambar opposition by giving economic aid to Paliwal traders who, it seemed, were rather impoverished. The family was bitterly reproachful of the wealthy Svetambar Oswals and Srimals for not supporting them in their dispute with the Digambars, claiming that the Svetambars refused to help because they did not want to damage their business connections with the Digambar community.

Despite these links, undoubtedly the greatest degree of economic co-operation remains within the sects. As noted above, among the Svetambars the two main castes of the Oswals and Srimals appear, nowadays, to be forming one social and economic group; we have also seen that caste divisions do not overlap sect divisions. So we see how the sect, in forming a boundary around the two caste groups, can also be seen as the boundary around the economic resource group. Thus the religious division of sect is, at the same time, significant in economic and social terms.

## *Sub-sects*

The religious divisions between the sub-sects have not led to social and economic divisions, or if they have at any time, then in Jaipur such divisions are overcome. As far as marriage is concerned, whilst there is a preference for sub-sect endogamy, marriages across the sub-sects are acceptable in Jaipur if a better match can be found outside the sub-sect than inside. In Jaipur, marriages between Sthanakavasis and Murti Pujas seemed to be relatively frequent. In cases of cross-sub-sect marriage the wife is expected to convert to the husband's sect. It appears that in the rural towns and villages marriage between the sub-sects is rare and not approved, so this is one instance where the rural and urban situations differ.

The *gacch* form the smallest division within the sect. My data here refer solely to the two *gacch* within the Murti Puja sub-sect. It is within the *gacch* that the level of religious co-operation and activity is greatest. Each *gacch* owns its own temples, *upasrays* and preaching halls and administers its own funds and property. The *gacch* are headed by their own ascetics who give daily preachings during *caturmās* (the four months of the monsoon period when, due to the abundance of insect and plant life, the ascetics are forbidden to travel but must remain in one place).

So it is within the *gacch* that people gather to hear preachings and attend ceremonies and it is the *gacch* that organises group pilgrimages for its members. On the frequent occasions when women perform group fasts together for a day or more it is with fellow *gacch* members that they perform the fast and it is the *gacch* which provides the meal by which the fast is broken at the end. It is to ascetics within their *gacch* that people show the most loyalty and the initiation ceremonies for the ascetics are organised on a *gacch* basis. Clearly, the *gacch* is the most important unit for religious activity, whilst the sub-sect and the sect are the units of shared beliefs and doctrines.

Because religious ceremonies and events are occasions when people meet, the *gacch* is an important group in terms of social interaction; in terms of marriage it is less significant, as marriages across the *gacch* boundaries are almost as common as marriages within the *gacch*, certainly in Jaipur.

As mentioned earlier, my lack of detailed information on Jain economic organisation allows me only to make suggestions, it seems that in economic terms the *gacch* is significant as a small resource group for its members. In order to see why, we need to look more closely at the Jain institution of *dān*, or donating.

Donating is a key Jain religious institution and in particular is practised on a large scale by the men, due to male control of economic resources within the family. In theory, donating should be performed in secret to prevent attachment to the act of donating itself. It is, in fact, a very public event. Decisions as to when funds are needed are made by the *gacch* committee. Donations are then requested at a special religious ceremony or after the Sunday preachings, when large numbers of both men and women are gathered. The preaching hall at such times resembles an English auction room, with two members of the committee standing at the front of the hall before microphones, encouraging people to bid increasingly larger amounts of money, often running into thousands of rupees. In this way huge sums can be collected and will either be put towards a specific cause, such as the building of a temple or *dharmsala*, or the cost of a pilgrimage or particular celebration; or it will be kept in the general fund to be used as and when it is needed. Those who donate have their names noted in a register; if the money is for a particular cause they will be publicly commemorated in some way. Donors' names can be found on the paving stones of temple floors or on a plaque outside religious buildings, and even the big metal donating boxes in the temples have the names of those who gave the boxes painted on them. One of the most spectacular occasions for donating takes place on the last day of Paryusan when the birthday of Māhavīr is celebrated. Silver symbols of the fourteen dreams of Māhavīr's mother are brought out and men bid several thousand rupees for the honour of garlanding a dream and being blessed by the ascetics under the gaze of the whole *gacch*, whose members gather for this event as one of the most important in the Jain religious calendar.

While the act of donating has a clearly religious rationale, and while the survival of the Jain religious infrastructure depends on the generosity of wealthy donors, *dān* clearly has a non-religious and economic aspect to it.

First, in terms of the individual businessman, the act of public donating serves to display his excess wealth and exhibits to other businessmen within his *gacch* his credit-worthiness. As Bayly points out in his detailed study of the Jain and Vaisnava merchant communities in India, credit-worthiness is vital for the survival of the businessman in such groups, without which he cannot trade or call upon the help of other businessmen (1983: 375). In this way the *gacch* constitutes a source of economic information used by businessmen belonging to it in later economic transactions.

Secondly, it is probable that the *gacch* forms a small economic resource group in that its businessmen would help out each other with loans and credit before they would help Jains from other *gacch* and sub-sects. Indeed, the *gacch* committees are headed by the wealthiest businessmen within the *gacch*. The *gacch* therefore could constitute a business resource group which at one level rivals similar groups. At another level of economic action the *gacch* groups possibly combine as members of the Murti Puja sub-sect against economic groups formed by other Svetambar sub-sects. Similarly, at another level the Svetambar sub-sects possibly combine as an economic group against, for example, the Digambars or the Vaisnava merchants.

Finally, it is possible that the large amount of money collected through public donations may, before it is used for religious purposes, form a pool of ready cash which can be loaned out to *gacch* members for business purposes and later repaid into the religious fund. This is only a supposition for which I have no evidence.

### *The community in Jaipur*

So, to sum up, the sect is the active social, economic, and religious community, in that within Jaipur the sect forms the boundary around the two main castes, within and between which marriage takes place. The affinal networks formed as a result constitute important lines of communication within the economic resource group. The sect is also sub-divided into decreasingly smaller religious units, the sub-sects and the *gacch*. Whilst these units are linked by common ties of marriage and economic transactions, each group in itself constitutes a dense network of religious, economic, and affinal links, with the density of internal co-operation and activity increasing as the sub-divisions get smaller. In fact it is possible that the various levels of division within the sect correspond to different levels of economic transactions and interaction.

It is likely that what seems to constitute the active Jain community in Jaipur may differ from what constitutes the active social and economic Jain community in the rural areas of Rajasthan. In Jaipur, criteria of wealth and status are of increasing importance in marriage arrangements as compared to criteria of sub-sect and, to a lesser extent, sub-caste and caste. Consequently, in Jaipur the castes, sub-castes, and sub-sects are linked by affinal and economic ties to form one community.

In the rural areas the dividing lines between sub-sect, caste, and sub-caste assume far greater importance as barriers to intermarriage; furthermore, in any one village or small town only one caste, sub-sect, or *gacch* may be represented. Unfortunately, lack of data prevents me from suggesting what affinal and economic links exist between the various divisions within any one rural locality and thus what actually constitutes the social and economic community in such areas.

*Women and the social reproduction of the Jain community*

The division of labour between men and women within the orthodox Svetambar community in the old city of Jaipur is clear-cut. Women are strictly confined to the domestic domain. Tremendous importance is attached to female chastity both before and after marriage and thus *parda* (purdah) norms restrict women's movement outside the home. Female employment within this group is not approved except for the women from the few poor Jain families for whom work is an economic necessity. Women are, therefore, economically dependent on men and have only a limited influence on the use of family economic resources.

A very marked characteristic of Jain women is that they are far more involved in overt religious activities and practices than the menfolk. As this is significant in terms of social reproduction it is worth considering in some detail the difference between male and female religiosity.

A woman's day begins between 4.0 and 5.0 am. Her first duty after bathing is to tend the household shrine. After this she sits before the shrine for 48 minutes and practices *samayik*, a form of contemplation which is regarded as an important means of encouraging worldly detachment. Once this is completed some women will take a set of vows called *cauda niyam*, or fourteen principles, which set a limit on the quantity of food, drink, clothing, household utensils, items of furniture, and means of transport used within the day. Another vow which most of the women take enjoins them not to eat or drink until 48 minutes after sunrise. It is believed that the sun's rays kill micro-organisms, so this vow controls the unwitting violence that a person might commit.

All women visit the temple daily, after which, if it is during *caturmās*, they attend the daily preachings given by the monks or nuns. During the rest of the year they attend preachings whenever the ascetics happen to pass through Jaipur. In the evening a small percentage of women perform *pratikraman*, a formalised confession of sins. Otherwise women perform this on their frequent fasting days and during Paryusan.

In a sense the daily preparation of food is also a religious act in that this, plus the actual food eaten, is governed by the religious injunction of *ahiṃsā*. This applies not only to meat and eggs but also to

2 Jain laywoman consults with a female ascetic from the Svetambar Kharataragacch. Photo: J. Laidlaw

vegetables.[2] Within the root vegetable category onions and garlic are strictly taboo and few women cook them. Other roots such as potato, carrots, and radishes are more widely eaten, although 50 per cent of my respondents had taken a vow not to eat them. Other women usually abstain from these during the four months of *caturmās*. Women also abstain from green vegetables and fruit on the eighth and fourteenth days of the lunar month which are regarded as auspicious. I

[2] There are a variety of interpretations as to why the consumption of root vegetables causes violence. My respondents explained that when the roots are pulled out of the ground the surrounding earth organisms are killed. Jaini (1979: 168) gives another explanation, namely that single-sensed creatures are believed to inhabit the tissues of certain plants, especially those of a 'sweet, fleshy, seed filled nature', and this explains the injunctions concerning the eating of roots and fruits.

With regard to green vegetables, my respondents informed me that as tiny insects shelter in the leaves the consumption of such vegetables incurs the risk of violence.

3 Svetambar Jain female ascetics of the Kharataragacch setting out on begging round, carrying bowls for food. Jaipur, Rajasthan 1987. Photo: J. Laidlaw

explained earlier how the injunction of *ahiṃsā* also affects the times when meals are taken in the evening. Three-quarters of my female respondents were careful to eat before sunset and the remainder followed this rule during *caturmās*.

Apart from these daily activities other religious duties exist, among which fasting is one of the most important. Fasts are a type of austerity and austerities are considered crucial to Jain religious practice in that they are meant to develop the quality of worldly detachment. The Jains have developed a huge variety of complex fasts, some of which can take years to complete. The women usually fast on at least two out of the five auspicious days in a lunar fortnight and for a minimum of three days during the eight-day festival of Paryusan. During the year they perform, in addition, several longer fasts. For example, in Jaipur many of the women perform the fast of *Naupad Oli* which lasts for nine days, during which time the women may eat once a day. It is performed twice a year for four and a half years in succession. They also perform the fast of *Aksaynidhi* which lasts for fifteen days and is performed once a year for four years in succession. Another popular fast is *Bis Sthanak Oli* whereby the individual must perform twenty individual days of fasting within a maximum period of six months. Each set of twenty fasts equals one unit and twenty such units must be completed. There are many more fasts, but these give an idea of their length and variety. As far as these longer fasts are concerned, the women often perform them together and will gather as a group in the *gacch upasray* to perform the lengthy prayers, hymns, and rituals connected with the fast.

Other religious activities include public *pūjās* which women attend in large numbers. They also join in several pilgrimages a year organised by the *gacch.*

By contrast to the women, the men are considerably less involved in religious activities. The most regular male activity consists of going to the temple daily. Few men attend the daily preachings during *caturmās* and in the Jaipur Kharataragacch Upasray there were usually 10 men to 200 women for week-day preachings, although men did attend in larger numbers on Sundays. Unless held on a Sunday, or during a ceremonial period, few men attend *pūjās.* Few practise *Samayik* and most men reserve *Pratikraman* to the last day of Paryusan when a special *Pratikraman* is performed to repent of the whole year's sins. Men follow the food taboos less strictly than the women and most of them tend to eat after sunset except during Paryusan. Fasting is also confined to the last day of Paryusan. The only religious activity where male participation is greater than women's is in the sphere of donating.

## *Women's role in the reproduction of the gacch*

In a sense the strength of the sect as a community rests initially with the unity and vitality of its smallest constituent part, namely the *gacch*, and thus I wish to begin my discussion of women's role in the reproduction of the Jain community at this level.

First, the maintenance of the *gacch* on a daily basis through time as a

,igious and social group is achieved by means of female religious ,ractice. By the regular attendance of women at the preachings, the *pūjās* and the *gacch* pilgrimages and their continuous performance of group fasts and the associated fasting rituals which are performed within the *gacch upasrays*, the *gacch* is maintained as an active religious entity. Moreover, as certain religious practices differ between the *gacch*, as, for example, the timing of auspicious days and their associated fasts, the women, in their observance of the auspicious day fasts, maintain the differences between the two *gacch* in Jaipur.

On a wider level, of course, the regular involvement of women in religious practice contributes to the maintenance and continuance of the religious traditions and practices upon which Jain identity partly depends. Significantly, as well as being actively involved, many of the Jaipur women take a delight in religious study and spend large amounts of time delving into religious literature from the temple libraries. Consequently, my experience revealed that the lay women often have a far deeper knowledge of the religion than the men.

To return to the *gacch*, however, not only do the women's religious observances maintain the *gacch* as a religious entity, but also they confirm the *gacch* as a social group in that the various religious gatherings, such as fasts and preachings, enable women to meet both relatives and non-relatives to exchange news. For example, after the daily preachings women gather in small groups to chat before going home. The fasting rituals also provide good meeting-places. In Jaipur women gathered in the *upasray* to perform the *Naupad* and *Aksay-nidhi* fasting rituals together. Invariably, they gathered half an hour before a nun appeared to lead the rituals, and they spent this time gossiping with one another. The large *pūjās* provide another occasion to gather, and often the decibel level of the music faces strong competition from the chattering voices of female devotees. Such religious occasions are particularly important for women, as *parda* restricts the frequency with which they can visit other women.

During these religious gatherings women are able to gather news about families within the *gacch* group. Of particular importance is the information which they may use later in marriage strategies. While men are actually responsible for initiating and conducting marriage negotiations, women exert considerable influence upon the husband in suggesting suitable spouses. It is the religious gatherings within the *gacch* which provide women with the necessary information. First, they are able to find out which potential spouses are available within their own *gacch*. Religious gatherings provide women with more frequent contact with the *gacch* as a group than the men gain through their more dispersed business contacts, hence the women play a vital role in reproducing the *gacch* through the information they pass on to their husbands. Should no suitable spouses be available within the *gacch*, then information about potential spouses may be gained from women with relatives in other *gacch* and sub-sects.

## *Women and socialisation*

Not surprisingly, women play a crucial role in the socialisation of the next generation of Jains. Due to their domestic-oriented role it is regarded as the mother's duty to instil into the children a sense of religious awareness which, in Jain eyes, is believed to increase moral awareness. Children are brought along to the temple at the age of five by their mothers and are taught the names of the twenty-four Tīrthaṅkars (the enlightened prophets who according to Jain belief have propogated Jain doctrine through the ages), together with the *namaskar mantra*, an avowal of faith in Jain doctrine. They are also told religious stories. From puberty girls begin to learn the more complex recitations which accompany *Samayik* and *Pratikraman* and begin to fast once a year. Through their mothers example they learn the religious role which they are expected gradually to adopt after marriage. In this way both the religious traditions together with the *gacch* as a religious unit are maintained through time by virtue of successive generations of dutiful, religious women.

Equally important is the effect which the religiously active woman has upon her sons. Boys are taught fewer actual rituals than the girls, but their mothers instil into them a pride in their religion and a strong sense of Jain identity by bringing them along to religious ceremonies and events. As they grow older and begin to help their fathers in the family business they learn that the religious world of their mother is in fact closely entwined with the business world of their father. The sense of Jain identity which they initially owe to their mother is significant economically because the very wealth and success of the Jain religious group as a business group appears to be predicated on the retention of wealth and resources within the religious group. At the very least, the Jain identity instilled into the men during childhood by their mothers contributes to the maintenance of these religious–business boundaries.

### *The role of the nuns in the reproduction of the gacch*

Although removed from physical reproduction, the female ascetics play an equally important role in the social reproduction of the *gacch*. The Svetambar Jains have both male and female ascetics who, as symbols of the Jain renunciatory ideal, are highly respected amongst the laity over whom they wield considerable influence. Amongst the Svetambars the female ascetics are considered to be spiritually equal to the monks, but in terms of temporal power they are subordinate. For example, the head of the nuns in a *gacch* (the *pravartanī*) must submit the travelling arrangements which she makes for the nuns to the *ācaryā*, the head monk of the *gacch*. Moreover, it is the *acāryā* who performs the final initiation ceremony for the nuns rather than the *pravartanī*. If both monks and nuns of a particular *gacch* are in the same town or village then usually it is the monks who preach rather than the nuns.

However, this difference in temporal power is frequently overcome by the very fact that there are far more nuns than monks within the *gacch*. This tendency seems to have been prevalent throughout Jain history. For example, the *Kalpa Sutra* quotes figures of the number of monks and nuns supposedly present under each Tīrthaṅkar and invariably the numbers of women far outweigh the numbers of men.[3] The practical consequences of this numerical disparity is that nuns wield the same degree of authority and power over the laity as monks, precisely because at any one time in any one area there may be no

[3] The *Kalpa Sutra* gives the following figures concerning the number of male and female ascetics under various Tīrthaṅkars:

under Rsabh (1st) 84,000 monks and 300,000 nuns
under Neminath (22nd) 18,000 monks and 40,000 nuns
under Parsvanath (23rd) 16,000 monks and 38,000 nuns
under Mahavir (24th) 14,000 monks and 36,000 nuns.

The references are taken from H. Jacobi's translation of the *Kalpa Sutra* (1884: 267, 274, 278, 284).

monks present to impinge on their authority. For example, only nuns visited the Jaipur Kharataragacch for the *caturmās* of 1983 and 1984. Not only did they preach daily to the laity but each Sunday they organised various religious ceremonies and celebrations. As the men tend not to work on Sundays, and because the ascetics wield tremendous authority over the laity, these religious events were heavily attended. So by virtue of organising such regular religious activities the nuns served to draw the members of the *gacch* together as a religious and social group, reinforcing *gacch* identity and solidarity and maintaining or reawakening in the devotees a sense of religious pride and fervour.

Also significant was the fact that the Sunday activities served as occasions for the men to donate publicly. Indeed, nuns were often instrumental in encouraging men to be generous with their bounty on such occasions and thus supported the economic aspect of the *gacch*.

Through their religious study and scholarship the nuns also play a vital role, together with the monks, in maintaining and transmitting Jain religious knowledge. Not all the nuns I came across were assiduous scholars, but those who had the ability and interest were given tuition, by both ascetic and lay teachers, in Sanskrit and Prakrit, so they could have access to the sacred literature. Several of the older nuns not only study but write books and pamphlets themselves, thus contributing to the already vast corpus of Jain literature.

On a more mundane level the nuns share with the lay women the task of educating young girls, and during *caturmās* they usually hold classes to teach the girls the *Samayik* and *Pratikraman* recitations.

## *The reproduction of the community through marriage*

At the level of the sub-sect and sect, women play a crucial, if passive, role in the reproduction of the wider community through the marriage system. To ensure the most advantageous match in terms of economic and status considerations it is essential to carefully guard a daughter's chastity. Through the arrangement of marriages between families of different *gacch* within the sub-sect and with different sub-sects within the sect, women constitute links between the various internal divisions of the wider sect. These affinal links form the basis not only for social ties and interaction between the different families but also for economic networks down which information and credit can flow. So, through the marriage of women, constituent groups within the sect are united, reinforcing existing links in the process or establishing new links. Consequently, female sexuality is strictly controlled to ensure that such links are not endangered by a careless liaison.

The careful arrangement of female marriages not only serves to unite the sect but also serves to conserve and retain economic resources within the sect as women are the channels through which tremendous wealth in the form of the dowry flows between families. As I said earlier, the very success of the sect as a business group is dependent on the fact that business transactions, support, and wealth are largely confined to the religious community which is at the same time the business resource group. Timberg shows in his study of the Marwari businessmen how essential this tight organisation is; he saw Marwari commerical success as due to the 'advantages which the Marwaris enjoyed as a community (or if you will a 'resource group') organised for commercial activity' (1978: 15). To retain both the integrity and wealth of the Jain community the marriages of women must therefore be controlled and arranged with due consideration to religious–caste–business boundaries.

Female marriages with non-Jains threaten to weaken both the boundaries and internal networks of the community and, therefore, threaten its success as a business group. Such marriages would lead to dowry wealth flowing out of the community which in turn would lessen the capital resources of the community as a whole. Similarly, while marriages within the religious group reinforce and maintain networks of economic communication, marriages outside the group would weaken and disperse these lines of communication, reducing the effectiveness of the Jains as a powerful business community.

In the same way one can see the control of female sexuality after marriage as a means of controlling and consolidating productive resources within the individual family, upon which the strength of the total community ultimately depends. As the woman gives birth to the next generation of inheritors it is seen as important to guard against the possibility of extra-marital affairs and the progeny of mixed parentage laying claim to the family's wealth.

In order to ensure female chastity upon which the survival and reproduction of the Jains as an effective business group is seen to depend, *parda* restrictions are enforced which constrain a woman's movement both before and after marriage.

Significantly, the religious system supports these *parda* norms and is therefore implicated in the reproduction of the community through the control of female sexuality. Female religiosity is encouraged as it is believed to be a means of ensuring a woman's sexual purity. This use of religion derives from the particular tenets peculiar to Jainism which stress above all the values of renunciation and the quiescent effect that religious activity is believed to have on the emotions. The copious 'religious story' literature, quoted in sermons given by the ascetics and avidly read by the women in their spare time, support and encourage this notion. These stories abound with religious heroines who are tempted to renounce their chastity but who withstand such temptation because of their piety, which has both quietened their inner passions and endowed them with a moral awareness as to what is right and wrong action for a woman.

The crucial point is that not only is sexual promiscuity seen to endanger the boundaries of the religious–business community, but that without sexual purity a girl cannot be married advantageously within the community. Moreover, the impaired reputation of one daughter in the family affects the marriage chances of all the daughters. As so much depends on a girl's reputation it is essential for her not only to be pure but to prove her purity publicly. As spiritual purity is equated in the literature and in Jain belief with sexual purity, women use public religious activity as a means of demonstrating their honour.

Indeed, the importance of religion as a symbol of female morality was demonstrated in Jaipur during the *caturmās* of 1983 in a case concerning two unmarried girls. One was twenty-three and the other twenty-nine, both of an age where to be unmarried leaves a girl vulnerable to local gossip and speculation regarding her morals. While neither of them indulged in regular religious activities, their mothers were adamant that for the duration of *caturmās* they should attend the daily preachings so as to be seen in public at religious gatherings and thereby maintain their moral reputations within the community.

Apart from being seen at large ceremonial gatherings and going daily to the temple, unmarried girls are not usually expected to be involved in religious activities to the same extent as their mothers. In fact it is the mother's duty to demonstrate not only her own moral purity but that of her daughters through her religious activity. The underlying logic is that if the mother is morally strong she will ensure that her daughters follow her example.

That religious activity signifies inner purity and honour is testified by its public nature. Particularly important are the longer fasts which all married women perform at some time. The end of the fast is invariably marked by some public celebration, either a feast or by an individual woman donating gifts to the temple and to the women who fasted with her. The most spectacular celebrations occur after *maskaman*, a fast when a woman eats nothing for thirty-one days. After such a fast the woman is dressed in her finest jewellery and sari, and taken through the streets of the old city of Jaipur in a horse-drawn chariot. She is publicly blessed by the ascetics and then taken to visit and make offerings at all five Murti Puja temples in the old city. Members of the woman's *gacch*, together with her natal and affinal relatives, join the procession and publicly garland her in recognition of her piety and spirituality. The husband will provide a huge feast for all the relatives and copious photographs are taken of the woman. The photographs are later mounted in a 'fasting album' which is shown proudly to visitors along with the wedding album. In a sense the fasting album forms a continuum with the wedding album, as at marriage a woman is given as *kanya dan* or the gift of a virgin to her new family. The fasting album shows that the woman has maintained her sexual honour after marriage and thus has also maintained and guarded the honour of her unmarried daughters. By these means she is recognised as helping to maintain the boundaries of the religious and economic community.

As well as the mother, the older women and grandmothers play a particularly important role in guarding and controlling the behaviour of the younger married and unmarried women and therefore contribute to the social and physical reproduction of the community. Past menopause, with their sexuality no longer suspect, they are free to come and go as they please, a freedom facilitated by the presence of daughters-in-law who undertake the household chores. These women keep a close watch on the behaviour of younger women and through their gossip and open chastisement they ensure that the younger women are seen at public religious gatherings, behave and dress demurely and remain within the domestic confines.

## *Conclusion*

This chapter has suggested various ways in which women play a role in contributing to the maintenance and continuance of both Jain religious traditions and the social divisions which constitute the Jain community: a role given recognition within the religious teachings themselves, both explicitly in the avowal that women are the spiritual equals of men, and implicitly in the literature which encourages that form of female behaviour upon which the boundaries of the community are believed to depend. In considering only women's role I have presented a partial, albeit important, aspect of the mechanisms whereby the Jain community is reproduced. In extending the examination begun in this paper it would be interesting to look at the role played by the ascetic community as a whole, for it is clear from my comments on the nuns that the ascetic community is closely implicated in the process of social reproduction. Another crucial aspect to look at, were the data available, is the way in which men and economic practices are implicated in this process.

# Part 2

# Local Jain communities

# 6

# Local Jain communities

Caroline Humphrey

All three of these chapters discuss relatively small local groups of Jains in Rajasthan, but they come to different conclusions as to whether these groups are 'communities' in terms of the criteria in the position paper (chapter 1). Howard Jones says that his circle of Jain businessmen does make a community, while Christine Cottam Ellis and N. K. Singhi, both discussing much larger groups, maintain that Jains in the final analysis have a dominant identity which derives from outside the purely Jain sphere.

The issue here is the differing contexts of these three studies. Although all are in rural Rajasthan, the three groups do seem to be rather different, even allowing for the individual emphases of our authors. It is not, perhaps, so important for us to state our opinion on the issue of whether these are, or are not, communities. Readers can make their own judgement. But what is interesting is to compare the materials we are given, look at the elements of cohesion and divisiveness among the three groups of Jains, and discuss whether these correlate with the local contexts.

To begin with, the papers deal with Jain groups of very different scale. Jones has a small group of 150 Jains, all of them engaged in business and finance, living in an isolated village with a total population of around 1,000. Cottam Ellis describes the 1,400 or so Jains of a small market town with a population of 11,000. Singhi deals with a yet larger group, the 5,000 Jains of a town which was earlier a mini-state, now with a population of nearly 24,000.

Both Jones and Cottam Ellis discuss long-established Jain groups which are essentially made up of businessmen, and the more profitable end of business at that. Chandrapur, Jones' village, is however in a region dominated by the tribal population of Bhils, and exists more or less to provide goods and services to these rather poor farmers. In Jain credit transactions there is a distinction between goods sold on account and pawnbroking, which in practice disbars Bhils from acquiring the former and Jains from borrowing through the latter. The other business people of the village are much less prosperous, and are engaged either in services or in trades, such as selling vegetables, which the Jains will not do for religious reasons. Thus, both in terms of their overt occupation, shopkeeping, and their more covert moneylending activities, Jains are distinct. Mandi, Cottam Ellis's market town, on the other hand, is located near the city of Jaipur, is surrounded by a prosperous farming hinterland made up of people from a variety of different castes, and is currently embarked on an economic upswing involving small-scale industry. Other merchants, Hindus and Muslims, are involved in the same kind of businesses as the Jains. While Jains in Chandrapur village completely dominate the business economy, the Jains in Mandi town are only half of the merchant community. In Mandi the shared merchant (Mahajan) identity predominates over the purely Jain one.

The differences in identity among the Jains in the two cases thus perhaps should be seen as contingent rather than necessary. Where the Jains are more or less the only businessmen, surrounded by the radically different Bhils, they are readily identified by others and themselves as a community. Where they are part of a burgeoning economy in a complex social environment they identify with other merchants and do not separate themselves off. This would suggest that scale and economic context are what determine Jain identity *vis-à-vis* other groups.

Things are more complicated, however. Cottam Ellis makes the interesting point that Muslim merchants are not really considered to be Mahajans, and that the Hindus and Jain businessmen share a common life style in terms of language (Marwari), food restrictions, and clothing. Belonging in many cases to the same castes, Jains and Hindus sometimes intermarry. What Cottam Ellis's chapter shows splendidly, more so than any of the other chapters in this volume, is the extent to which Jains enter the wider Indian social world, the ascetic, exclusive, and yet philanthropic culture of middle-class Western India. This is a matter not just of economic factors, but of socially defined groups ('castes') and what we might call religious style, excluding Muslims and Saivite Hindus.

Cottam Ellis shows how Jains join in activities together with Vaishnavas (business associations, the cow-sanctuary, even picnic parties) and it appears from her account as though these have the same weight as purely Jain institutions. Carrithers, however, observed in Kolhapur (to some extent this can also be seen in Banks' material) that many older and less cosmopolitan Jains regard the Jains as a community apart. Moreover, many very well-educated people will throw themselves wholeheartedly into Jain, but not into other, voluntary associations. In very large populations of Jains, such as in the city of Jaipur, Humphrey noted that even all-Jain institutions, for example, those which organise all-Jain parades through the city, are less fervently supported than similar organisations based on particular Jain sects. In other words, we should not forget that religious activity itself, whether defined at the 'Jain' or the sect level, is a potent motivating force for many people.

This leads us to a discussion of the internal divisions of Jain society. Singhi makes the significant observation that the role of Jains in the premodern state may have some bearing on the matter (see also M. Carrithers' chapter). In his town of Sirohi some Jains were not businessmen but mainly officials in the service of the state government. This group coincided with the Bisa 'sub-caste' of the Oswals. Even now, he says, there are marked differences in life style between the two groups. The modernity, stress on education, and free-spending ostentation of the Bisa Oswals contrasts with the conservative and restrained habits of the actually rather richer merchants, the Porwals and Dasa Oswals. We are led to wonder, given that there are persistent differences in life styles between Jains of different occupations, how this correlates in general with distinctions of caste and sect?

This is no easy question to answer. It might appear, for example, that one could make the generalisation that the larger the Jain population the more likely it is to be divided by sect and sub-sect. However, the southern Jains, although farmers as well as businessmen, are virtually all Digambar. Differences of sect occur among the northern Jains of Rajasthan, Madhya Pradesh and Gujarat (Cottam Ellis notes that there are three sects and three castes among the merchant Jains of Mandi, but does not say how they interrelate). But even in Rajasthan, Singhi's chapter shows that a comparatively large community may lose its sectarian divisiveness. His Svetambar Murti Puja Jains were formerly divided into a number of sub-sects (*gacch*s) and supported a large number of temples, but recently sectarian divisions have disappeared, the *Tapagacch* prevails, and people attend any temple near their home. One could speculate that this might have been due to lack of religious leadership in the other *gacch*s. Certainly, it was not caused by the rabid attacks on the Jains from Hindus, since Singhi records that although the Jains were forced to unite to defend themselves physically and legally, integration was only temporary and their social internal divisions into 'castes' remained intact.

Singhi describes carefully how the Jains of Sirohi nevertheless maintain an identity as Jains. For a start, Singhi states that Jain 'castes' (*nyat*) are not real castes. Rather they are non-hierarchical residential groups which maintain several reciprocal and equivalent symbolic exchanges with one another. They exist to specify social rules, for example on widow remarriage, which the Jain religion does not concern itself with. We should note that unlike the castes in Cottam Ellis's town, the Sirohi *nyat*s are made up only of Jains. *Nyat*s are endogamous groups. (Singhi does not discuss the relation between endogamy and hierarchy, but see the chapter by Sangave in this volume.) Whatever status differences might have existed between the *nyat*s in the earlier political economy have now been eradicated. It is the little gifts made to all three castes, when someone gets married, at a serious illness, and when the parents die, which indicate membership of the Jain community. These are ritualised. There is much criticism if they are not reciprocated. Most important of all, perhaps, is the fact that the size of these gifts is fixed. In other words, there is no competitive giving here, otherwise so prominent and divisive a feature of Jain donations, and this preserves a sense of equality. Equality between the castes is also maintained in the religious sphere by the insistence that all three groups should have equal representation on temple management committees (*pedhi*) despite their actual differences in size and wealth. Such obligations contribute to the reproduction of the community, since they are inherited at birth, are tied to kinship, and should not be disavowed even if a person moves away from the locality. They presume, in fact, that people will not move away.

Singhis's paper also gives us the most detailed picture in this book of the extraordinarily elaborate series of fasts, rituals, religious activities such as pilgrimages, and various associations which Jains go in for. It may well be that a community of a certain scale is necessary before these are developed to full complexity, but note that Jones and Cottam Ellis have put their emphases elsewhere. As Singhi mentions and we should stress, larger Jain festivities, such as fairs, the inauguration of a statue, or the taking of orders by an ascetic, are widely publicised in the region and often draw tens of thousands of Jains from the neighbourhood. It is a duty and a pleasure to attend these, even if one has to travel into a different state to do so. Thus tiny groups of Jains are not in fact as isolated as they might seem.

One point made in both Jones' and Singhi's papers is the opposition which exists between Jains and neighbouring tribal peoples (see also C. Humphrey's chapter for a discussion of this). We seem to be dealing here not only with an economic relation which may have persisted for centuries (Jones), but also with a radical difference in life style and values, in which Jainism becomes the archetype of the merchant ethos (Cottam Ellis) in general.

Such distinctions rise above the purely local and make it impossible finally to conclude that Jain identity is entirely context-dependent. In fact, these three chapters, particularly those of Cottam Ellis and Singhi, raise a new criterion for the existence of a community: the intensity of interaction through various institutions and the consequent issue of a dominant identity in the range of possible identities. Only Jones describes the dominant identity as Jain. For Cottam Ellis it is the wider merchant (as opposed to purely Jain) identity, and for Singhi it seems to rest with the local 'caste' (*nyat*). It is clear from both of these chapters that the situation has not been historically constant. In particular we may speculate on the role of the premodern state in organising and dramatising local communities, which now have fallen back on other resources, or found new ones. What is apparent in rural India, however, is that the Jain identity has been continuously present as an option, and that the religious and cultural features which distinguish it have not changed all that much for a very long time (see Carrithers, chapter 17). In the cities, however, and in Jain groups outside India, as we shall see in Part 5, the presence of alternative 'models' of Jainism as a religion introduces a further set of issues.

# 7

# The Jain merchant castes of Rajasthan: some aspects of the management of social identity in a market town

Christine M. Cottam Ellis

## *Introduction*

The traditional merchant castes of India have a total population of about three million, located for the most part in western India and especially in the adjacent states of Rajasthan and Gujarat. In this region, they constitute a small number of associated castes, commonly called Bania[1] by the indigenous populace, though the castes in question tend to prefer the more honorific appellation Mahājan. About half the Mahājans of Rajasthan are probably Vaishnava Hindu and the remainder Jains. Collectively, Mahājans have dominated the industrial and commercial life of India for at least the last 100 years. As Erdman (1975) has indicated, they are popularly believed to possess an economic and political power quite out of proportion to their small numbers in the sub-continent. According to Timberg (1973) the greatest family firms in the sub-continent today trace their ancestry to Rajputana and Saurashtra, the former princely states now known as Rajasthan and Gujarat. These expatriates are also called Marwari, presumbly because the Marwar area of Rajasthan experienced the most sizeable outmigrations of the traditional merchant castes to the burgeoning colonial cities of Bombay, Calcutta and elsewhere in the second half of last century (Timberg, 1978; Kling, 1966). Consequently, in these places particularly, but also throughout India generally, the categories Bania, Mahājan and Marwari have become

This paper redrafts ideas originally presented to a seminar held at the Oriental Institute, Oxford University, on 11 November 1983. I am grateful to the academic staff and postgraduate students of that institution for their perceptive remarks and especially grateful to Richard Gombrich for his very kind invitation and thoughtful hospitality.

[1] From the Sanskrit *Vanij*: merchant or trader. Almost everyone in India will say that Banias are business people, though not necessarily knowing the derivation of the word. It is also written in English as *Baniya* (Fox 1967; 1969; etc.) and even as *Wani* (Michaelson 1976: pers. comm.) according to regional differences in pronunciation.

synonymous, usually with Jain, though obviously not all merchants are Jains, just as all Jains are not necessarily merchants. As I have mentioned elsewhere (Cottam, 1980: 331) the traditional merchant castes are rather like a mirage, in that they are more easily perceived as a social category from a distance. Not only does the business of buying and selling today involve castes whose hereditary vocation is not trade or commerce, but pruning away all of these leaves a residue which does not call itself Bania or Marwari (see also Millman, 1954: 5–7).[2] It may or may not be Jain.

This general problem of delineating the social identity of the traditional merchant castes is raised in connection with a key question in the consideration of the Jains as a community: to what extent are Jains as businessmen significantly different or organised separately from other businessmen? As the position paper (chapter 1) points out, some have argued that the Jains are culturally distinct as businessmen, or that they organise themselves more effectively as businessmen, whilst others have asserted that there is an Indian business community which transcends the barriers of caste and religion. The present study attempts to find a middle way between these opposing points of view, perhaps even to reconcile them, by suggesting that social identity is not a discrete, permanent thing, but can be and indeed is changed according to the exigencies of context. To put that another way, social identity can be managed as self-interest dictates. There is nothing particularly iconoclastic about this theoretical perspective in general sociological and anthropological terms. A whole school of thought has devoted itself to the problem of ethnicity, for example, particularly but not always in urban areas (Cohen 1969; Leach 1977). However, in the context of South Asian studies, the concept that social identity may fluctuate or alternate and that this is normal or usual seems not to have been taken on board. Nici Nelson (1980: 19), one of the few Africanists[3] to have studied South Asian society, complains

[2] This is because *Bania* is also a term of abuse implying thief, cheat, or miser and is synonymous with black-marketeering, smuggling and so on. This is similar to the usage of Jew or equivalent labels to mean both a specific ethnic group and someone who is sharp with money. These cultural characteristics comprise the traditional stereotype of the Bania reported elsewhere in India (Lamb 1955, 1959; Fox 1969; Hazlehurst 1968; and others).

[3] Compare this with Meillassoux (1973: 108) who finds that Indianists use caste tautologically, stress religious status rather than political power and hence fail to penetrate the dominant ideology: 'The attempt we see today to give it a structuralist coherence seems more like an ideological patching-up operation than a scientific exercise.'

that anthropologists have been 'mesmerised' by Indian caste or ritual systems, and she is right. For years, stress has been placed on delimiting interactional and/or attributional criteria for identifying castes and constructing caste systems (Marriott 1959; Mayer 1960; and others), futile searches for the 'true' or 'real' caste, when in reality socially sustained categories are far more fluid.

What follows is divided into three major sections. The first section deals with the nature of caste segmentation within the overall category of Mahājan and shows that the identity 'Jain' is merely one of several responses to the question, 'What is your *jāti?*' The second discusses the function of Jain or Jain-influenced beliefs and practices in the management of social identity amongst Mahājans as a whole and also the role of various committees, associations and organisations in integrating disparate Mahājan households into a moral community. The third looks at the question of the cultural distinctiveness of Jains as businessmen, focussing on the ritualisation of business practices in particular. However, it is necessary to describe the ethnographic setting before proceeding with these ideas.

## *Basic ethnographic data*

Field research was conducted in a market town in the Jaipur region of Rajasthan[4] which, in order to preserve the privacy of its inhabitants, I have earlier called 'Mandi' (Cottam 1980; 1983;). It means a market-place, especially for food grains. In 1971 (more recent figures are not yet available) the population was a little over 10,000, of whom approximately 5,500 were male and 4,400 female. According to the official town handbook[5] Hindus compose 74 per cent of the resident urban population of the Notified Area of the Township, Jains 14 per cent and Muslims 13 per cent, whilst Scheduled Castes and Tribes formed 25 per cent, mostly residing in the outskirts of the town

[4] Just over one year's fieldwork in Rajasthan was kindly made possible by a Social Science Research Council Fieldwork Award. The SSRC also supported a postgraduate studentship in social anthropology held at the School of Oriental and African Studies (SOAS), London University. A. C. Mayer, currently Head of the Department of Anthropology and Sociology at SOAS, was my supervisor for several years, including fieldwork. To him, many thanks are due.

[5] Rajasthan *District Gazetteers* (NS) *Town Handbooks* published by the government of Rajasthan in collaboration with the Central Gazetteers Unit of the Government of India, 1970–.

proper. Assuming that the Jains and Vaishnavas constitute approximately equal numbers, the Mahājans would be 28 per cent of the urban population.[6] Since independence, the census has not recorded caste affiliation and it would not have been possible to attempt a complete survey of Mandi's 1,861 occupied residential houses in the time available. The most significant 'groups' according to the town directory are (in descending order) Mahājans, Jats, Chamars, Minas, Gujars, Bhils, Shaikhs and Pathans.[7] Table 1 gives a list of all the *jāti*s encountered during fieldwork which were resident in the Notified Area. The traditional occupational speciality of each caste, or its customary association with an occupation locally, are indicated. Where more than one occupation is listed it is to be understood that the last is the current occupation. This applies also to the tribal population, represented in Mandi by no more than a handful of households.

The town is located in a region which supports one of the lowest population densities of Rajasthan and therefore of India (Nand 1966). Apart from a small area of cultivated land to the south of Mandi, the desert comes up to the town boundaries. Its origins, which are very ancient (Jain 1972: 203–4), can be traced to the importance of a permanent water supply in an arid environment for long-distance trade and military strategy. Mandi has both a walled *bāzār* and separate *kasbah* (fort) which, according to Weber (1962: 78) reveals the essential Islamic character of such settlements. Fox (1971) asserts that in India much of the history of urban formation is concerned with a local *rājā*, *nawāb* or *zamindār* who created a market-place and ensured peace so that trade would prosper. In the case of Mandi, legend has it that a Rajput chieftain named Naruka founded the new town and its reservoirs near ruins of an earlier city which was obliterated by a sandstorm. Partly because of its great antiquity, Mandi is regarded as a holy place and is a pilgrimage site. It has seven sacred springs and four famous tanks, one of which is reputed to cure leprosy. Its mountain is revered and circumambulation of it is an act of religious merit. There are three mosques, two Jain temples, innumerable Hindu temples and

[6] This figure excludes the Muslim merchants, since they are not indigenously regarded as belonging to the Mahajan category, despite the fact of their antiquity. The Muslim traditional merchant castes found locally are listed in table 1.

[7] It is clear that this information is taken from the *Imperial Gazetteer of India* (Provincial Series), 1908.

shrines, as well as gardens, *dharmśālās* (pilgrims' hostels) two *sati* sites and a Buddhist monastery. The impact of long-distance trade, pilgrimage and recent immigration has resulted in a variety of languages and dialects being spoken, the principal languages being Hindi, Urdu and Rajasthani, which sub-divides into at least sixteen major dialects. Other languages include Afghani, Sindhi and Punjabi, in sizeable numbers, and Malwi, Marathi, Nepali, Bihari, Tamil and Telugu by no more than one or two individuals. The Sindhi-speakers are displaced persons from Pakistan.

Although Marwāris have an India-wide reputation for arriving penniless but within a few years making fortunes from land deals (Millman 1954; Timberg 1971; Gupta 1976) the acquisition of farmland in Mandi is not perceived as a priority. Only one Mahājan household owned a farm, which was cultivated by tenants. All the Mahājan households living in the town are associated with business in one way or another. Whereas twenty-five castes, tribes and ethnic groups were enumerated as employed in business activities, the Mahājan category as a whole has a near monopoly of the trade in food grains, oil seeds, unrefined sugar, clarified butter, vegetable oil and cloth, that is to say the staple commodities. It completely monopolises timber and builders' merchants, transport agencies and government contracts for deals in cement. Jains predominate in the most profitable businesses: commission agencies (brokers) for the city dealers in food grains, oil seeds and spices, the wholesale and retail cloth merchants, the wholesale grocery trade and, most significantly, fringe banking (confirming, guaranteeing and insuring transactions) as well as the newly developed and very profitable vegetable oil mills. The Jains in this part of Rajasthan are essentially an urban population, as might be anticipated, with two-thirds (66 per cent) of the Jains of the *tehsil*[8] living within the Notified Area. This compares with one-third of the Muslims (31 per cent) and 12 per cent of the Hindus. The rural Jains are also businessmen, employed as village shopkeepers and travelling salesmen between hamlets, conducting their trade from bullock carts as they did a century ago (Bayly 1973; 1975).

The main Jain sects in Mandi consist of the Digambar, whose

[8] A *tehsil* is an area unit of local government generally consisting of somewhere between 50 and 200 villages, plus a small town which is the headquarters of the *tehsildar*, who is responsible for revenue collection and the administration of elections.

Table 1. *Castes and tribes resident in the Notified Area*

| Hindu | Jain | Muslim |
|---|---|---|
| *Ritual specialists* (and allied castes) | | |
| Brahman (priest) | | Syed } Descendants of the Prophet or his original followers |
| Vedh (apothecary) | | Sheikh } |
| Joshi (astrologer) | | Qureshi } |
| Bhat (genealogist) | | Fakir (wandering mendicant) |
| *Landowners* | | |
| Rajput (thakur) | | Pathan (khan) |
| Jat (farmer) | | |
| *Merchants* | | |
| Agrawal } Mahajan | Agrawal | Sarafa (bullion dealer) |
| Khandelwal } | Khandelwal | Bohra (financier) |
| Maheshwari } | Oswal | |
| *Tradesmen/craftsmen* | | |
| Sonar (goldsmith) | | Sunhar (goldsmith) |
| Lakharia (banglemaker) | | Manihar (banglemaker) |
| Lohar (blacksmith) | | Lohar (blacksmith) |
| Halwai (confectioner) | | Halwai (confectioner) |
| Darzi (tailor) | | Darzi (tailor) |
| Kyasth (scribe) | | Siklinghar (armourer/knife sharpener) |
| Teli (oil presser) | | Patthar (stonemason) |
| Kumhar (potter) | | Kumhar (potter) |
| Khati (carpenter) | | Khati (carpenter) |
| Chipa (dyer) | | Bharbhunja (grainparcher) |
| Balai (weaver) | | Barai (weaver) |
| Khatik (butcher) | | Qasai (butcher) |
| *Service castes* | | |
| Nai (barber) | | |
| Dhobi (washerman) | | |
| Mali (gardener) | | |
| Bhand (singer) | | |
| Reghur (leatherworker) | | Paldar/Kalal (wineseller) |
| Chamar (shoemaker) | | Mochi (leatherworker) |
| Bhangi (sweeper/scavenger) | | |
| *Tribal* | | |
| Gujar (herdsman/farmer) | | Meo/Mewati (Muslim Mina) |

Table 1. *Cont.*

| Hindu | Jain | Muslim |
|---|---|---|
| Mina (robber/farmer) | | |
| Bhil (witchfinder/distiller/farmer) | | |
| Pindara (robber/woolcarder/ ropemaker) | | |
| Koli (basketmaker) | | |
| Nat (acrobat/prostitute/tattooist) | | |
| Kanjar (basketmaker/ birdcatcher/labourer) | | |
| Katuga (beggar/scavenger) | | |
| *Others* | | |
| Sindhi ('business') | | |
| Maratha ('business') | | |
| Gujarati ('business') | | |
| Bengali ('business') | | |

*Source:* Cottam (1983: 82–5). Note that the ordering of categories is not meant to represent a fixed status hierarchy but a paradigmatic model of social stratification which is stochastic.

images of Mahāvīr are unclothed, whose ascetics are naked and who assert that women cannot attain salvation, and the Śvetāmbar, who hold precisely the opposite view regarding women's status and drape their images in white. The Dhundia are a sub-sect of the latter and carry the common doctrine of *ahiṃsa* (non-violence, harmlessness, or absence of the desire to kill) to extremes. They also follow the teaching of *gurus*, who may be female (at least one female *guru* was resident in the town). Paradoxically, more published data is available concerning the ancient history of the Jains than is available on Jainism (or indeed merchants) today. No figures are available, for example, in any of the official publications on the town concerning sectarian affiliation amongst the Jains, but informants asserted that the three groupings mentioned here were approximately equally divided in the their followers. As in Gujarat (Pocock 1976) the trading community is associated with the orthodox, scriptural traditions and the Hindus amongst the Mahājans belong almost entirely to the Vallabhacharya branch of Vaishnavism. This is a *bhakti* cult, devoted to the practice and development of the love of the deity, in this case the infant Krishna. As Dumont says (1972: 236) Jain influence 'would account for the vegetarianism' and also for the aspect of renunciation (non-attachment) which characterises Vaishnavas. Again, like the Jains, Vaishnava worshippers form bands attached to a spiritual guide or *guru*, who visits them occasionally and whom they support financially. The Jains, however, are enjoined not only to vegetarianism but also to a detailed and fastidious taxonomy of appropriate behaviour, too complex to reproduce here, though examples of dietary restrictions in operation locally are reproduced below (see table 2). Suffice it to say that, unlike Buddhism and other renunciatory sects, the model for the monk or *guru* is also applicable to the layman, and has remarkably affected lay thinking and behaviour.

Because of the overarching orientation towards Jainism, intermarriage between Jain and Vaishnava Mahājans is sometimes permitted. In other instances, intermarriage is prohibited and here the sect-based caste segments mutate into sub-castes, since they are in effect the primary endogamous units. Therefore, although in theory caste and sect operate on different levels, in practice the sect can appear caste-like. So, for example, Khandelwal Vaishnavas and Khandelwal Jains prohibit intermarriage whereas Agrawal Vaishṇavas and Agrawal Jains permit it. This complex but interesting phenomenon is discussed in the following section, which outlines the merchant caste category in more detail.

## *The merchant caste category: a framework*

Belonging to the traditionally authenticated category of castes which are collectively styled 'Mahājan' implies recruitment by birth into a small number of named, endogamous social units called *jāti*s. *Jāti* is used interchangeably with *biraderi* locally, although there are certain differences in implicit meanings.[9] By tradition, there are twelve *jāti*s of

[9] *Biraderi* literally means brotherhood. As Alavi (1971) has shown, the term has two connotations in popular usage: a collection of agnatically related households, and fraternal solidarity between such households as shown in collective action e.g. gift exchange and an endogamous group. *Zāt* or *jāti* by contrast is an endogamous hereditary social group which has a name and is occupationally linked to a fixed position in the local status hierarchy. In the case of Hindus, concepts of purity apply.

Mahājans in Rajasthan, though no one in Mandi could list all of them. Millman (1954: 16) records fourteen Marwari *jāti*s which can be classified as traditional merchant castes.[10] However, in Mandi itself there are just four *jāti*s which are indisputably Mahājan: Agrawal, Khandelwal, Oswal and Maheshwari. Of these, Khandelwals and Agrawals sub-divide into sect-based segments, but the Oswals (all Jain) and the Maheshwaris (all Hindu) do not. Generally speaking, each *jāti* in an Indian village possesses an individual combination of economic and religious characteristics which denote a particular rank in the local status system. In the case of the Mahājan *jāti*s of Mandi this status is shared, or common, hence their designation here as a 'caste category', that is, a collectivity of similar *jāti*s or castes.[11]

Although there is a tendency for outsiders to perceive the Mahājan *jāti*s as more or less unitary, each is sub-divided into further, smaller groupings, with segmentation proliferating according to the spatial context of the social relations under consideration. Dumont comments: 'If one asks, "What is your caste?" (*jāti*) he may indicate either which of the four *varṇas* he belongs to, or a caste title, or his caste, or his sub-caste, or even the exogamous section to which he belongs' (Dumont 1972: 101). Thus, following this framework, a respondent from the traditional merchant castes in Rajasthan might reply that he is Wesh (Vaisya *varṇa*) Mahājan, Agrawal, Khandelwal Vaishnava, or Todwal. He might also give a caste nickname, such as 'Vaishnu' for Vaishnava Hindu and *gaccha* (sectarian affiliation) is yet another possibility. In answer to this question, 49 out of 245 *malik*s of family businesses gave 'Jaina' as their *jāti*, whilst 29 gave 'Vaishnu'. Social identity is therefore situational – as Mayer (1960): 5–6) expresses it, 'only in relation with other castes is the caste a significant unit'. But if identity is situational, what are the situations? The diagram (p. 84) attempts to summarise the nesting degrees of

[10] These are as follows: Agrawal Vaishnavite, Agrawal Jain, Oswal Vaishnavite, Oswal Jain, Maheshwari (all Vaishnavite), Khandelwal Vaishnavite, Khandelwal Jain (Saraogi – Digambar Jains), Vijay Vargra (all Vaishnavite), Tikkewal (all Vaishnavite), Jaiswal, Paliwal, Porwal, Sreemal, Shreshshreemal (all Jains). Millman also mentions that 12.5 castes are popularly supposed to constitute the Marwaris who belong to the Vaisya *varna*. Presumably this lack of clarity implies that the classification is finite – whilst open to negotiation? Compare it with the 17.5 *gotra*s amongst the Agrawals.

[11] Note that this usage differs from Mandelbaum (1970) who interprets *varṇa* as caste category. However, *varṇa* is not used locally, except by educated persons eager to demonstrate their familiarity with the scriptural traditions of Hinduism.

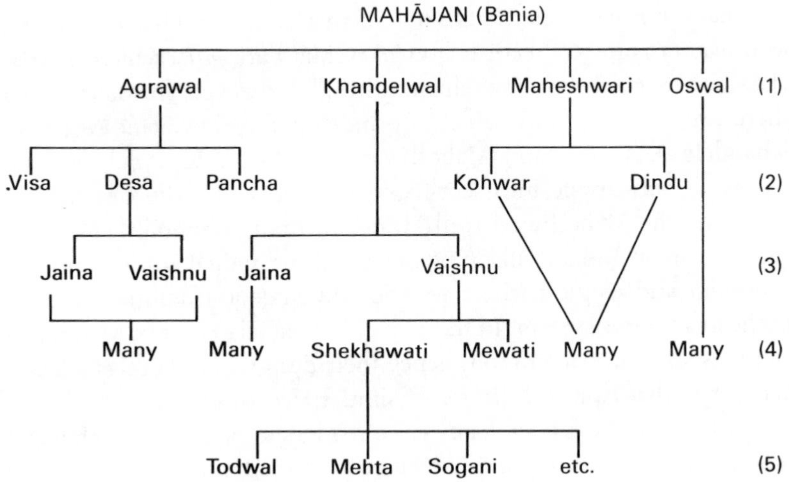


Caste segmentation amongst Mahājans in Mandi

segmentation found within the Mahājan caste category in Mandi. Commencing with Mahājan, we find that this is, in fact, the caste title, the hereditary occupation being denoted by 'Bania'. As mentioned earlier, in common parlance 'Bania' means anyone who is in business, regardless of caste, and it sometimes carries negative connotations (see Fox 1969; Hazlehurst 1966; Millman 1954; Mines 1972; and others). For this reason, the merchants of Mandi are uncomfortable with the appellation, since it suggests a lower social status than they would like. Consequently, whilst they are not ashamed of their customary vocation in the way that a scavenger or graveyard attendant might be, they generally use a different term of reference for themselves. This is 'Mahājan' and out of deference to their sensibilities this is the name given to the caste category in the present study.

Within the caste category, the first order of division is primarily on the basis of place. According to Hemchand Jain (1972: 566ff) several *jāti*s amongst the Vaisyas (*sic*) are known to have come into existence after the seventh century AD, taking their identity from the ancient towns and cities of the desert. Jain suggests that the Oswals, Srimals and Paliwals came into being after the Jain saint Ratnaprabha Suri visited the towns of Osia, Srimala and Pali and made converts there. Similarly, he argues, the Khandelwals take their name from Khandela, the Bagherawals from Baghera, and the Maheshwaris' nickname

'Dindu' from Didwana, by which they have been known since very early days. The Jaiswals originate from the twelfth century AD in Jaisalmer and the Agrawals from Agroha in Hissar District, according to Gupta (1976). Gupta argues that because of the place-name connection, Aggarwal, as it is often written, should be pronounced Agrawal, which is indeed how it is said in Mandi. Shah (1978) has devised a similar scheme for Brahmans in Gujarat and argues that, ideally, each caste division is supposed to match up with spatial segmentation in other *jāti*s. For example, Paliwal Brahmans ought to be *purohit*s (family priests) to Paliwal Mahājans or Paliwal Rajputs, Khairawal Brahmans for Khairawal Mahājans or Rajputs, and so on. However, in 'the real world' the elegant synchronicity of caste divisions is not so apparent as it is in indigenous theorising. As asserted earlier, Jain '*paṇḍit*s' are not necessarily Brahmans and can, on occasion, be women, the acquisition of ritual status working according to achieved rather than ascribed criteria. What then is the point of this imaginary blueprint of caste connections? It would seem that at the level of ideology, the perceived correspondence of *jāti*s serves three functions: (a) it attempts to come to terms with urban complexity and spatial mobility; (b) it reflects the national, even international orientation of Mahajans; (c) it illustrates the felt needs for extra-local associations, for example caste associations, some of which will be discussed subsequently.

The second degree of segmentation consists, oddly, of numbered, not named, units of endogamy. Dumont (1972: 164) cites Blunt (1931) on the Agarwals (*sic*) of Punjab and Gujarat 'who have the "20" superior and "10" inferior' (Visa and Desa) and deduces that this level of segmentation is the sub-caste, as these units are the primary basis of endogamy. The problem with this argument is that the same exogamous units are found in both divisions, therefore it is difficult to see how his assertion is substantiated. In Mandi, informants were uncertain and confused as to the significance and implications of numbered categories and lack of a name is especially problematic in that naming (or 'labelling') is basic to the process of identity formation in all societies. It is most likely that numbering is indicative of indigenous recognition of the essentially fissiparous nature of the Mahājan caste category and especially with regard to differences of standing between maximal patrilineages within the *jāti*s. The logic of hierarchy between castes presupposes equivalence within each caste – which is patently not the case where status differentiation is pronounced on economic grounds. Not all Mahājan households are rich; some can be very poor indeed and especially by comparison with their *lākh-pati* (roughly translated as millionaire) caste fellows.

The third level of segmentation is into *ekda*s or *gol*s (units or circles). Each has distinctive myths of origin (see Millman 1954: 18–30), individual tutelary deities and separate *purāṇa*s (holy scriptures), or so informants believed. They also have different marriage regulations, corresponding to differences in diet, commensality habits and practices concerning contact with and avoidance of other castes. Shah (1978) insists that in Gujarat *ekda*s and *gol*s often reside in separate streets in the towns and cities, thus stressing their social compartmentalisation. But this was not observed in Mandi, possibly because of the relative smallness of its population and the rapidity in which it is growing (Cottam 1983: 74). *Ekda* and *gaccha* are approximately equivalent social categories and it is here that the sect-based caste segment finds its true meaning. As noted above, the Agrawals subdivide into Agrawal Vaishnava and Agrawal Jain and the Khandelwals into Khandelwal Vaishnava and Khandelwal Jain. It may be guessed that Maheshwari and Oswals would similarly sub-divide were their populations large enough. (No more than two or three families are represented in the town at present.) Sometimes marriages are arranged contravening *vania kapta* (commensal relations); for example, cases of intermarriage between Agrawal Vaishnavas and Agrawal Jains were reported by informants to exist, and did so, whereas they were unanimous that Khandelwal Vaishnavas and Khandelwal Jains might not intermarry locally, even if they did in Jaipur. This qualification would appear to indicate a possible readiness to dispense with the absolute prohibition dictated by local custom and certainly the prohibition of intermarriage is more severe at higher levels of segmentation, between Agrawal and Khandelwal Jains, for example. It would also seem likely that further fragmentation is possible, or, conversely, two *ekdas* could combine (see Karve, 1953: 157–8 on the unification of 'sub-castes'; Parry 1979 on *patti*s in the Kulu/Kangra region).

The last level of segmentation above the exogamous lineage is the *tat*. This can be translated as 'third', 'split' or 'faction', suggesting that this level of segmentation may derive from the conflicts of *jāti* leaders or possibly the combination of patrilineages to form interest groups. Difference, not status, is emphasised at this level: alleged differences of customs and habits, of likes and dislikes, of personality and character, as if household inclinations were responsible for the proliferation of small groupings within the overall caste framework. Perhaps a general sociological hypothesis may be put forward here: the greater the degree of segmentation, the less the stress upon hierarchy as a principle of social interaction. This might help to explain why in regions of India such as Punjab, where there are many castes, purity and pollution are much less of an issue than in South India, where castes are fewer (see Pettigrew 1975; Beck 1973). Finally we come to the exogamous lineages themselves. Every household head is head of a minimal patrilineage or *khāndān* and so regards himself as a petty chief or *malik*. The term asserts the structural equivalence of individual households and only on a personally negotiated basis can a *malik* extend his leadership throughout the wider community. There are no hereditary leaders or *chaudhari*s such as exist in other castes, for example the Jats. From the perspective of any individual Mahājan, his cognitive map reveals five levels of integration into the business 'community' (to beg the question for a moment):

1 with his lineage (*khāndān*)
2 with his marriage circle (*ekda/gol/tat*)
3 with his caste (*jāti* or *gaccha*)
4 with other Mahajans in Mandi
5 with other Mahajans elsewhere, including overseas

Thus for a cloth merchant like Bajrang Lal, his *khāndān* is Bhanjia, his *ekda* Shekhawati, his *gaccha* Agrawal Jain, his caste title Mahajan and his affiliations in a wider world Rajasthani Vani. Any of these labels might be adduced as his *jāti*, according to the social context of the enquiry and the identity of the inquisitor.

By way of summarising this section it may be mentioned that a mixture of levels of social identity seems typical of urban areas and situations of social change through spatial mobility. It is suggested that the nesting segmentation system outlined above is in fact functional, for the following reasons. First, it provides a cognitive framework, based on kinship, into which exogamous maximal lineages can be inserted. Secondly, it permits and regulates the fluidity of marriage alliances within the general rule of caste endogamy. Thirdly, it facilitates and legitimises both spatial and social mobility, by stressing separation and exclusiveness – as opposed to hierarchy – as the prime principle in social relations within the category.

### *Jain community or business community?*

The question now arises of the extent to which the schematic framework of segmented social identity devised above from informants' own perceptions is representative of any kind of social reality. To put it another way: if there is a business community, does it include or exclude the Jains? 'Community' is a fashionable word and is used in such a variety of ways that, before any assessment can be made, it must be clear what is involved in the sociological use of the term (it is from this perspective that I am writing). Frankenberg's authoritative study *Communities in Britain* takes as an operational definition MacIver's and Page's assertion that community is 'an area of social living marked by some degree of social coherence. The bases of community are locality and community sentiment' (Frankenberg 1971: 15; MacIver and Page 1961: 9). He comments that the word community implies having something in common: economic interests that are the same or complementary, shared religious or recreational activities, and so forth, and that their common interest in things gives them a common interest in each other. 'They quarrel with each other but are never indifferent to each other' (Frankenberg 1971: 238). In fact, as he shows, disputes may be a form of cooperation, since people work together to solve conflicts, or at least to keep them manageable. So far so good; however, unless one is describing truly rural localities (villages, hamlets, etc.) the community must be delimited in some way. In urban areas, particularly the places characterised by spatial and social mobility, this becomes a problem for both the insider and the outsider – the researcher. How is community membership decided and proclaimed in these situations?

A newcomer business household to Mandi will not be accepted as a Mahājan unless the behavioural characteristics of the family members (both male and female) are perceived to be conformable with socially sustained conceptions of appropriate life style for the traditional merchant castes. In the case of women, this means observing seclusion and veiling and a particular style of dress within the home, by which they will be evaluated by female neighbours. Language and diet are equally important factors in social recognition, immediately apparent diacritical features. Marwari is one of the four major dialects of Rajasthani and is associated with merchants both inside and outside Rajasthan. It is similar to Gujarati, though it possesses its own script and is often written in Persian by older Mahājans. It is the language in which the traditional account books (*vahi*, or sometimes *bahi* or *wahi*) are kept, and *hundīs* (letters of credit) are drafted. By judicious management of vocabulary and pronunciation, Mahājans can render themselves unintelligible to outsiders, whilst continuing to understand the latter, a fact which amazes rustic clients and customers. Language is in fact basic to the process of identity management, since it is a cultural feature of interactions within the group, a boundary around it and a barrier against penetration by outsiders. In the shop, the immaculate white *dhoti-kurtā* of Mahājan businessmen, their embroidered slippers and pale pink, mop-like turbans publicly proclaim an exclusive identity. Wearing white (*safed poshnā*) has connotations of high ritual status throughout the whole of the subcontinent, as well as scriptural learning, an image which all Mahājans judiciously encourage by the elaborate ritualisation of business practices (for example seating arrangements and the entertainment of customers; see Fox 1969: 54 and Cottam 1983: 181–2).

However, it is diet which is subject to the greatest degree of elaboration and perhaps the most significant in the management of social identity. A Muslim merchant, for example, may speak Marwari, dress in white, keep his accounts and conduct business correspondence as the Mahājans do, arrange his shop and entertain customers in exactly the same way[12] but is subject to absolutely different ritual prescriptions concerning food habits deriving from Islam. The diet of Mahājans is subject to a complex system of rules and regulations, clearly influenced by Jain philosophical ideas even in the case of the Vaishnava Hindus amongst them. For example, all Mahājans avoid leafy vegetables and root vegetables because they would inadvertently consume grubs and insects. Self-germinating plants, such as onions and garlic, and seed-bearing plants, such as tomatoes, are also avoided

[12] See Mines for further details.

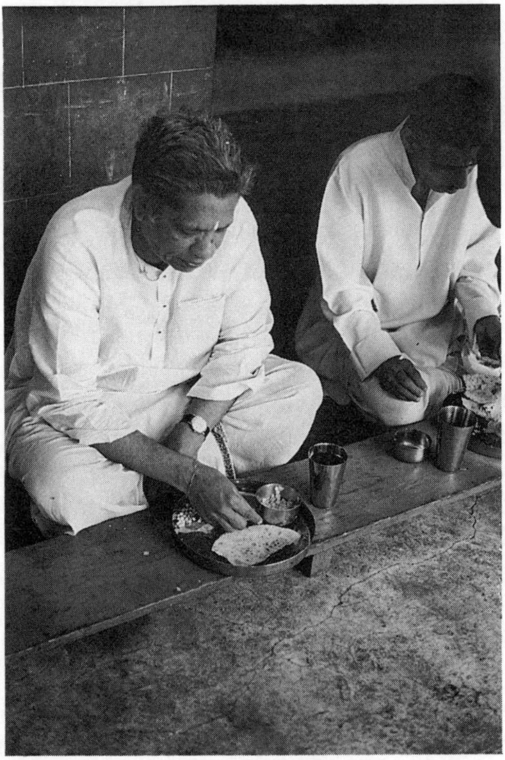

4 Svetambar Jain businessmen wear ritually pure clothing to eat restricted food during a fast, Jaipur 1983. Photo: C. Humphrey

so that life will not be taken. All permitted food items should be washed carefully in strained water before cutting and cooking, again to avoid accidental harm to living things. For this reason, too, the Mahājans of Mandi avoid the greengrocery business, since the task of picking over and discarding fruit and vegetables automatically involved harm to animal life. Sectarian affiliation causes differences in the explanations of specific food habits, a list of which (by no means exclusive) is presented in table 2. Jains assert that food should be prepared and consumed before dusk and after dawn because the effect of sunlight is beneficial, and that food is washed carefully to avoid accidental killing of grubs, worms and so on.[13] Vaishnavas say that the

[13] The influence of monachistic practices is apparent. That the doctrine of *ahiṃsā* is taken by Jain monks to extremes, for which the Buddha himself rebuked them (Dumont 1972: 193), is clear. The Jain monk should sweep the path as he walks in order to avoid crushing minute living things underfoot, breathe through a gauze mask, drink water that someone

significance of thorough washing lies in the purification which water brings and the effect of sunlight (if any) is to enable the eater to see what he is eating. But it is clear that the main thrust of both Jain and Vaishnava ideas is to avoid accidental violence to living things. Hence intermarriage between Hindus and Jains, where it is permitted, is not at all problematic.

Of course, it could be argued that in view of the special characteristics of food exchanges in social interaction in South Asia, which have been the subject of an extensive literature, there is nothing particularly remarkable about all this. However, the rigidity and comprehensiveness of dietary rules and the austerity and asceticism of Mahājans' general life style are such that, in a country renowned for its ability to tolerate alternative life styles, other castes do single them out for comment. This is especially the case in Rajasthan, where meat-eating is prestigious and a sign of high social status. Mahājans are nicknamed *kanjus* (misers) and *makkijus* (fly-suckers) because of their 'poverty stricken' diet and concern for small living things in their food. They are called *dhāl bāttis* (rice and lentils) because this is just about what remains, it is believed, when all the prohibited vegetables are avoided. The somewhat innocuous phrase in English has a hidden sting, in that rice and lentils are regarded as an invalid diet or a weaning food for children. But is not their supposedly preferred diet of rice and lentils also life-bearing? This is a very difficult question for Mahājans to answer. It is worth quoting the response of one informant, Gyan Chand Jain: 'Food is the cause of all sin and disease in this life. It is like the rust which rots iron. The only way to achieve good health in mind and body is not to eat.' It may be recalled in this connection that the good death for a Jain monk is to fast to death, providing that no social or religious merit is anticipated to accrue from the action.

The results of this exclusivity of life style are (a) the erection of a boundary based on mutual negative stereotypes between Mahājans and other castes;[14] (b) a self-sustaining separateness of the traditional merchant castes which resembles ethnicity more than any other social

else has boiled, etc. The elaboration of taxonomic orders regulating his conduct is truly remarkable, for example, detailing how to get into/out of a boat.

14 As Fox puts it: 'In many ways the Bania stands apart from society, partially by his own choice, partially by the distaste by him for other castes, so that his social life, other than business dealings, is relatively unknown to the general populace' (Fox 1969: 43). It should be asserted that the dislike is mutual.

Table 2. *Prohibited, permitted and preferred food items*

| Prohibited | Permitted | Preferred |
|---|---|---|
| *Meat and meat-type* | | |
| Meat H/L/P | | |
| Fish H/L | None | None |
| Eggs H/L/P | | |
| *Food grains* | | |
| None | Rye | Rice C |
| | Wheat | White flour C |
| | Barley | |
| | Oats | |
| | Millet H | |
| *Pulses* | | |
| *Kesari dal* Po | *Mung* C | *Channa* H |
| *Kabuli channa* H/P | *Moth* H | *Channa-dal* C |
| | *Mash* C | |
| | *Masur* H | |
| | *Malak* H | |
| | Gram H | |
| | Red beans H | |
| | Blackeye beans H | |
| | Peas H | |
| *Leafy vegetables* | | |
| Cauliflowers L | *Kariphulia* H | Coriander leaves C |
| Leeks L | Spinach | Mint C |
| | Mustard H | |
| | *Cabbage | |
| *Root vegetables* | | |
| Carrots S | Potatoes H | Sweet potatoes H |
| Turnips S | *Radishes C | |
| Onions S/P | | |
| *Seed-bearers* | | |
| Aubergines H/P | *Tomatoes H | Bananas C |
| Paw-paws H/P | Capsicums C | Apples C |
| Pomegranates H/P | Melons C | Grapes C |
| | Cucumbers C | Oranges C |
| | Squashes C | Lemons C |
| | Mangos H | |
| | *Guavas L | |

Table 2. *Cont.*

| Prohibited | Permitted | Preferred |
|---|---|---|
| *Dried fruits* | | |
| Dates H | Apricots H/P | Sultanas C |
| Figs H/L | Peaches H/P | |
| | Raisins H | |
| *Nuts and seeds* | | |
| Walnuts H/P | Coconut H/R | Almonds C |
| Pine nuts H | *Groundnuts H | |
| | Poppy seed C | |
| | *Ajwain* C | |
| | *Sunflower H | |
| | Sesame C | |
| | Cashew H | |
| *Spices* | | |
| Garlic H/L | Coriander C | Saffron H |
| Ginger H/L | Cumin C | Black cardamom C |
| Chillies | Cardamom C | |
| | Cinnamon H | |
| | Nutmeg H | |
| | Cloves H | |
| | Tamarind H | |
| | Turmeric H | |
| *Preserved food* | | |
| Bottled industrially D | Home prepared pickle chutney and preserves | Clarified butter H |
| Tinned industrially D | Dried milk H | |
| | *Vegetable oil H/D | |
| Vinegar D | Brown sugar H | White sugar C |
| Honey H/L/D/P | | |
| *Stimulants and drugs* | | |
| Alcohol H | *Bhang* R/C | *Kulfi* C |
| Coffee H | Tea? C | *Sherbet* C |
| Tobacco H | | |
| *Milk products* | | |
| Cheese H/D | Yoghurt C | All of these (except buttermilk) |
| Non-cows milk H/Po | Buttermilk H | |
| | Milk C | |
| | Cream C | |
| | Butter H | |
| | *Lassi* C | |

Table 2. *Cont.*

Key:

| | |
|---|---|
| H | Hot/heating |
| C | Cold/cooling |
| L | Life-bearing |
| D | Decaying |
| P | Passion-inducing |
| Po | Poisonous/bitter |
| R | Ritual use only |

*Notes:* All preferred foods are permitted; to avoid repetition, items have been included only once in the table.

Some items such as honey, sugar and clarified butter are not strictly preserved foods as such, but because of their preservative function have been allocated to that category.

Items marked with an asterisk are not consumed by Jains, though they are eaten by Vaishnavas.

process; (c) to cause Mahājans to resemble other marginal or minority groups, who are excluded from the general activities of the majority and associated with a particular economic niche in society; (d) the monopoly of a privileged social and economic position, since they are freed from the demands of friends and acquaintances in the wider society for preferential treatment in business.

These factors isolate the traditional merchant castes of Mandi as a distinctive category amongst the urban population as a whole. However, to be termed a community, as opposed to a category, some degree of social coherence needs to be demonstrated. The subsequent two sections discuss the role of various associations and collective activities in welding together common interests.

### *Religions and voluntary associations*

These play an important role in determining and managing social identity, demonstrating community membership and providing means for acquiring and displaying leadership functions, for example by forming committees to maintain schools, temples, widows, orphans, and so on. The most important committees and associations in Mandi are the Rāmlīlā Committee, the Gaushalla Committee, the Chaturbhuj Temple Committee, and the Old Jain Temple and New Jain Temple Committees, of which only the last two are exclusive to Jains. There are also various *ad hoc* committees got up from time to time to organise picnics and outings to religious sites and quasi-religious beauty spots in their appropriate season. These may or may not be all Jain in their composition. For example, an outing to Padampura (see Humphrey, chapter 13) would be organised by Jains, the conveyance provided free of charge, in all probability, by the Jain transport companies and any Hindus (or others) present assuming the role of guests. However a ladies' picnic at the hot springs could include Jain, Hindu and Muslim neighbours. Collections and contributions to the maternity hospital, the veterinary hospital and the dispensary/clinic are similarly important. Lists are kept of the significant contributors, which form a record, in a sense, of fully paid-up community membership.

The Rāmlīlā Committee is a fairly informal grouping of the unmarried or newly married adult sons of the wealthiest Mahājan households. Its sole purpose is to organise the festivities connected with *Dasera* (September/October). Both Jains and Hindus could be found on the self-selected committee, which collects funds from the family firms along the two main bazaars. Since the festival is a Hindu one, it is the Vaishnava firms which are the most generous, although many Jain firms do contribute (as they do to the *Eid-ul-Fitr* celebrations amongst Muslims in the same month). A grant is also made by the municipal board annually to the Rāmlīlā funds. These are administered by a *seth* (community leader) who pays for the plays, dancers, musicians and processions. The names of subscribers are recorded in advance and announced at the start of every play.

The Gaushalla Committee also receives the moral and financial support of both Jains and Vaishnavas, its purpose being to maintain a sanctuary for cows on the outskirts of the town. An annual subscription is levied to pay for the supplementary fodder, cowherds, stabling facilities and veterinary fees. Once a year in *Kartika* (November/December) there is a *gavāṣṭami* (cow festival) when the cows are painted and adorned with bells and garlands and a special *pūjā* of chickpeas is made to them. Leading members of the committee make speeches about the necessity for cow protection and veneration, a programme is circulated with the names of the subscribers, their business interests and the amount given. Finally there is another collection of money and the name and amount announced to the audience. This type of occasion provides the opportunity for all Mahājans to play the politics of respect with municipal, state and national bureaucrats and politicians. Guests of honour during fieldwork included the chairman of the municipal board, the new Jain temple *paṇḍit* (*sic*), the block development officer and the home minister of Rajasthan from the legislative assembly in Jaipur, for example. Not surprisingly, this is an altogether more serious affair than the Rāmlīlā Committee and membership of the committee is restricted to the two or three dozen *maliks* around whom the economic organisation of the market revolves. It is by invitation only.

Merchants gain religious merit (*punya*), social prestige, economic gain and credit-worthiness in business from their contributions to and participation in these activities. Giving financial support to the three main temples and their temple schools, the myriad of small shrines and temples, hostels for pilgrims and so on is a specially meritorious act and Jains as well as Vaishnavas figure prominently in this regard. Every major religious institution has a committee to administer its finances, composed of six or seven prosperous *maliks* of Mahājan families, and their organisation is essentially similar. For example, the new Jain temple committee is composed of Manak Chand, Kesar Chand, Phul Chand, Rattan Lal, Gujar Mal and Bajrang Lal, the last two individuals heading two of the most wealthy and well-connected family firms in town. The committee is reviewed every three or four years by the Maharaj Guru, in consultation with the opinion leaders of the temple congregation. As in the case of the Vaishnava *guru*s, his visits are sponsored by leading Jain families. The size of the temple funds is kept secret, but they must be quite considerable, judging from the expenditure on special occasions. For example, on the occasion of Mahāvīr Jayanti (April) Rs 20,000 was collected in one morning from Jain family firms. This paid for the streets of the Mahājan *mohalla* to be decorated with gold and silver bunting and specially washed so that an image of Mahāvīr could be paraded from the old Jain temple to the new Jain temple and back again. The festival itself, which included two bands with dancing 'girls' cost 'more than that' to stage. The highlight of the celebrations was when a young married couple from the Jain household who donated the most money (Rs 11,000) rode through the streets on the back of an elephant, sponsored by the Jain firm of Gambhir Mal-Rattan Lal. Jain informants asserted that it was a relatively minor event compared with the three day *mela* (fair) held every third April. Shops close from dawn to dusk for six days so that Jains can attend plays on the life and teachings of Mahāvīr at the Jaina Samaj ground near Jhillai. They said that, during the last *mela* the Maharaj Guru had landed by helicopter on the forecourt of the new Jain temple whilst a light aircraft showered the town with rose petals. It is impossible to assess the veracity of such a story and it should be noted that there is, in fact, a good deal of indigenous controversy surrounding showy donations, despite the meritoriousness of the gift in ritual terms in South Asia. Prakash Chand, a leading Jain merchant, pointed out that 'Jain religion says not to give money to temples. Instead it should be given to a school or maternity home. The reason behind all this [showy donations] is first to gain publicity and second to avoid income tax.'

Picnics and outings can also be classified under the heading of ritual and voluntary associations for the sake of convenience. Particularly during the monsoon season, friends and neighbours make trips to local places of interest, either walking or going by *tonga*. Often they are all-male affairs, but ladies also go on *pardā* picnics and very occasionally there are mixed parties of young married couples from the more modern Jain and Vaishnava households. These are considered outrageous by the traditionalists. Outings to more distant places are more structured. Certain Jain households might club together to pay for the conveyance of 'everybody', or alternatively the arrangements are made in the name of the Jaina Samaj (actually the same households). These are double picnics, since men and women travel separately. Food is provided by an approved *halwai* (confectioner) and paid for out of temple funds or by auctioning garlands. Management of these enterprises provides another outlet for community service and demonstrates both participation and leadership characteristics to either an all-Jain or mixed audience of Jains and Vaishnava.

Religious and voluntary associations have proliferated as the town has grown in size and prosperity and provide the means by which the newly rich can flaunt their wealth in a socially approved manner. The committees and associations discussed above are especially important for aspiring politicians, since the festivities reach the entire urban population. They also intersect with caste associations and business associations, since the membership of all of these more or less corresponds.

### *Caste and business associations*

Whereas the religious and charitable organisations are localised and traditional in scope and spirit, caste and business associations are modern phenomena organised on a regional or national basis. Again, whilst the religious and charitable organisations covertly serve the general interests of merchant families by advertising their business activities, the caste and business associations overtly express their specific self-interests. Each of the four Mahājan *jātis* present in Mandi has some families who are members of a larger caste association. These organise conferences, either regularly or occasionally, to discuss topics with a modern focus and with the aim of raising the public image of the caste, such as raising the *de facto* age of marriage or improving educational levels. In order to achieve some kind of media coverage, caste association journals are published to popularise the issues, which underscores the point that a critical criterion for membership in the *sabhā*, *sangha* or *samāj* is use of a common language. One example is sufficient to describe their common features, though obviously some associations are more dynamic than others.

The Khandelwal Mahāsabhā is an organisation to which both Vaishnavas and Khandelwal Jains in Mandi belong. It is a caste association with an all-India membership, which publishes a monthly magazine, the *Khandelwal Mahāsabhā Patrika* which gives news of births, deaths and marriages and of educational grants for religious and business studies abroad. There is also a flourishing matrimonial column, organised on a city-by-city basis. The governing body of the Mahāsabhā is elected every two or three years by means of a ballot; the regional headquarters for organising this are located in Jaipur. The committee takes members from both north and south India and meets in Bombay, Madras or Calcutta. As in the case of the temple committees, fund-raising is a significant index of group commitment, since lists of benefactors are published in the magazine. For example, the *Khandelwal Mahāsabhā Patrika* might record that a certain family firm, residing in Mandi, gave Rs 10,000 to the caste association on the occasion of their youngest son's marriage, or that a Mahājan family firm, in Jaipur, offered scholarships for overseas study worth Rs 100,000 per annum to eligible Khandelwals. In this way, ascribed status by birth is transformed into achieved status within a wider arena, a process which is instrumental in welding together localised *jātis* into a nation-wide organisation. Caste associations have thus much in common with business associations.

In Mandi there are four business associations: the grain brokers and traders (Aaret Vyapar Mandal), the cloth merchants (Kapre Vyapar Mandal), the shopkeepers (Kirana Sanstha Sangha) and the District Oil Mill Association. The last, at the time of fieldwork, was barely a year old and in order to emphasise its assertive modern outlook sported an English title. The other organisations may be quite ancient. The social and economic functions of the business associations are basically similar. They ensure that labour charges are regulated, buying and selling charges to clients are reasonable, commodities are properly cleaned, weighed and delivered and payments are made correctly. They also effect commercial introductions through their connections with the city chambers of commerce and act as confirming houses or guarantors. The government-operated Krishi Upaj Mandi is supposed to oversee the workings of any local trade association – and indeed of the market – but none of the local-level institutions involved in the regulation of trade was registered with it. Each institution has a committee of three: a president (*adhayaksha*), a cashier or treasurer (*munim*) and a secretary (*munshi*). Funds are raised from the annual subscriptions of approximately Rs 50 and also on *sawal* (request). They are used for assistance to members during financial difficulties, hospitality to visiting dignitaries and delegations to Jaipur's Legislative Assembly.

A most important aspect of the work of the trade associations is to resolve conflicts between businessmen. The emphasis is upon solving disputes amicably, by discussion and debate to achieve consensus amongst the parties involved, but severe economic sanctions can be imposed occasionally. For example, a certain local businessman was accused of using money, deposited with him for safe-keeping, to finance his own commercial transactions. (This is a serious offence in

Mahājans' eyes, since it undermines the relationships of trust between merchants without which trade is impossible.) As he was unable to satisfy the Aaret Vyapar Mandal that he was not taking unnecessary risks with other people's money and always consulted his clients before using their money and names in business deals, the association advised other business organisations against further transactions with him. Under this kind of pressure, the grain broker had no option but to sell up and leave town altogether. He now runs a trinket shop in another town, in partnership with relatives residing there.

Looking again at the main points covered in this section, if the kinship system provides a frame of reference by which Mahājans can identify each other as equivalents, religious and para-religious institutions and organisations provide an opportunity for them to express social unity through collective action in a variety of different ways. These range from informal and spontaneous events such as picnics to formal social institutions such as the temple committees. Caste and business associations also permit disparate Mahājan households to come together in joint activities, thus welding together competing family firms into collectivity. The Mahājans of Mandi have a strong sense of communal identity and of a shared purpose in life, through a perceived common cultural heritage. This said, however, the Mahājans of Mandi are not, in the strict sociological sense of the term, a real group and it would be wrong to treat them analytically in any way other than a status category, within which the potentiality for group action, when occasion advises or dictates, can be motivated. The Jain temple committees, the collection of funds from and participation by Jain households and family businesses in various religious or religiously inspired activities form such a focus in the process of community formation. But there are other organisations which Jains can belong to and these, according to context, are likely to be much more significant than merely being a Jain, pure and simple.

## *Jains as businessmen*

In this section I turn to the question of the cultural distinctiveness of Jains as businessmen. Much has been written (following Weber) on the relationship between religious ideology and business organisation and it is not the purpose of this paper to contribute further to the

5 Jain businessmen of the jewellery trade at home in Jaipur 1985. Photo: C. Humphrey

debate.[15] Jain merchants themselves identified three areas of significant difference from other Mahājans in Mandi – the way they arranged or set out the place of business, the way in which the account books were written and the importance of public or community service. It is proposed to deal with each of these in turn. Space precludes any detailed analysis, which can however be found in Cottam (1983).

The assiduous cultivation of a religious atmosphere in the *dukān* (shop/place of business) was noted earlier. Every sizeable Mahājan shop has a *pūjā* room; even hawkers decorate their barrows with religious pictures and images, and every morning begins with *Lakshmipūjā*, amongst the Jains as well as the Vaishnavas. A picture of the goddess is dusted, along with other revered ritual objects including photographs of earlier *maliks* and perhaps a picture of Mahāvīr in the case of the Jains. Incense is burned and a new page is opened in the daily cashbook. This is decorated with sacred symbols, such as the swastika sign for Ganesh, and the names of ancestors. At home, both Jain and Vaishnava women perform *ārtī* (presenting a tray

[15] See Gellner (1982: 527–42) for a recent statement of the points at issue.

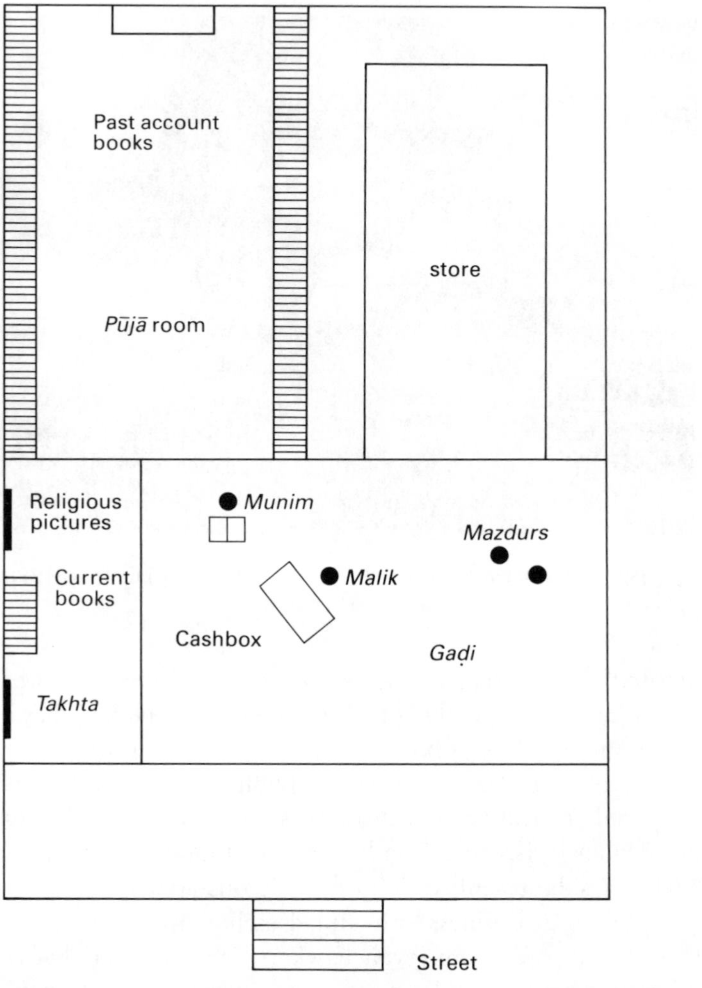


The spatial arrangement of the shop

of little earthenware lamps) to the *kuldevis* (lineage goddesses) and sacred pictures and images to complement the rituals in the shop. Often these are garlanded, whereas in the shops they are not, usually. Women sometimes perform *ārtī* in the temples or burn incense or take garlands to neighbourhood shrines. Reverence for the *kuldevis* is not, it must be pointed out, an exclusively Mahājan activity, though it does connect the family with its forbears, stresses the social status of the patrilineage and also emphasises the timelessness and continuity of the firm. (In this way, it maintains the exclusivity of the maximal patrilineages and prevents assimilation of Jain and Vaishnava households into a wider world.) Seating arrangements within the shop are highly ritualised (see the diagram) with nearness to the *malik* indicating relative degree of social standing. Despite the fact that Jains think their *dukāns* are different, no difference was found between Jain and Vaishnava, or for that matter between them and the Muslim shops. The most honoured guests and valued customers are invited to sit upon the *gaḍi* ('seat' or 'throne' – white padded floor covering) and to recline, on the right hand of the *malik*, against bolsters. This area is called the *takhta*. Tea and snacks will be offered and even fetched by the *malik*'s own sons if the client is sufficiently esteemed. Less honoured customers squat facing the *malik* or on his left hand and the least esteemed of all are not invited to enter, but must make their purchases from the street through one of the *maẓdurs* (literally, labourers). Neither of these are offered hospitality. The *malik* and his sons do not even speak to such customers if they can avoid it, nor hand items to them nor receive money from them directly. In this way the purity of the shop and especially of the cashbox is maintained. For this reason, all who enter the place of business must remove their shoes and refrain from smoking (see also Fox 1969; Bayly 1975; and others).

Throughout the day someone will be constantly adjusting the books. Whereas the cashbox is the responsibility of the *malik*, the bookwork is that of the next eldest (unless he is incompetent). Usually two sets of books are kept, one for the family records and the other for concerned government agencies, and there are five books per set. If the family firm employs a *munim* (accountant), unless he is a totally trusted employee (which many Mahājans asserted is impossible) his work is restricted to that of checking figures and making neat copies. The books are between 2 and 3 feet long and 6 to 12 inches wide, with a red cloth cover, folded over into three parts and tied with a black and white thread. The books are written in the Marwari or Persian script and set out in precisely the opposite way to wooden ledgers, which makes them hard to read for unpractised eyes. It is a common belief that Mahājans use a secret language for business transactions (see Coren 1967; Millman 1954) and Mahājans themselves believe that their books are unique. This is not the case, however. The Muslim merchants also keep *vahi* and so do the genealogists (Shah and Shroff

1959). Perhaps it is the complicated nature of Mahājans' accounts which differentiate them, since all family or household expenditure is noted as if it was an expense of the family firm. Bayly (1975) says that in the nineteenth century books of merchants in Benares expenditure on family shrines in ancestral villages, on *ghat* retainers at the cremation grounds, and on gifts to cows have all been recorded. In Mandi, the cost of special *pūjās* at *Dasera* and *Dīwālī*, on dowries and *trousseaux* for daughters and, conversely, any incoming wealth, such as houses or shops or jewellery, is mixed in with 'straightforward' business accounts, as if they were one and the same thing. In addition to the daily rituals which involve the account books, a special *pūjā* is made to the oldest book, the inkpot and the cashbox either on *Dasera* or *Dīwālī*, according to the individual family traditions of Mahajan firms. This involves preparing a *thali* of dried fruits, seeds and flowers and performing *ārtī* and is called *saradapūjā* (ancestor worship). Although *Dasera* and Dīwālī are important Hindu festivals, and have little or no significance for the Jain religion as such, both Jains and Vaiśṇavs performed *sarada pūjā*. Sometimes in the Jain family businesses *Durgapūjā* (worship of the goddess of death), which forms an otherwise sizeable part of the performance of the rituals, was omitted. In others, pictures or images of Mahāvīr took equal place with Durga, or indeed a variety of other objects of reverence. Beginning the new books for the year similarly follows a generalised pattern in all the Mahājan shops – the word *srī* is written in red or yellow paste repeatedly, to form a triangle on the front page, a silver rupee, preferably the oldest in the family's possession, is placed on the page and *ārtī* is again performed. The rupee is kept there overnight and then removed for safekeeping till next year. (Compare Stevenson 1915: 261.)

For all Mahājans, the patrilineage and its economic endeavours are synonymous. Doing business is *dharmik*, that is to say, their religious duty and therefore a source of merit. Mahājans say that if one has faith, business will prosper and almost any faith will do, though it is wisest to comply with family traditions. Jains say that they are especially successful businessmen because 'Jainism is simple and easy to follow'. Vaishṇavas explain their success as being because 'they are the followers of Vishnu'. Both agree that if a business fails, despite every effort, it must be due to sin and/or lack of faith. Bad luck or ill fortune can be removed through the acquisition of *punya* (religious merit) either by *dāna* (the free gift) to temples, hostels, wandering mendicants and so on (as described earlier) or by means of *sevā* (public service). Public or 'community' service, to be meritorious, should be selfless or disinterested and if sufficient time and effort are invested this will bring about the energy or power needed to overcome all obstacles in the material world. Therefore, according to Mayer (1978) building ten temples will cause ten times the merit of one temple, ten times the power to do business and ten times the success, provided that it is not anticipated because the action would no longer be selfless. Similarly, can we deduce that serving on ten committees would be ten times as efficacious on the supernatural plane as serving on one committee? However, despite the emphasis of Jain informants on the specific necessity for public service in their religion, *sevā* as a concept is found in practically all South Asian religions, though not necessarily with the *dharmik* implications that it has in Jainism. As Millman (1954: 47) somewhat cynically remarks of Marwaris' 'philanthropic' activities, 'every one of their religious deeds has a price tag on it and is based on the ideas of assets and liabilities'. The point here is that the Marwaris studied by Millman consisted of both Jains and Vaishnavas, and it may be added that amongst Muslim merchants there is a similar belief that success in business is due at least in part to participation in the religious life of Islam. Mines (1972: 55–63) shows how Muslim merchants in South India establish borrowing and lending relationships and draws attention to the fact that commonly cooperating merchants are close associates in other activities as well as business, but especially in religious matters. Religious merit and social credit, which subsumes economic credit-worthiness, are thus self-reinforcing social processes, making it irrelevant to argue whether the traditional merchant castes are primarily concerned with ritual status, family prestige, economic power or political influence, as Bayly (1983) argues. Credit and merit are cumulative, self-fulfilling and with concrete effects upon survivability, especially where competition is oligopolistic – which is the typical situation of a small market town.

## *Conclusion*

The purpose of this study has been to discuss to what extent Jains are significantly different, or organise themselves separately, from other businessmen. It should be reasonably clear from the foregoing that, in

Mandi at least, Jains are not culturally distinct as businessmen, nor do they form a separate economic interest group. Only the Jain temple committees and the committees of the attached temple schools are specifically Jain social institutions, amongst a plethora of organisations and associations present in the town and in which (except for the Chaturbhuj temple committee) Jains freely participate. 'Jain' is therefore merely one of several social identities available to a Mahājan household which happens to be Jain. According to context, lineage, marriage circle, hereditary occupation and ethnic origin are equally important or more significant as personal 'labels'. Moreover, in terms of the structuring of interpersonal interactions the details of language, diet and dress may be much more critical features than religious affiliation. It was noted above that merchants were keen to stress the cultural similarities, rather than the cultural differences, between Jains and Vaishnavas in the town. 'Being a Mahājan' would appear to be a more dominant social identity than either of these. It is concluded, therefore, that the Jains in Mandi do not form a community, since they neither have an exclusive social identity nor demonstrate collective action in support of common interests on the basis of that identity, as such.

This is not to say that Jainism is not now and cannot ever be an effective symbol for the focus of community identity in South Asia (or anywhere else for that matter). Sufficient studies have been made of the role of religious identity in raising political consciousness for that idea to be quickly discounted. The point is that perhaps Mandi is neither big enough nor small enough for religious identity to constitute much of a social issue. It possesses neither the anonymity of the city, where a felt need for the development of some kind of exclusive social identity is likely, nor the face-to-face social relationships of a village, where Jains may be the only merchants in the vicinity and thus perforce constitute a discrete social entity which, because of the homogeneity of its specific interests, becomes a community. Moreover, Mandi is growing quickly due to the recent development of small-scale industry operated by local families. The black economy is also flourishing (see Cottam 1983). There is business enough for everybody and although some of the older Mahājan households complained that the *ānewālās* (newcomers) were taking their trade, it is difficult to see how their complaints could be substantiated in economic terms. Therefore, there is no need for the Jains to form an economic pressure group in defence of their particular interests and every reason for them to participate in the trade organisations already existing. Furthermore, because of the high status which Mahājans enjoy in Rajasthan as a whole and in the Jaipur region especially (to the extent that it is nicknamed Baniaraj: the kingdom of the merchants) the motivation to combine together to raise their social status, a process which Timberg (1973; 1978) documents for expatriate Mahājans, is superfluous.

8

# Jain shopkeepers and moneylenders: rural informal credit networks in south Rajasthan

J. Howard M. Jones

The typical Marwari moneylender was not by nature a landowner, his Jain faith and distinct life style marking him out as an alien who was as unassimilable outside his own profession as the medieval Jew.

Eric Stokes, *The Peasant and the Raj. Studies in Agrarian Society and Peasant Rebellion in Colonial India* (Cambridge University Press, 1978)

## *Introduction*

The supply of informal credit is recognised to be an extremely important component of overall credit provision in India. Habib (1964) in his analysis of usury in the medieval Indian economy demonstrates the long history of moneylending in the sub-continent. Numerous studies (e.g. Bailey 1964; Desai 1979; Michie 1978; Timberg and Aiyar 1984) show the continued importance of such moneylending practices in both the rural and urban areas of India. However, it is also recognised that there is little precise data to give us an accurate economic account of the extent and operations of the informal credit markets.

A similar situation exists with regard to Jain studies. The Jains are rightly regarded as an important and very influential merchant community in India. However, apart from rather general studies of Jain ethics and business practices we have no detailed economic accounts of their business and commercial activities.[1] Furthermore, this paucity of economic information is particularly pronounced with respect to the many Jain communities in the rural areas of India.

Carrithers and Humphrey (this volume) have identified five criteria

[1] Fox (1969), Hazlehurst (1966) and Timberg (1978) provide accounts of urban businessmen, traders and shopkeepers rather than specific studies of Jain shopkeepers and businessmen. Nevaskar (1971) does concentrate on Jains but provides no detailed information regarding their business interests or practices.

by which they feel the Jains may be described as a community. The five criteria include: a common set of beliefs and practices; the distinctiveness of these from the surrounding society; a consciousness of identity as Jains; an effectiveness as a collectivity in social, political and/or economic life; finally, the ability for enduring existence. This chapter concentrates on examining the economic component of the fourth criterion. That is, can the Jains be regarded as a distinguishable community by virtue of their effectiveness as a collectivity in economic life? This question is examined by reference to the Jain population of a village in south Rajasthan and the position of these Jains as financial intermediaries in the local credit market.

Economists usually contrast informal credit to formal credit by reference to the former's private supply and the lack of government control over the informal credit market (see Timberg and Aiyar 1984). L. C. Jain's comprehensive survey (1929) of indigenous banking in India opened the way to analysing the many different kinds of informal credit. Subsequent studies have enlarged upon the distinction he made between indigenous banking and moneylending and also upon the different types of moneylending.[2] Moneylending can vary with respect to location, span of operation, the creditors and debtors involved, the nature and size of loans, the security required and the interest rates charged. Discussion has also focussed on the use of informal credit (whether for production or consumption purposes), the advantages informal credit may have for the borrower and the often hostile attitudes expressed by the rest of the population towards moneylenders. Economists have paid particular attention to the determination of interest rates charged in the informal credit markets,[3] the effect these markets can have on a government's monetary policy

[2] Jain (1929), Desai (1979). Indigenous banking is distinguished from moneylending by virtue of its use of bills of exchange (*hundīs*) and the taking of deposits. A distinction is also made between professional and non-professional moneylenders. The former category includes individuals who work exclusively as moneylenders. The latter category is reserved for those individuals for whom moneylending is a 'subsidiary' activity and is further sub-divided into landlords, merchants, agriculturalists and 'others'. This distinction between professional and non-professional moneylenders does not seem completely satisfactory. In Chandrapur, the Jains are not exclusively concerned with moneylending but they are very professional about this activity.

[3] Bottomley (1964). Economists have been concerned to identify which variables are responsible for the relatively high rates of interest in the informal money markets e.g. administrative costs, opportunity costs of capital, risk premiums, monopoly profits etc.

(Sundaram and Pandit 1984) and the effect interlinkage of factor markets (land, labour and credit) may have on agrarian development (Rahman 1979). However, there are still few studies which provide detailed statistical accounts of rural informal credit. Furthermore, not enough attention has been paid to the provision of such credit from the perspective of the moneylenders themselves.

The Jain shopkeepers and moneylenders referred to in this chapter live in a village called Chandrapur which is situated in Dungarpur District, south Rajasthan.[4] By borrowing and working through the account books of the Jain moneylenders, details of each loan were obtained and recorded. This data enables us to consider three areas. First, the working of the rural informal credit markets in south Rajasthan. Second, the economic relationships these village Jains have with non-Jains. In particular, the economic relationships they have with the local tribal people, the Bhils. Third, the extent to which these village Jains can be regarded as a distinguishable community by virtue of their economic occupations. Focussing on the Jains as suppliers of credit not only clarifies the workings of rural informal credit markets but also adds, from an economic perspective, to our understanding of these Jains as a community. As we shall see, the extent and span of the credit networks clearly demonstrate that the Jain community in this rural part of Rajasthan does have a very real economic effect.

The rest of this chapter is divided into seven sections. The first gives a brief outline of Dungarpur District in south Rajasthan. In the second section, a description of Chandrapur village is presented, giving details of its population, the bazaar area and the business activities of the village's Jain families. The third and fourth sections give detailed accounts of the credit networks of two Jain moneylenders, while, in the fifth section, this data is extrapolated to provide a total picture of credit supplied by the Jains in Chandrapur. The sixth section examines the credit supplied by non-Jains in the village and finally, in section seven, the question of whether these Jains form a distinguishable community by virtue of their economic occupation is discussed.

[4] This is a fictitious name for the village. Fieldwork was conducted in Chandrapur for eighteen months in 1975 to 1977 and for three months in 1983. I am grateful to the SSRC for their support during the initial fieldwork period and to my supervisor, A. C. Mayer.

## *Dungarpur District*

Dungarpur District is a former princely state, which until 1948 was ruled by the Maharawal of Dungarpur. It is the smallest of the districts in Rajasthan comprising just 1,460 square miles. Dungarpur District lies in the southern part of Rajasthan State, bounded to the north by Udaipur District, to the east by Banswara District and to the south by the state of Gujarat. The topography of Dungarpur is formed by the offshoots of the Aravalli mountains and is characterised by a consistently rugged, rocky and hilly terrain, though within certain areas of the district we find a more fertile habitat. The area has few industries (some mining concerns, saw mills, printing presses and the like) and the agricultural sector is dominated by small and poor-quality holdings which are subject to the uncertainties of the monsoon.

Although Dungarpur was ruled by Rajput chiefs of the Sisodia clan from the thirteenth century, the majority of the area's population belong to a tribal people called Bhil. The Bhils form 64 per cent of the district's total population according to the 1981 census and for the most part these people reside in 'dispersed' settlements called *pals*. These *pals* are scattered across the whole of Dungarpur District. The different *pals* are usually associated with particular Bhil clans and may cover very considerable areas of land.

In contrast, the non-Bhil villages in Dungarpur District are nucleated settlements which are for the most part inhabited by caste Hindus, Jains and in some instances by Muslim and Bhil households as well. The nucleated settlements form a network, across the district, of what geographers term 'service centres' (Sundaram 1977; Wanmali 1975). These villages vary in the range of services and functions they provide, but it is not the purpose of this chapter to identify a functional hierarchy of such centres as suggested by Sundaram and Wanmali. It is sufficient to note that Chandrapur, the village from which the following data is drawn, is typical of a rural service centre in this district which has extensive economic links with numerous Bhil *pals*. Furthermore, it is the Jains in Chandrapur who supply the great majority of credit loans that go to the Bhil households in these *pals*.

## *Chandrapur village*

Chandrapur is an old-established village. Moreover, the fifteenth-century inscriptions in the village's *Pārśvānāth* temple is evidence of a long history of Jain settlement in this rather remote part of Rajasthan. The village is situated in the rural part of Dungarpur *tehsil*,[5] an area in which over 80 per cent of the population are Bhils, according to the 1981 census. Chandrapur itself is a 'mixed' village containing Caste Hindu, Jain and Bhil households within its boundaries. However, the Bhil households do not live in the nucleated part of the village, but in a separate area of land called Pholeri where the settlement pattern is of a dispersed kind.

Chandrapur has a permanent market area which has extensive trade links with many neighbouring Bhil *pals*. The village has a complex economy in which agriculture is but one of many sources of income and four main components to this economy can be identified. First, the large amount and variety of non-agricultural activities in the village; in particular, the large number of Jain shopkeepers in the village who have extensive trade and credit networks with the surrounding Bhil villages. Second, the extremely small cultivated land areas in the village, particularly the irrigated land areas. Third, the importance of work undertaken outside the village and migration from the village. Fourth, the large number of government servants working in the village. These four components have important implications for the credit networks, but before examining these credit networks in detail, we should note the information below on Chandrapur's population and the business activities of the Jains in the village.

### *Population*

Table 1A shows that the population of Chandrapur is just over 1,000 persons. More than a dozen different caste groups are represented in the village along with a substantial number of Bhil households and a few Muslim households. The extensive government services in the village are shown in table 1B and the small land area of the village is shown in table 1C. The cultivated land area for the whole village is

[5] A *tehsil* is an administrative division. There are three such *tehsils* in Dungapur district.

Table 1A. *Chandrapur population structure, September 1983*

| | | Chandrapur residents | | On service in Chandrapur from outside | | | Daily commuting to village |
|---|---|---|---|---|---|---|---|
| | | HH | Pop. | HH | SP | Pop. | |
| Brahman | Priest | 12 | 55 | 6 | 1 | 26 | 2 |
| Sevak | Temple Servant | 7 | 46 | 1 | — | 2 | 1 |
| Rajput | Warrior | — | — | 1 | 1 | 6 | — |
| Jain | Merchant | 20 | 150 | 1 | — | 4 | — |
| Sikh | | — | — | 1 | — | 2 | — |
| Panchal | Blacksmith | 17 | 104 | — | — | — | — |
| Derzi | Tailor | 7 | 36 | — | — | — | — |
| Bhoi | Gardener | 5 | 29 | — | — | — | — |
| Patel | Farmer | — | — | — | 2 | 2 | 1 |
| Sutar | Carpenter | 2 | 10 | — | — | — | — |
| Kumhar | Potter | 2 | 4 | — | — | — | — |
| Nai | Barber | 2 | 9 | — | — | — | 1 |
| Haraniya | Knifemaker | 1 | 2 | — | — | — | — |
| Hazuri | Servant | — | — | — | 1 | 1 | — |
| Jogi | Religious mendicants | 20 | 123 | — | — | — | — |
| Chamar | Leather worker | 1 | 4 | — | — | — | 1 |
| Bhangi | Sweeper | 2 | 14 | 1 | 1 | 3 | 1 |
| Bohra | Muslim | — | — | 1 | — | 5 | 2 |
| Bhil | Tribal | 66 | 368 | 1 | 11 | 13 | 9 |
| Caste unknown | | — | — | 3 | 3 | 11 | — |
| Total | | 164 | 954 | 16 | 20 | 75 | 18 |

Table 1B. *Government services in Chandrapur, September 1983*

| |
|---|
| Mini-Health Centre, Ayurvedic Hospital |
| Veterinary Dispensary |
| Primary, middle and secondary schools |
| Agricultural Extension field staff |
| Forest Department Office |
| Soil conservation staff |
| Police post |
| Village accountant |
| Post Office |
| Panchayat Office |

Table 1C. *Land in Chandrapur, September 1983*

| | Acres |
|---|---|
| Government land suitable for cultivation | 1.28 |
| Government land unsuitable for cultivation | 104.32 |
| Khatedari – cultivated | 340.70 |
| New Allotments | 54.66 |
| Cattle Grazing – Gram Panchayat | 86.36 |
| Other Departments – Police, Hospital | 1.54 |
| | 588.86 |

only just over 340 acres and, on average, the per household irrigated land areas are below one acre.

In table 1A a distinction is made between 'Chandrapur residents' and those persons 'on service in Chandrapur from outside'. The former category refers to those families who reside in the village and would regard Chandrapur as their 'permanent' abode. Some of these families have a long history of settlement in Chandrapur and belong to lineages stretching back for up to eight generations. The latter category refers to mainly government servants from other parts of India who live and work in Chandrapur. This distinction is not completely satisfactory but it serves to emphasise the large number of 'outsiders' in Chandrapur and the 'service' nature of the village. Furthermore, these 'outsiders' all have regular monthly incomes and this has implications for the Jains' credit networks. A third category of people commute to the village on a daily basis. This group totals eighteen persons and includes government servants, two Muslim shopkeepers and a barber.

From table 1A we can see that the Jains are numerically the second most important group in the village. They have a resident population of 150 persons divided into 20 households. In fact, in the nucleated part of Chandrapur the Jains are numerically the most important group. These 150 Jains are Digambar Jains and they all belong to the Humada caste. This caste is concentrated in Dungarpur, Banswara and Pratapgarh Districts in south Rajasthan. This particular Jain caste is associated with the Kashta Sangha and is divided into eighteen named exogamous *gotras*. Five of these *gotras* are found in Chandrapur, and one distinctive feature of the Jain community in the village is the significant number of Jain marriages arranged within the village. There is one Śvetāmbar Jain household in the village. However, this household is from Udaipur and the household head works in Chandrapur for the Irrigation Department.

*The bazaar*

The Jains in Chandrapur are not just numerically important but are also pre-eminent in the business activities of the bazaar. Table 2 shows the number of retail shops, mills and services in the bazaar in 1977 and 1983; the table also shows the ownership of these concerns in 1983. Of the twenty-seven retail shops in the village, twenty are owned and run by Jains. Not only do the Jains run the majority of the shops in the bazaar, but their shops, with a few exceptions, are the most important and successful retail businesses in the village. The Jains own all five cloth shops, two metal goods shops, the silver shop, the combined cloth/provision shop and eleven of the fifteen general provision shops. Furthermore, only the Jains have families with multiple retail interests in the village. Many of these Jains also advance credit of various kinds and we may now examine the number of Jain families engaged in this kind of business and the types of loan they advance.

*The Jain moneylenders*

Of the thirteen Jain families running retail shops, eight families are involved in moneylending. It is very likely that the other five families

Table 2. *Shops and businesses in Chandrapur May 1977 and September 1983*

| Type of shop/business | May 1977 | September 1983 | Ownership September 1983 |
|---|---|---|---|
| *Retail Shops* | | | |
| General provision shops | 11 | 16 | 11 JAIN |
| | | | 2 Bohra |
| | | | 1 Sevak |
| | | | 1 Panchal |
| | | | 1 Jogi |
| Cloth shop | 4 | 5 | 5 JAIN |
| General provision & cloth shop | 1 | 1 | 1 JAIN |
| Metal goods shop | 1 | 2 | 2 JAIN |
| Silver shop | — | 1 | 1 JAIN |
| Medical store | — | 1 | 1 Jogi |
| Pan shop | 1 | 2 | 1 Blacksmith |
| | | | 1 Bhil |
| Fruit/vegetable sellers | — | 3 | 2 Bhoi |
| | | | 1 Jogi |
| *Mills* | | | |
| Flour mills | 2 | 3 | 2 Brahman |
| | | | 1 JAIN |
| Flour & oil mill | 1 | 1 | 1 JAIN |
| *Services* | | | |
| Cycle store | — | 1 | 1 Bhil |
| Hotels (teashop) | 3 | 6 | 1 Brahman |
| | | | 2 Sutar |
| | | | 3 Bhil |
| Barber | 3 | 2 | 2 Nai |
| Tailor | 7 | 8 | 6 Derzi |
| | | | 2 JAIN |
| Blacksmith | 12 | 11 | 11 Panchal |
| Potter | 1 | 2 | 2 Kumhar |
| Knife-maker | 1 | 1 | 1 Haraniya |
| Shoe repair | — | 1 | 1 Chamar |

are also involved, but either their recent arrival in the village or their reticence thwarted information being collected. Furthermore, an elderly Jain widow also lends money; indeed, she is one of the most important moneylenders in Chandrapur. The involvement of these nine Jain households in moneylending varies with respect to the number and size of the loans they advance and also with the type of loan they advance. Four main types of loan are given by these Jain moneylenders; shop goods given on credit, cash advances on the security of jewellery, cash advances on the security of land or property and finally various grains needed for cultivation. This paper will concentrate on examining the first two types of credit as these form the most extensive of the Jains' credit networks.

To fully appreciate the complexity and extent of credit networks operated by Jains we need to consider individual Jain shops and examine questions such as the following. What is the geographical and numerical spread of the credit networks? What kind of credit is advanced and under what conditions is this credit given and repaid? Who are the Jain shopkeepers advancing credit to? Are the informal credit networks servicing seasonal, periodic or chronic credit requirements? What is the size of these loans and how long does it take the borrower to repay them? What is the attitude of the non-Jains towards the Jain moneylenders? To what extent are these moneylending activities exclusive to the Jain community?

Many of these questions are not easy to answer. Most shopkeepers, and Jains are no exception to this, have no intention of supplying accurate information regarding their business interests. To obtain information on the credit networks, it is necessary to work through the shopkeeper's account books. This is clearly not an easy task. However, it was eventually possible to do this with certain Jain families in the village. In particular, two Jain shopkeepers furnished a great deal of information regarding their credit networks. The first shopkeeper, Mr B. Jain, ran a general goods shop and the data relating to this shop and his moneylending activities is shown in tables 3A to 3F. This was the shop from which the most accurate and comprehensive information was obtained. The second shopkeeper, T. Jain, owned a cloth shop in Chandrapur and table 4 shows the credit network for this particular shop. The data from these two shopkeepers forms the basis of the two examples presented below.

## *B. Jain general provision shop*

B. Jain is a young shopkeeper in Chandrapur whose shop is one of the most profitable in the village. The data from his shop demonstrates the key role these village Jains play as traders and moneylenders in this rural part of Rajasthan. Although his establishment is small and unpretentious, it has an excellent turnover and a very extensive network of credit transactions. The shop was started in 1972 with capital of Rs 1,500 from B. Jain's father and it has been increasingly successful since that date. To illustrate the retailing and credit activities of this shopkeeper, the data on his shop is divided in the following way:

the shop's stock;
the goods on account credit network;
the pawnbroking credit network.

### *The shop's stock*

An inventory of the stock is shown in table 3A. The wide variety of more than 200 goods sold in this shop has a retail value of just over £1,000. The food and clothes items account for just over 60 per cent (by value) of this stock. Many of the food items are quick-selling goods such as sugar, oil, ghi, tea and various grains. Cigarettes (particularly beedis) have a very quick sale. All of these provisions are bought by the shopkeeper on a cash basis; he is not part of a 'ladder of indebtedness' stretching back to the wholesalers (see T'ien 1953). Most of the goods he buys from Dungarpur (Rs 2,000 – £131 weekly) and from Udaipur (Rs 5,000 – £328 monthly). Very few of the items sold are produced locally. Stock is also purchased from agents who visit Chandrapur. In addition, grain in small amounts is bought daily from the mainly Bhil customers and tobacco is purchased from his father's shop.[6] The retail mark-up varies considerably from item to item. A general indication of the retail mark-up for the food items and clothes is shown in the notes to table 3A. For the food items the shopkeeper has a retail mark-up which varies from 5 per cent to 33 per cent. Similarly, for the food items he has a retail mark-up which generally varies from between 10 per cent to 34 per cent.

[6] The Bhils regularly purchase small items from the shop by first selling to the shopkeeper very small amounts of grain.

Table 3A. *B. Jain – general goods shop*

Stock (retail value) September 1983

| | No. of items | Shop Rs | Godown Rs | Total Rs | Total £ | Percentage |
|---|---|---|---|---|---|---|
| Food | 56 | 2,709 | 3,159 | 5,868 | 386 | 36.7 |
| Clothes | 22 | 3,916 | 100 | 4,016 | 264 | 25.1 |
| Electrical goods | 23 | 1,880 | — | 1,880 | 124 | 11.8 |
| Toiletries | 28 | 1,012 | 665 | 1,677 | 110 | 10.5 |
| Medicine | 9 | 169 | — | 169 | 11 | 1.0 |
| Household goods | 26 | 1,287 | 109 | 1,396 | 92 | 8.8 |
| Stationery goods | 29 | 675 | 87 | 762 | 50 | 4.8 |
| Miscellaneous | 8 | 194 | — | 194 | 13 | 1.3 |
| | 201 | 11,842 | 4,120 | 15,962 | 1,050 | 100.0 |

*Notes:*

(i) Stock purchases (cash basis)
Dungarpur weekly Rs 2,000 – £131
Udaipur monthly Rs 5,000 – £328
Average monthly Rs 3,250 – £213

In addition
(a) daily purchase of grains from customers
(b) purchase of stock from visiting agents
(c) purchase of tobacco from father's shop

(ii) Retail mark-up – *Food items* – 43% of goods between 5%–14%
33% of goods between 15%–29%
*Clothes* – 28% of goods between 10%–19%
28% of goods between 20%–34%

Credit – value of goods given on credit September 1983

| Chandrapur | No. clients | Amount credit: Rs | Percentage | | £ | | Average (£) |
|---|---|---|---|---|---|---|---|
| Chobissa Brahman | 5 | 1,521.95 | 10.3 | | 100.13 | | 20.02 |
| Other Brahman | 1 | 25.10 | 0.2 | | 1.65 | | 1.65 |
| Sevak | 3 | 433.60 | 2.9 | | 28.52 | | 9.51 |
| Jain | 12 | 2,162.75 | 14.6 | | 142.29 | | 11.86 |
| Blacksmith | 5 | 831.90 | 5.6 | | 54.73 | | 10.95 |
| Tailor | 1 | 119.45 | 0.8 | 85.7 | 7.85 | | 7.86 |
| Gardener | 1 | 177.90 | 1.2 | | 11.70 | | 11.70 |
| Barber | 1 | 148.25 | 1.0 | | 9.75 | | 9.75 |
| Potter | 1 | 40.00 | 0.3 | | 2.63 | | 2.63 |
| Jogi | 4 | 6,277.55 | 42.5 | | 412.10 | | 103.02 |
| Service | 11 | 915.9 | 6.2 | | 60.26 | | 5.48 |
| *Outside* | | | | | | | |
| Service | 9 | 1,737.65 | 11.8 } | 14.3 | 114.32 | | 12.70 |
| Other | 5 | 372.8 | 2.5 } | | 24.53 | 4.91 | |
| Total | 59 | 4,764.80 | 100.0 | | 971.36 | | 16.46 |

*Notes:*

(i) Value of goods given on credit in May 1977 = Rs 2144.41 (£141)

(ii) Dislike of giving much goods on credit – especially to people outside Antri – because of difficulties in getting the money back. Usually no interest charged

*Goods sold on credit*

The extent and characteristics of this particular credit network are shown in table 3B. The extent and span of this credit network are not very great because the shopkeeper is unwilling to advance this kind of credit on a general basis. Only fifty-nine clients have such accounts and the amount of the credit totals just under £1,000 (Rs 14,764 – £971). If a client regularly takes credit and also regularly clears his account then no interest is charged on these accounts. If, however, repayments become long overdue, then an interest charge of 1 per cent monthly is made by the shopkeeper.

The striking feature of this credit network is that over 85 per cent (by value) of these credit accounts are for clients within Chandrapur itself. Furthermore, only those individuals inside the village who have a reliable income and who are regular customers will be given this type of credit. The only exception to this rule may be fellow Jains for whom it would be difficult to refuse such accounts. This credit is advanced to a number of different caste groups in the village, but the majority of these loans (by value) go to the Jogis (42%), the Jains (14%) and the Chobissa Brahmans (10%). Many of the Chobissa Brahman families have regular income from government employment. The Jogis are traditionally a very low caste of religious mendicants. However, credit is advanced to these four Jogi clients because they have a regular income from government service or income from migration. Eleven of the fifty-nine accounts are for outsiders 'on service' in Chandrapur. These are mainly government servants with a regular monthly income and consequently the shopkeeper is keen to secure their custom. Fourteen accounts are for individuals who live outside Chandrapur, mainly Bhils from neighbouring *pals*. Nine of these Bhil clients are in 'service' and therefore have a regular income, and it is very likely that the remaining five clients also have some kind of regular income.

Although this credit network has been expanded since 1977, the expansion has largely taken place within Chandrapur. In 1977, twenty-seven clients had accounts with a combined total of £141 (Rs 2,144). This compares with fifty-nine clients in 1983 whose combined accounts totalled £971 (Rs 14,764).[7] The demand for this type of

[7] Throughout this chapter prices are expressed in nominal terms and have therefore not been adjusted for inflation.

credit would be considerable, particularly from the Bhils. However, because of the difficulties that would arise in retrieving the money owed to him, B. Jain is reluctant to expand this credit network into the surrounding Bhil *pals*.

*The pawnbroking credit network*

The pawnbroking credit network of this shopkeeper is shown in table 3C. Bearing in mind that Chandrapur is a small village in a remote part of Rajasthan, the extent and span of this credit network is quite spectacular. Indeed, pawnbroking is the major type of moneylending that this shopkeeper engages in. In September 1983 the total number of outstanding loans was 350. These loans were spread over forty-seven villages and had a present-day (redeemable in September 1983) value of over £5,500 (Rs 83,807).[8]

The most striking feature of this pawnbroking network is that over 82 per cent of all these loans (by original value) go to Bhils from the neighbouring *pals*. This is in great contrast to the much more limited geographical span of the goods on credit network. There are certain *pals* that have a relatively high number of loans, for example, Baragaav, Moja, Padla and Surta. This is due to their close proximity to Chandrapur and/or to the fact that B. Jain's shop is situated on the route from these *pals* into the bazaar area. This pawnbroking network has expanded considerably in size and span since 1977. In that year the number of loans outstanding was just 99 and the total value (original value) was only £485. Even in 1977, only 9 out of this total of 99 loans were for clients within Chandrapur. The capital required for this expansion has come from B. Jain's own profits and not from the formal money market.

With very few exceptions, cash loans in this credit network are only advanced on the security of silver and gold jewellery. As M. Harris (1983) correctly points out, jewellery is easy to value, easy to store and easy to sell. Over thirty different types of jewellery are pawned to the shopkeeper, most of which are made of silver. When a client comes to the shop for a loan, the jewellery is taken and details of the loan are written on a small piece of paper which is tied to the ornament concerned. These details include the client's name, his village, the type

[8] The importance and extent of these pawnbroking systems are far greater than is usually recognised by economists and have important implications for the economic analysis of rural informal credit.

Table 3c. *B. Jain – general goods shop (cont.)*

Credit – money loans still outstanding in September 1983

| Villages | Number of loans | Value of original loans | | Present value of original loans | |
|---|---|---|---|---|---|
| | | Rs | Percentage | Rs | £ |
| Chandrapur | 45 | 9,249 | 17.6 | 13,285 | 874 |
| Baragaav | 38 | 6,047 | | 9,451 | 622 |
| Moja | 31 | 3,591 | | 5,510 | 363 |
| Padla | 19 | 3,059 | | 4,734 | 312 |
| Surta | 19 | 3,407 | | 5,098 | 335 |
| Valota | 18 | 2,495 | | 3,951 | 260 |
| Selez | 16 | 1,266 | | 1,992 | 131 |
| Ojri | 16 | 1,146 | | 2,074 | 136 |
| Pagora | 12 | 1,776 | | 2,476 | 163 |
| Margia | 11 | 2,249 | | 5,546 | 365 |
| Mal | 11 | 1,744 | | 2,179 | 143 |
| Navaghara | 11 | 1,463 | 82.44 | 2,319 | 153 |
| Dol. Oda | 9 | 1,007 | | 1,425 | 94 |
| Bhandighati | 9 | 1,475 | | 3,997 | 263 |
| Teleya | 8 | 644 | | 869 | 57 |
| Golambha | 7 | 622 | | 1,480 | 97 |
| Dungra | 7 | 824 | | 1,031 | 68 |
| Bhavadi Kheda | 7 | 1,074 | | 1,202 | 79 |
| 2 villages | 10 (5 × 2) | 1,619 | | 2,582 | 170 |
| 4 villages | 16 (4 × 4) | 3,126 | | 4,955 | 326 |
| 1 village | 3 (3 × 1) | 390 | | 774 | 51 |
| 5 villages | 10 (2 × 5) | 1,542 | | 2,482 | 163 |
| 17 villages | 17 (1 × 17) | 2,850 | | 4,395 | 289 |
| 47 villages | 350 | 52,665 (£3,465) | 100.0 | 83,807 | 5,514 |

*Notes:*

(i) 341 loans given with mainly silver and some gold jewellery as security; 9 loans with watches as security

(ii) Not more than 30% of the value of the silver or gold will be advanced as a loan

(iii) Interest charged; an initial 10% cut will be made in the sum advanced and 3% monthly (simple interest) charged thereafter on the principal, e.g. if Rs 100 is lent, Rs 90 will be advanced and Rs 3 a month charged as interest.

(iv) Jewellery will not be returned on the same day as a repayment of the loan, but on the following day. If the creditor also owes money for goods from

Table 3C. (*cont.*)

the shop, this money will have to be paid before any ornaments are returned

(v) In May 1977 the outstanding loans stood at Rs 7,377 – £485 (original value).

(vi) K. Jain estimates two other Jain moneylenders with larger money-loan credit accounts:

(a) H. Jain Rs 200,000–Rs 300,000–£13,157–£19,736

(b) D. Jain Rs 100,000–£6,579

and weight of the jewellery, the size of the loan and the date. Every few days, or whenever the shopkeeper has half a dozen or so of these pawned items, he transfers the information from the slips of paper into two account books. The jewellery is kept in two separate and very secret places. Consequently, which of the two account books the details are written in depends on which place the jewellery is deposited by the shopkeeper.

Generally speaking, not more than 30 per cent of the scrap value of the jewellery will be advanced to a client. An initial 10 per cent cut will be made from the loan and an interest charge of 3 per cent a month made thereafter. For example, if a loan of Rs 100 is lent, only Rs 90 will actually be advanced and Rs 3 a month charged as interest.[9] Simple interest and not compound interest is charged. The pawned jewellery will not be returned except by a full repayment of the original loan and the interest which has accrued. Moreover, if a client also owes money for goods taken on credit, the money will also have to be repaid before the jewellery is returned. According to B. Jain, quite a lot of the goods on credit money returns to him in this way. Even when the money is repaid to the shopkeeper, the jewellery will not be returned to the client on the same day. The shopkeeper will return the jewellery on the following day to safeguard the whereabouts of his collection of pawned items.

We have already noted that in contrast to goods given on credit, the vast majority of clients in the pawnbroking network are Bhils from outside Chandrapur. However, there is a further significant difference

[9] There is a remarkable similarity to the way these pawnbroking systems work, the interest rates they charge and the 'shame' attached to using them compared to the pawnbroking business in England (Harris 1983).

Table 3D. *B. Jain – general goods shop (*cont.*)*

Credit – money loans within Chandrapur by caste/tribe September 1983

| Caste/Tribe | Number of loans | Original loan | | Present value original loan | |
|---|---|---|---|---|---|
| | | Rs | Percentage | Rs | £ |
| Sevak | 3 | 537 | 5.8 | 1,388 | 91,31 |
| Blacksmith | 4 | 1,675 | 18.0 | 2,070 | 136,18 |
| Tailor | 3 | 1,213 | 13.0 | 1,860 | 122,36 |
| Gardener | 1 | 80 | 0.9 | 179 | 11,77 |
| Jogi | 8 | 3,441 | 37.0 | 4,228 | 279,15 |
| Bhil | 10 | 2,303 | 24.8 | 3,560 | 234,21 |
| Total | 29 | 9,294 | 100.0 | 13,285 | 874,98 |

Table 3E

Credit: size distribution of money loans (original value) outstanding in September 1983

| Size of Loan (Rs) | No. of loans | Percentage |
|---|---|---|
| 1–49 | 95 | 27.1 |
| 50–99 | 57 | 16.3 |
| 100–149 | 59 | 16.9 |
| 150–199 | 36 | 10.3 |
| 200–249 | 46 | 13.1 |
| 250–299 | 20 | 5.7 |
| 300–349 | 9 | 2.6 |
| 350–399 | 4 | 1.1 |
| 400–449 | 6 | 1.7 |
| 450–499 | 3 | 0.9 |
| 500–549 | 2 | 0.6 |
| 550–599 | 4 | 1.1 |
| 600–649 | 5 | 1.4 |
| 650–699 | 1 | 0.3 |
| 900–949 | 1 | 0.3 |
| 1,000–1,049 | 2 | 0.6 |
| Total | 350 | 100.0 |

*Notes:*

89% of the loans (313) are of a value between Rs 1–Rs 299, i.e. up to a value of £19.67

Table 3F

Credit: Age distribution of money loans outstanding in September 1983

| Duration of loan (months) | No. of loans | Percentage |
|---|---|---|
| 1–5 | 100 | 28.6 |
| 6–11 | 53 | 15.1 |
| 12–17 (1 year–) | 59 | 16.9 |
| 18–23 | 23 | 6.6 |
| 24–29 (2 years–) | 37 | 10.6 |
| 30–35 | 16 | 4.6 |
| 36–41 (3 years–) | 23 | 6.6 |
| 42–47 | 13 | 3.7 |
| 48–53 (4 years–) | 7 | 2.0 |
| 54–59 | 7 | 2.0 |
| 60–65 (5 years–) | 3 | 0.9 |
| 66–71 | 4 | 1.1 |
| 72–77 (6 years–) | 2 | 0.6 |
| 96–101 (8 years–) | 2 | 0.6 |
| 114–119 | 1 | 0.3 |
| Total | 350 | 100.0 |

*Notes:*

$>$ 50% $>$ 12 months
43.7% of the loans between 1–11 months
23.4% of the loans between 12–23 months
15.1% of the loans between 24–35 months
10.3% of the loans between 36–47 months

between the two credit networks. Table 3D shows the breakdown by caste/tribe of the clients in Chandrapur who have taken cash on the security of jewellery. It is noticeable that no Jains and no Brahmans within Chandrapur have borrowed money on this basis. To do so would involve 'loss of face' for the families in these two communities. Similarly, ten Bhil families in Chandrapur (Pholari) have pawned jewellery with this shopkeeper but not one Bhil family in this village has a credit account for goods from the shop. The question of why these people pawn their jewellery to this Jain shopkeeper can be considered more clearly after examining the size and age distribution of the 350 loans.

In table 3E the size distribution (by original value) of the 350 loans is given. It is immediately apparent that the great majority of these loans are for very small cash advances. Once more, we need to bear in mind that these are Jain traders in a relatively poor and remote part of Rajasthan. Ninety-five loans (27%) are for cash advances of between Rs 1 and Rs 49. Furthermore, 313 loans (89%) are for cash advances of between Rs 1 and Rs 299, that is, up to a value of just under £20. However, even though the majority of the 350 loans are for such small amounts of money, the difficulties experienced in repaying them is indicated by table 3F.

The data in table 3F shows the age of each loan at one point in time – September 1983. Over 50 per cent of the 350 loans are over twelve months old. Furthermore, 115 loans (33%) are over two years old and 62 loans (18%) are over three years old. With interest charges of 3 per cent a month, this makes pawning jewellery a very expensive way to borrow money.

The data on this shopkeeper's moneylending business was undertaken on the strict understanding that the information would not be discussed with anyone else in the village. In any case, it would have been impossible to enquire from the 350 clients why they had pawned their jewellery with this shopkeeper. However, it was apparent that the great majority of these loans are for consumption purposes: in particular, the need to meet a cash crisis very quickly. The need to meet marriage costs, to meet hospital costs, to meet the costs of a small bribe were examples of cash requirements that could not be met by the formal money market. Moreover, the Jain shopkeepers offer a service which can have distinct advantages over the village cooperative and the banks in Dungarpur city. The Jain shops are open from dawn to dusk and are therefore highly accessible. They offer a service which is extremely quick, requires no awkward questions to be answered and no complicated forms to be filled out. Also, these loans can be used for any purposes. In M. Harris's (1983) article an English pawnbroker's customer accurately remarked: 'It's the fastest way around to get your hands on a small amount of money . . . you're just in and out.' The same can be said for the Jain pawnbrokers in Chandrapur.

### *T. Jain cloth shop*

The Jains in Chandrapur have a monopoly on the sale of cloth in the village as they own all of the five cloth shops. The data from T. Jain's shop provides an example of a Jain's credit network for this type of retail concern. His shop is the third most successful cloth shop in the village. It was quite impossible to obtain information from the families running the two most profitable cloth shops and certainly their credit networks will be larger than the one described below. Furthermore, there was a good deal of quarrelling between T. Jain and his eldest son M. Jain concerning the latter's lack of application to the running of the shop. However, it was the one cloth shop from which it was possible to borrow the account books and these do give an indication of the credit networks for this kind of retail shop. In contrast to the previous example, this Jain shopkeeper has a very extensive goods-on-account credit network and he himself is part of a credit chain which reaches back to his suppliers in Ahmedabad.

*The stock*

The shop sells quite a wide variety of cloth for both men's and women's clothes and also sells a number of ready-made items. Most of these goods are of rather poor quality and are relatively inexpensive. Nevertheless, all of these items are imported to Chandrapur and this again illustrates the key role village Jains play as suppliers of manufactured goods in this rural part of Rajasthan. M. Jain estimated that in September 1983 the total value (wholesale) of the stock amounted to around Rs 25,000 (£1,645). The two most successful cloth shops he estimated to have stocks worth Rs 40,000 (£2,631) and Rs 30,000 (£1,973) respectively. A month before Dīwālī and Holi, the stock in all the cloth shops would be increased by between Rs 5,000 and Rs 10,000 (£329–£658) worth of goods. This is to cater to the increased demand for new clothes at these times in the year.

Most of the stock is bought from Ahmedabad or from agents who visit Chandrapur. Yearly purchases are put at around Rs 70,000 (£4,605) worth of stock. If the shopkeeper falls short in certain items he can replenish the stock of these goods from Dungarpur city. About half the shop's stock is bought with cash and about half on credit. The wholesale price the shopkeeper has to pay for his stock varies according to which of these two methods he uses to pay for the goods and whether he buys direct from the wholesaler or through an agent. If the shopkeeper settles this account after three months then an interest charge of 1.5 per cent a month is made by the wholesaler. A similar system operates if the shopkeeper buys through an agent, but now an additional commission charge of 10 per cent must also be added to the bill.

The retail mark-up charged by this shopkeeper is generally around 25 per cent. However, this can be reduced to 20 per cent for cash sales and is often increased to 30 per cent for credit sales. In recent years, this shop has reduced the proportion of its sales made on a credit basis. The shopkeeper felt it was becoming too difficult to retrieve the money owing to him and reported that not more than 10 per cent of his sales would now be on a credit basis. A similar situation was expressed by at least one other of the cloth-shop proprietors. Certainly, the credit network illustrated in table 4 is not as 'healthy' or lucrative as the credit network illustrated in table 3C.

*The goods-on-account credit network*

From table 4, we can see the total amount of goods given on credit by this shopkeeper over a three-year period. The extent and span of this credit network is quite considerable. In Dīwālī 1983 the goods on account had a value which totalled more than Rs 5,500 (£3,779) and the number of clients at this time was 625. The vast majority of the clients in this credit network are Bhils from the surrounding *pals*. Consequently, this goods-on-account credit network is similar in its span to B. Jain's pawnbroking credit network.

However, a striking feature from table 4 is that over the three-year period the total amount of each Dīwālī is remarkably similar. There has not been an extensive growth in the credit network like that illustrated in B. Jain's pawnbroking network. In Dīwālī 1983 the total number of accounts had increased to 625 compared to 611 in 1981. The value of these accounts had increased from Rs 51,908 to Rs 57,435 over the same period. Although more than Rs 57,000 is owed to T. Jain he has no security to back these accounts and he is finding it difficult to retrieve the money. In table 4 the columns 'Loans' and 'Credit' refer to new loans given and repayments taken between each Dīwālī. Between Dīwālī 1982 and Dīwālī 1983 he had advanced credit to a value of Rs 13,251 (£871) and obtained repayments to a value of Rs 11,211 (£738). Over a twelve-month period this does not amount to a great deal of business. The shopkeeper employs a Jogi man to work in the shop and to go out into the *pals* to try and retrieve money owed to the shop. Until the old accounts are cleared the shopkeeper is reluctant to advance any further credit. So this shop seems to have reached something of an impasse. A great deal of money is owed to this Jain shopkeeper and he is finding it very difficult to secure repayments. At the same time, new advances are not being given to those clients who have failed to repay their debts. The son is in favour of writing off all accounts which have a value of under Rs 25 (£1.64) and starting afresh. His father is very reluctant to adopt this policy and an analysis of the size distribution of the accounts indicates the reason.

The size distribution of the accounts is given in the notes to table 4. The most striking feature is the small size of the great majority of the loans. Over 65 per cent of the accounts are for amounts of less than Rs 50 (£3.29). Furthermore, over 95 per cent of the 625 accounts are for amounts of less than £20.25. This is another Jain shopkeeper whose credit network consists of a multitude of small advances spread over many Bhil *pals*. The largest single account is for Rs 2,887 (£190). This is for a Chandrapur Jogi man who incurred substantial expenses for the marriages of his daughters.

Interest charges of 1.5 per cent a month are made for certain accounts. The shopkeeper reported that if accounts were for amounts of over Rs 100 then interest would be charged when these accounts were over three years old. For 'large' accounts interest would be taken after a year. These interest charges are not shown explicitly in the account books. An ingenious system of entering fictitious new accounts and repayments is used so that interest is effectively charged but is impossible to detect. This system is shown in table 4, note (ii). Here we can see how Rs 500 interest is charged to an account by means of a fictitious new loan of Rs 3,000 and a fictitious repayment of Rs 2,500. In reality, the client had taken no further loans or made any repayments, but the books now show him owing this Jain shopkeeper a total of Rs 3,500.

In the case of B. Jain and T. Jain we have two examples of Jain shopkeepers whose credit networks extend over wide areas and link hundreds of families (mostly Bhil) to a particular retail shop. We can now try to estimate how extensive these credit networks are for the rest of the Jain traders and moneylenders in Chandrapur.

### *The total amount of informal credit supplied by the Chandrapur Jains*

By extrapolating from B. Jain's own data and the information he gave concerning other Jain pawnbrokers, we may obtain a rough estimate

Table 4. *T. Jain, cloth shop*

Credit: value of goods given on credit and repayments, Dīwālī 1981, 1982 and 1983

| Villages | Dīwālī 1981 | Loans | Credit | Repayments | Dīwālī 1982 | Loans | Credit | Repayments | Dīwālī 1983 | Loans |
|---|---|---|---|---|---|---|---|---|---|---|
| Chandrapur | 9,837 | 71 | 4,807 | 4,567 | 10,077 | 76 | 1,143 | 1,613 | 9,507 | 79 |
| Pholari | 2,323 | 20 | 240 | 245 | 2,318 | 20 | 502 | 362 | 2,458 | 20 |
| Valota | 5,415 | 68 | 2,625 | 1,060 | 6,980 | 68 | 1,729 | 2,030 | 6,679 | 69 |
| Doja | 5,344 | 50 | 1,162 | 998 | 5,508 | 51 | 864 | 861 | 5,511 | 52 |
| P. Gokal | 4,728 | 32 | 2,457 | 2,302 | 4,883 | 33 | 3,519 | 1,733 | 6,669 | 33 |
| Kahari | 4,353 | 59 | 2,998 | 1,993 | 5,358 | 57 | 2,779 | 2,101 | 6,036 | 58 |
| 3 villages | 3,824 | 16 | — | 525 | 3,299 | 16 | — | — | 3,299 | 16 |
| P. Moru | 2,952 | 39 | 270 | 502 | 2,720 | 38 | 340 | 275 | 2,785 | 39 |
| Verda | 2,523 | 23 | — | 40 | 2,483 | 23 | 367 | 120 | 2,730 | 23 |
| Biliya | 2,332 | 23 | — | — | 2,332 | 23 | — | — | 2,332 | 23 |
| Telaya | 2,346 | 53 | 1,782 | 1,167 | 2,961 | 52 | 985 | 914 | 3,032 | 53 |
| Pasoor | 1,249 | 24 | 474 | 286 | 1,437 | 24 | 151 | 93 | 1,495 | 24 |
| Naar | 1,231 | 20 | — | — | 1,231 | 20 | — | — | 1,231 | 20 |
| Gorgha | 1,140 | 40 | 949 | 668 | 1,421 | 41 | 311 | 337 | 1,395 | 41 |
| D. Oda | 1,054 | 26 | 650 | 532 | 1,172 | 26 | 403 | 722 | 853 | 30 |
| 6 villages | 1,032 | 26 | 95 | 75 | 1,055 | 25 | 158 | 60 | 1,153 | 25 |
| 3 villages | 225 | 21 | — | 55 | 170 | 20 | — | — | 170 | 20 |
| 26 villages | Rs 51,908 | 611 | 18,509 | 15,012 | 55,405 | 613 | 13,251 | 11,211 | 57,435 | 625 |
| £ | 3,415 | | 1,218 | 988 | 3,645 | | 871 | 738 | 3,779 | |

| | Size | Number of loans | Percentage |
|---|---|---|---|
| Rs 1–49 | (up to £3.22) | 402 | 64.3 |
| Rs 50–99 | (£3.28–£6.51) | 81 | 12.9 |
| Rs 100–149 | (£6.57–£9.80) | 48 | 7.7 |
| Rs 150–199 | (£9.86–£13.09) | 25 | 4.0 |
| Rs 200–399 | (£13.16–£26.25) | 40 | 6.4 |
| Rs 400–599 | (£26.31–£39.40) | 9 | 1.4 |
| Rs 600–799 | (£39.47–£52.56) | 8 | 1.3 |
| Rs 800–999 | (£52.63–£65.72) | 5 | 0.8 |
| Rs 1,000–1199 | (£65.79–£78.88) | 3 | 0.9 |
| Over Rs 1,200 | (£78.94– ) | 4 | 0.6 |
| | | 625 | 100.0 |

(ii) Interest (1.5% monthly) is taken when account is above Rs 100 and over 2–3 years old – this interest is not shown explicitly in account books but in terms of fictitious further transactions – e.g. Rs 500 interest

| Dīwālī 1982 | Credit | Repayments | Dīwālī 1983 |
|---|---|---|---|
| Rs 3,000 | 3,000 | 2,500 | 3,500 |

(iii) Retail mark-up higher for goods on credit (30%) than goods bought for cash (20%–25%)

(iv) Total for Dīwālī 1975 – Rs 61,975.77 – £4,077.

(v) In comparing this table with 3C note that in 3C Chandrapur includes Bhil settlement of Pholari

for the Jain pawnbroking networks as a whole. There are at least eight Jain shops which advance this type of loan, as well as the Jain widow mentioned earlier. B. Jain estimated that three of these shops and the Jain widow had pawnbroking accounts which were by value 50 per cent of his own. This gives a total of approximately Rs 105,330 for all four. He also estimated that three Jain shops had pawnbroking accounts which were of similar value to his own shop. For these four shops the total is Rs 210,660. One Jain shop was estimated to have a pawnbroking network twice as large as his own and, finally, one Jain shop was estimated to have a pawnbroking account five times greater than his own. For these two shops the total is Rs 368,655. This gives a grand total for all the Jain moneylenders of Rs 684,645, that is, £45,042. Furthermore, if we extrapolate from the per capita value of B. Jain's pawnbroking account (Rs 150,47) this would give a grand total of 4,550 clients, most of whom would be Bhils in the neighbouring *pals*. Even from this one small village the extent and span of the Jains' pawnbroking networks are quite considerable. Across the district as a whole, the extent of these pawnbroking networks and the number of clients must be very large indeed.

If we use a similar extrapolation to estimate the total of the goods-on-account credit networks, then a figure of Rs 245,435 (£16,147) is reached for the Jain shops in Chandrapur. Although the extent and span of this type of credit network are smaller than that for the Jains' pawnbroking business, it is still an impressive figure and it is undoubtedly an underestimate. Furthermore, over the district as a whole, the extent of these goods-on-account credit networks will be very considerable. We may now consider two further questions. First, is the supply of informal credit exclusive to the Jain shopkeepers and moneylenders? Second, are these Jains advancing credit as individual moneylenders and traders or are they advancing credit as a community?

### *Non-Jain shopkeepers and moneylenders*

In Chandrapur there are a few non-Jains who lend money on the security of gold and silver jewellery. These pawnbrokers include two blacksmiths, two tailors and a gardener caste (Bhoi) man. It was impossible to obtain direct information on the extent of these pawnbroking concerns. However, B. Jain did estimate that the two blacksmith moneylenders had pawnbroking accounts amounting to Rs 44,765 (£2,945) and Rs 26,332 (£1,732) respectively. That is, these two accounts amount to 85 per cent and 50 per cent of his own pawnbroking business. No estimate was available for the two tailors' pawnbroking concerns, but as far as the gardener caste man is concerned his pawnbroking business totals no more than a few hundred rupees.

From table 2 we note that just over half a dozen retail shops in Chandrapur are owned by non-Jains. We note also that these shops tend to be much smaller and have a lower turnover than the Jain shops. It is therefore no surprise that only one of these non-Jain shops has a goods-on-account credit network of any importance. This shop is a *pan* shop owned by a young blacksmith caste man. It September 1983 he had a total of Rs 13,491 (£917) owing to him for goods given on credit. Just over 75 per cent of this £917 was owed to him by clients from Chandrapur itself. Consequently, in his reluctance to extend this kind of credit outside the village this shopkeeper has a credit network very similar to the goods-on-account credit network of B. Jain.

Clearly, the supply of informal credit in Chandrapur is not the exclusive concern of the Jains in the village. However, in total the amount of credit supplied by the non-Jains is very small indeed compared to the extensive credit networks of the Jain shopkeepers and moneylenders. Furthermore, are we now able to argue that these non-Jains are advancing credit as individuals while the Jains are advancing credit as a community?

## *Informal credit and Jains as a community*

In this chapter, we have examined a local group of Jains in a small market village in south Rajasthan. In what sense, from an economic point of view, can these twenty Jain families be regarded as a distinguishable community? Certainly, it is clear that these Jain families do have a very real economic effect. Moreover, by the extension of their credit networks into the surrounding Bhil *pals*, this effect is felt by literally thousands of Bhil families. However, do these Jains form a community of traders and financial intermediaries or do they simply comprise a number of individual shopkeepers and moneylenders who happen to be Jain?

Before looking at the economic aspects of community it is

important to consider two preliminary points. First, the particular position of the Jains in Chandrapur. Second, how the non-economic criteria for a community as identified by Carrithers and Humphrey (see chapter 1) relate to these Jain families. It is essential to recognise that this paper has not been discussing city- or town-dwelling Jains, but Jains who live in a small village in a remote part of tribal Rajasthan. Consequently, it is relatively easy to identify these Jains as a separate social entity, especially when we bear in mind that they all belong to one particular Jain caste and that there are no other trading castes present in the village. Furthermore, if we recognise that a community can be distinguishable by collective inaction as well as by collective action, then the non-economic criteria of Carrithers and Humphrey are also evident with respect to the Jains in this village. The Jain temple of Pārśvanāth is the largest and most imposing temple in the village. In addition to their daily worship at this temple, the Jains in Chandrapur also have their own distinctive and separate religious festivals. The most dramatic of these culminates in the annual procession of the Pārśvanāth *mūrti* (image of the deity) through the village. This religious distinctiveness is further enhanced by the non-involvement of the Jains in certain major Hindu festivals in the village. For example, the Jains do not participate in the worship of Amba Mata which takes place during Navratri, the annual nine-nights festival. Similarly, the Jain women are conspicuous by their absence in the annual worship of Sitala, the 'smallpox goddess'. Thus, the Jains in this village collectively display beliefs and practices which are distinct from their neighbours. Furthermore, they are clearly conscious of their identity as Jains. A very tangible example of this consciousness is a recent public appeal made by the Chandrapur Jains for funds to restore the Pārśvanāth temple.

With regard to the economic aspect of community, the relative importance of economic occupation in identifying a collectivity will vary from local Jain community to local Jain community. At one extreme, the Jain moneylenders may *act* collectively and distinctively and thereby form a distinguishable community of shopkeepers and moneylenders. At the other extreme, the Jain shopkeepers and moneylenders may already form an effective community by virtue of non-economic criteria (e.g. Jainness) and their business interests and practices may be no different from other merchant castes involved in similar commercial pursuits. As far as Chandrapur is concerned, it is argued that the Jains are effective as a collectivity in economic life and that this plays a key role in identifying these village Jains as a distinguishable community. In a very real sense, the Jains do act collectively through their sheer dominance of the informal credit markets and retail businesses. Furthermore, this collective economic action is given ritual expression at certain times in the year. For example, on the first, fifth, eleventh and thirteenth days of *paryūṣaṇ* all the Jain shops in the village, and only the Jain shops, must be closed. The Jains in this village are distinguishable as a community in terms of the extent, span and success of their business interests and by their concentration in these lines of activity. In particular, only the Jains have as a community such extensive credit links with the tribal Bhils. Furthermore, it is only within the Jain community that these credit links are given ritual expression at the time of *Dīwālī*, with the opening of the new account books.[10] The Jains in this village have a clear sense of identity as Jains and they also have an identity of economic interests. From an economic point of view, these Jains make up a functional community (Plant 1974), a community of traders and moneylenders which plays a key role in the economy of south Rajasthan.

The economics literature is full of criticisms levied against rural moneylenders and, in particular, the quotation from Stokes at the beginning of this chapter exemplifies a popular conception of Jain moneylenders. Such views are often exaggerated and as Wilmington (1983) points out, more attention should be paid to the problems moneylenders themselves have, for example, in mobilising capital and in retrieving their credit advances. However, having said this, it is true that the pre-eminence of Jains as shopkeepers and moneylenders in this rural area of south Rajasthan does affect how they are regarded as a community by the non-Jains in the area. Not only do the non-Jains express the usual kinds of prejudices levelled against middlemen (Bonacich 1973) but the colloquial name for Jains in this part of Rajasthan is a particularly abusive term, which reflects the wealth the Jains are felt to earn from their retailing and usurious activities.

L. C. Jain (1929) in his survey of indigenous banking expressed the

[10] I am grateful to C. M. Cottam Ellis for reminding me of this fact.

view that whereas indigenous banking is the preserve of 'banking castes', as far as moneylending is concerned 'everyone does it'. However, an analysis of the rural informal credit markets in south Rajasthan shows that the examination of particular communities can be just as important for the study of rural informal credit as for the study of urban indigenous banking. The important point about moneylending in Chandrapur is not that 'everyone does it', but that no community 'does it' quite like the Jains.

# 9

# A study of Jains in a Rajasthan town

N. K. Singhi

### *Introduction and overview*

Cultural pluralism is a basic characteristic of Indian society. The structural openness of Hinduism explains the pluralism. It is in this context that we need to examine the question of whether or how the Jains are a community.

Let us first examine the features common to all Jains. Jainism is a religion with a distinct and abstract philosophical basis. Its philosophy has given rise to schools of logic, mathematics, geography and literature, architecture and painting. Most of the Jain literature is in the form of manuscripts written in Prakrit or Sanskrit, and very little of it has been translated or published. The ordinary Jain is largely unaware of his philosophical heritage, and emphasises the overt/manifest dimensions of practices in daily life. At a certain level, Jains also share a value system, despite sectarian differences. Dietary practices are commonly shared, for example. Based on the non-killing of animals or insects, these practices are distinct from those of Hindus or people of other religions in India. To eat before sunset, to eat dried vegetables especially on the eighth and fourteenth day of every fortnight, to use boiled water on these days, also during *paryūṣaṇ* (a period of intensified religious observance), and not to use root vegetables such as potatoes, onions, garlic, or those which have a multiplicity of seeds, have been dietary universals of Jains throughout the country. Vegetarianism is the accepted pattern of food consumption among Jains.

The *nokar mantra* (= *namaskāra mantra*) is another universal feature. All Jains remember it by heart. The meditative and confessional practices of *sāmāyik* and *pratikramaṇ*, as well as fasting, are other universal dimensions. Common pilgrimage sites, despite sectarian claims for ownership, reveal the shared symbol of the *Tīrthaṇkar* (founding exemplar of Jainism) in which all repose faith.

Consciousness of identity is another dimension which makes a community. The routinisation of identity often makes it less visible and leads to a lack of consciousness. On the other hand, identity is negatively buttressed by threats to the Jain community. On some occasions when Jain *sādhus* have been beaten up, a common cause was made by all Jains. But the Jains have taken up common causes on only a few occasions. The declaration of Mahāvīr Jayanti as a national holiday, a restricted holiday during *paryūṣaṇ*, and celebrations of the 2,500th anniversary of Mahāvīr have been such occasions.

We can see the notion of identity is woven in a concentric circle. The individual has several identities, namely, familial, regional, religious and national. The emergence of each identity is contextual and has to be examined in that sense. Apart from the self-perception of identity, the shared quality of such an identity is significant in giving a distinct character at the level of the collectivity. The Jains in this connection have to be viewed differently in villages, towns and cities. Regional differences also have to be taken into account.

This chapter deals with Jains in Sirohi, which is a small town in Rajasthan. Let us first summarise the general characteristics of Jains in this district. Most Jains here are entrepreneurs. Business as an occupation is highly self-oriented, and thus it is a negative factor in the formation of a common dominant Jain identity. The business ethos has created competition in the ritualistic and institutional dimensions of religious practice. Auctions at the time of *paryūṣaṇ* and *pratiṣṭhā* (consecration of a new image), and the competitive organisation of pilgrimages, are illustrations of this. Those who have achieved affluence in business display their acquisitions, which gives them heightened social status, a fillip in business and a social position from which to get better matrimonial offers for their children. In the religious sense, this binds people and does give a sense of identity, but socially it is divisive.

In Sirohi, the Porwal and Dasā (Oswal) castes have been associated with business and Bisā Oswals with service. This has led to the development of distinct sub-cultures and styles of life among these Jain castes. Caste affiliations have been buttressed by occupational specialisation. The great sense of difference among these castes has been emphasised by the fact that the Bisā Oswals have a higher rate of literacy, have taken to modern occupations and life styles, their women have more education, and they have taken employment in government work. In contrast, Dasās and Porwals have more wealth but have been very slow in accepting new styles of life and progressive measures. However, the differences between these castes are most pronounced in day-to-day life. Physical proximity in residence and frequency of interaction enhance this. Folklore, consisting of proverbs and sayings, reveals mutual perceptions in terms of stereotypes.

There have been only a few instances of crises when all three castes have united. But other communities do not perceive Jains as divided, since they view all Jains as one collectivity. This creates a duality, in which the perception by others tends to regard all Jains as a 'whole', while the Jains themselves emphasise the 'parts' more than the whole.

Jains were very active in the freedom movement. Brahmins and Jains were the leaders in these movements. The leaders had formal education in colleges and universities and were influenced by the national leadership. Support for this movement also came from the middle castes. Both Oswals and Porwals provided leadership, went to jail and had their property confiscated.

After Independence, however, in the first elections there was a contest between a Rajput and a Jain candidate. The lower castes supported the Rajput candidate, despite the fact that the Jain candidate had made great sacrifices in the freedom struggle and was a leader of long standing. The Rajput fought as an independent candidate and used the strategy of uniting all the lower castes on an anti-Jain theme. In the 1985 election, again, a Jain candidate who stood as a BJP candidate against a Congress (I) party candidate lost. The Jains were divided and did not support the Jain candidate on caste or religious grounds.

## *II*

The present chapter analyses the Jains in Sirohi town in the south-west of the state of Rajasthan, India. The town was founded five centuries ago by Maharaja Sahasmal, a scion of the Dera Chauhan dynasty. The population of Sirohi town, according to the 1981 census, is 23,903. The total population of Jains in Rajasthan is 513,548. The population of Jains in Sirohi District is 4.53 per cent of the total population. The number of Jains is 19,197, of which 41.65 per cent reside in urban areas.

In Sirohi town all the Jains are Śvetāmbar and all are *Mandir-mārgi* (*Mūrtipūjāk*). The three castes break down by household as follows:

| | |
|---|---|
| Bisā Oswal | 601 families |
| Dasā Oswal | 161 families |
| Porwal | 256 families |

The total number of Jains is around 5,090, which constitutes nearly one-fifth of the total population. Compared to other castes, their concentration in the urban area is very high.

Sirohi was a princely state ruled by hereditary kingship. Feudalism was the dominant ethos of social life. The Oswal Jains of Sirohi were associated with the administration of the state in different capacities at the higher levels of the hierarchy. Dasās and Porwals were in business. These occupational diversities created distinctive life styles. The Oswals tended to live lives of ostentation and luxury, while the Porwals and Dasās maintained a simple style of life.

## *III*

M. Carrithers and C. Humphrey (this volume) have proposed five criteria for characterising a populace as a community. These criteria envisage sharing of a common culture, beliefs, and practices, as well as common interests, which ought to be significantly different from the surrounding society. The consciousness of identity is necessary for any section of a population to be termed a community. A community should be effective as a collectivity in social, political and/or economic life – and should indicate cultural continuity and not merely a temporary constellation.

The construction and applicability of the concept of 'community' to the Jains necessitates analysis of the empirical reality as expressed at the following levels:

a ascetic/religious – non-social
b ascetic/religious – social
c institutional/secular
d habitat/locale
e crisis management

The above classification is intended to help examine beliefs and practices in terms of their coverage of these levels. The dimensions of shared consciousness as a subjective indicator of identity can be constructed through the objective and manifest actions of the Jain population in different institutional and non-institutional spheres of activity.

## *IV*

Let us first examine (a) the 'ascetic/religious – non-social' level. *Poṣadha* and *oli* are religious *tapas* (acts of religious self-mortification) which do not involve any social ceremonies. They are popular among Jain women in Sirohi. The normal *oli* is a period of restricted eating (fast) which lasts for nine days. But there are many more elaborate forms. The *bari oli* (great *oli*) has 100 periods of restricted eating (*ambil*) followed by a fast (*upavasa*).[1] The great *tapa*, with 600 such periods, takes 14 years, 3 months and 20 days. There are no ceremonies associated with *oli*. Prestige is attached to the persons who undertake *oli*, but it is confined to older women and does not add to prestige at a wider level.

*Poṣadha* means sinlessness. It is taken in an *upāśraya* (residence for ascetics and general religious meeting-place). It can be taken for 24 hours or 12 hours. In *poṣadha* one lives like a *sādhu* for the period, that is, the routine of the *sādhu* is followed by the *śrāvak* (lay person). A particular *tapa* necessitates its *pacchakan* (vow). The following *pacchakans* are common:

1 *Nokarsi* – not to eat or drink till 48 minutes after the sunrise
2 *Porsi* – till one and a half hours after sunrise.
3 *Sadh porsi* – till one and a quarter hours after sunrise
4 *Parimudh* – till 12.45 p.m.
5 *Avadh* – not before 4.0 p.m.
6 *Choviar* – not to eat four types of eatables: the four *ahars* (types of nourishment) are *asanam* (part meals), *panam* (water), *khyanam* (meals) and *saynam* (medicine)
7 *Tiviyar* – only water can be taken after sunset
8 *Duviviar* – milk can be taken after sunset for medicinal reasons
9 *Pona* – for those who fast

[1] *Ambil* permits a particular food to be taken once a day. No oil, ghee, sugar, salt, or curd is permitted, nor dry or green fruits. *Upavasa* requires that no food be taken throughout the day.

*Poṣadha* cannot be taken for more than a day or so at a time. Besides *akasana* fasting, permitting food only once a day, *Pratikramaṇa* (confession) and threefold *dev-vandanā* (image worship) must be performed during *poṣadha*. The *śrāvak* or *śrāvikā* (layman or laywoman) should carry a *sarwara*,[2] which symbolises *ahiṃsā*.

The lack of ceremonial in these *tapas* of *oli* and *poṣadha* can be explained by their frequency. Generally, old women undertake them. Since *oli* is done in the *ambilkhana*, where one gets meals free of charge, and *poṣadha* requires staying in the *upāśtarya*, it is widows and older women who prefer to participate, as it enables them to get away from the daughter-in-law, with whom they may not be getting on well. Essentially, these are *tapas* devoid of post-performance gaiety. Thus, despite the limited amount of prestige which does accrue to the performer, social prestige tends to follow a reverse pattern: people tend to think that participation in these *tapas* is an indication of familiy problems which require the performer to retire for a time from the family scene. Thus the 'part-prestige' (religious) gained is also a 'part-prestige' (social) lost. It is interesting to note that fear of losing social prestige prevents some people from taking up these *tapas*. So even at the purely ascetic-religious level social considerations may outweigh the religious.

## *V*

The category of (b) 'ascetic/religious social' activities includes *upādhyana*, *varsitapa* and collective *pratikramaṇa*, all of which reveal the social dimensions of ascetic *tapa*. They are manifest at two levels: (1) organisational; (2) ritual occasions.

*Upādhyana* and *varsitapa* are considered to be *yoya*s. There are three *upādhyana*s undertaken for 48, 35 and 28 days respectively. During this time the *śrāvak* undertakes the *akasana* fast (one meal a day) alternately with other fasts, followed by special dietary restrictions on the eighth and fourteenth days of the lunar fortnight. *Upādhyana* involves adopting the routine of the *sādhu* or *sādhvi* and is undertaken in the *upāśraya*. The *varsitap* involves *tapasya* for 13

2 *Sarwara*(*oroga* in the case of sadhus) is a brush made of thick woollen threads with a wooden handle. It is carried by the sadhus to clean the space where they sit. The insects are not killed by these thick woollen threads.

months and 14 days, during which there is fasting followed by *ambil* (see glossary). Two consecutive fasts follow if there is a *tithi* (sacred date) falling immediately after a fast. This *tapasya* is undertaken at one's home residence. The *upādhyana* is done collectively and is open to all the *nyats* (local caste group) of Jains. The expenses of this *tapa* are met by the individual in whose name it is organised. After its completion, social functions follow. For example, all those who undertake this *tapa* are given gifts. In one *upādhyana* a gold chain was given to all the participants. The participants also gave *prabhāvana* (small gifts). Relatives give money called *neg* to the *tapasvi*. In one ceremony (the *mela*) the brother puts a golden necklace round the neck of his sister. A further ceremony, *palana*, is done at the pilgrimage sites of Palitana or Hastinapur. Close relatives go to this place and the ceremonies of *mela* and *prabhāvana* are performed. There is a *boli* (auction) for the first, second and third performance of the *mela* ritual. *Neg* is given, and then there is a return gift from the *tapasvi*. Songs are sung and new dresses are worn; this is a social festivity. Friends from other communities join in, offering *neg*, further small prestations, and receiving return gifts.

In religious terms *pratikramaṇa* signifies a ritual for penance of the '*pāpa*' (sin) done during the day. Any *miradhana* (small transgression) done in the night similarly necessitates *pratikramaṇa* in the morning.

*Pakki pratikramaṇa* is performed once a fortnight; that is, those who cannot do *pratikramaṇa* every day compensate by doing it once a fortnight. *Pratikramaṇa* can also be performed once a year, during *paryūsaṇ*. This is for those who cannot do *pratikramaṇa* either daily or once a fortnight.

*Pratikramaṇa* when performed in the *upāśraya* is held in a group under the guidance of a *sādhu* or *sādhvi*. Women in Sirohi attend these regularly in great numbers. They are occasions for gossiping, exchange of information, conversation about engagements, marriages, deaths, *promnas* (relations), in-laws, particularly the mother-in-law/daughter-in-law theme. So in the absence of any institutionalised place for women to hold group conversation outside the home (which is available to men), the *pratikramaṇa* in the *upāśraya* serves that purpose. These days the *upāśrayas* are used by women who live in their close vicinity, as a matter of convenience. *Baiyon-ka-upāśrayas* (women's residences) are managed by women.

Some of the organisationally oriented institutions of the Jains are concerned with the management of society at large, while others act as self-help associations. Thus, the institution of the *gota* is concerned with the running of the Jain temple. Each temple has its own *gota* (management). This consists of representatives of two or three *gotras* (kin groups within surnames, such as Singhis, Hirans, Mardias). Those families who constructed the temple continue to manage it. The *gota*s are not constituted by the castes (Dasā Oswal, Bisā Oswal and Porwal), but they are, rather, independent units specifically and traditionally organised for the management of temples. There are eighteen temples in Sirohi.

The *pedhī*[3] is also concerned with the management of temples but with other related religious matters as well. There are fifteen members of Ānanda Kalyāṇjī *pedhī* which manages temples at Dilwara and Bamanvadji. There is an equal representation of all the three castes in the *pedhī* – five members are elected from each caste, despite the fact that the castes are significantly different in size. About ten years ago, the Oswals wanted representation according to the size of the caste. But two of the prominent Bisā Oswals (numerically the majority group) tendered their resignation on this issue and the proposal was rejected. This reveals their desire to maintain the identity of the Jains as a whole, despite their numerical strength. The president of the *pedhī* for the last twenty years has been a Porwal. The post of secretary has been held by either a Bisā Oswal or a Dasā Oswal.

The influence of the individual has been the criterion for selection as president or secretary of the *pedhī*. The Dasās have sent *tilayats* (heads of family groups) as *pedhī* members, the Porwals have sent their leaders and the Oswals have held formal elections. In this realm, religious interests have dominated over caste interests. Although some younger people have resented the continuation of one person as president for such a long time, his influence has preserved continuity.

The Jain Sangh is a general association of all the Jains. It is a religious body consisting of every head of all the Jain families in Sirohi. It manages the *Vishi*, which is a complex consisting of a dharamsala, a bathing-ghat, an *upāśraya* and a temple. Invitations to *sādhus*, performances of *prathiṣṭhā*, *paryūṣaṇ*, and *dīkṣā* (initiation of

[3] The *gota* is internal to Sirohi and constituted by local gotras, while the *pedhī* is an organisation which operates on a wider regional scale as well as inside the town.

ascetics) ceremonies are organised by the Sangh. The executive committee of the Jain Sangh consists of twenty-one members, seven from each caste. The Jain Sangh also takes religious decisions.

The *upāśrayas* are places where *sādhus* stay and group activities such as *pratikramaṇa* are performed. There are four '*Baiyon-ka Upāśrayas*' (for ladies) and three for men. Their names indicate the regional, *gotra*, caste and *gacch* (sub-sect) character of the *upāśraya*; but in practice these characteristics have been lost. Now, people living in a specific area patronise that *upāśraya*. Goaliji-walon-ka Upāsraya was built by people from a small village 3 km from Sirohi town. There is a Kharataragaccha *upāśraya*, a Tapāgaccha *upāśraya*, a Lokagaccha *upāśraya* and one which is managed by the Jain Sangh. But all *gacchas* have lost significance and identify themselves with the Tapāgaccha (a prominent sub-sect of Śvetāmbar Jains). There was one Baiyon-ka Upāśraya in Singhi Lane which was largely patronised by Porwal women. About forty years ago the '*baithakas*'[4] of four Oswal women were thrown out by Porwal women from the Singhi Lane *upāśraya*. The Oswals vowed to construct a new *upāśraya* for themselves (Oswals) and took up the task of buying an adjacent building. But today the Oswal/Porwal distinction has been lost at this level, and irrespective of caste both Oswals and Porwal women join in the collective activities of *pratikramaṇa* and *poṣadha* in the *upāśraya*.

The Jain temples in Sirohi are places which people from all Jain castes visit every morning. A smaller number visit in the evening also.

Apart from these, there are three associations, the Mahāvīr Navyuvak Mandal, the Pārśvanāth Mahila Mandal and the Śantināthji Mandal, that undertake and organise arrangements at religious functions involving collective participation. Volunteers are drawn from these organisations; they provide a band which heads processions such as the *varghoda* (a term deriving from the marriage procession, but used for all processions of this type) and look after arrangements during *pratiṣṭhā* (consecration of a statue) and *swamivatsala* (communal gathering).[5] There are also a few charitable organisations which provide medicines to the needy and sick, irrespective of caste or religion.

[4] *Baithaka* is a woollen cloth mat used for sitting on at the time of *pratikramana*.

[5] *Swāmivatsala* literally means the community of believers in Lord Mahāvīr. But locally the term is also used to apply to the feast given for all the three *nyats*.

Some other religious functions also significantly project into social life. During the *paryūṣaṇ* festival, for eight days women and children wear their best attire and women wear their heavy jewellery, that is, there is high social exhibitionism. People gather together to listen to the *sādhus* at sermons. There are *bhajans* during *Śānti pūjā* in the afternoon and *prabhāvna* is given at the end of the *pūjā* (sweets, coconuts, utensils or similar gifts given by a patron).

The institution of *ghee bolna* (literally 'butter-calling')[6] is a form of auction for the right to perform a religious activity first. Bidding occurs for many religious items on different occasions. For example, there are bids for *pakal* (the anointing with milk which initiates the *pūjā*) and for *pūjā ārtī* (light waving) in the temples on important occasions. During *paryūṣaṇ* in particular there are many occasions for bidding. The *boli* or bid goes up according to the importance of the event. During *paryūṣaṇ* the bidding for the *palna* (cradle) of Lord Mahāvīr fetches high *ghee*. At the time of consecrating a statue (*pratiṣṭhā*) the price for *dhvaj chadhana* (putting up the flag) and *kalash chadhana* (making the ritual purification) goes very high. At the last *pratiṣṭhā* it was the bids for *swāmivatsala nokarsi* and *phera chunari* which were the most prestigious.

*Swāmivatsala nokarsi* signifies bearing all the expenses for meals (breakfast, lunch and dinner) for all the three castes of Sirohi. A separate *boli* was called for the honour of providing for each meal. *Phera Chunari* is an institution which enlarges the scope of *swāmitvatsala* beyond the Jain castes, as it extends to all the castes of the town/village. A piece of yellow cloth is hung at the outskirts of the town and all the people are thus informed of the invitation to meals. In the March 1985 *pratiṣṭhā*, instead of meals 0.5 kg of sweets (*nugdi*) was sent to all the houses of the other castes. Thus there is the enlargement of the collectivity on the basis of the locality. The town itself is provided with an identity through this activity.

The institution of *sangha* (pilgrimage) provides the opportunity for communal ritual journeys to different *tirthas* (pilgrimage places). One individual bears all the expenses and he gets the title of *sanghapati*. The *sanghas* go either on foot or by van. Invitations to join the *sangha* are sent, and the people observe the necessary *vratas*

[6] Bidding is done in terms of units of *ghee* (clarified butter).

(vows) during their sojourn. Charitable inns, eating-halls, and dormitories (*ambilsals*, *bhojansals*, *dharmsalas*) provide opportunities for people who might not otherwise have the means to undertake such journeys. It is believed that the *saṅgha* helps to check *parigraha* (the sin of taking satisfaction in possessions) as it involves spending large sums of money in its organisation.

However, it would be interesting to examine the economic benefits which accrue to people who organise *sanghas*. For one thing, 'black' money (illegally acquired money) can be used through the expenditure incurred. Even the *pedhīs* who keep accounts, it is alleged, give receipts which do not mention the actual money given and thus help the donors in converting 'black' money into 'white'.

The social consequences of *sangha* and *ghee bolna* are many. On the one hand, prestige is acquired by the *sanghapati* and donors and, on the other hand, the financial reputation earned through spending large sums of money begets investment and credit facilities which lead to the expansion of business. Matrimonial alliances made at this time allow daughters and sons to rise in the caste hierarchy.

The consecration of a statue, although essentially a religious occasion, has great social importance. The last *pratiṣṭhā* in Sirohi consisted of ceremonies lasting for eleven days. There were thirty-three *swāmivatsalas* and also *phera chunari* for the thirty-six castes in the town. Sermons were held for fifteen days, attended not only by Jains but also by people from other castes. The festivities were like a marriage. The *varghoda* ceremonial procession was the grand finale. About 4,000 people from other places joined in. The new rich who are doing business in Madras, Bombay, Bangalore, Hyderabad, etc. came back to Sirohi and spent much money. An exhibition depicting the life of Lord Mahāvīr and other *tīrthankars* was organised. Bhajan Mandals came from outside. A large *pandal* (marquee) was erected in the place where these functions were held, and dramas about the life of Mahāvīr were performed. Around 40 lakhs rupees were collected through auctions. The expenditure was estimated at around 20 lakhs. Jain participation involved deep commitment, but other communities also participated. The *varghoda* procession is a feudal practice involving people from many communities. It starts with elephants, horses, *rath* (a chariot), sepoys and a music band, and is followed by men and then women. The procession displays status, aristocracy and royalty.

The *masa khamana* (fast for one month), *athai* (eight days) and some other *tapasyas* are also followed by social festivity, for example, a feast after *masa-khamana*. The *tapasvi* (female faster) is taken to the temple with a band, good clothes and heavy jewellery, she is given a sari and other gifts from her *pihar* (father's house), and a feast is given to relatives, caste or community, depending on the economic status of the individual. *Neg* (money symbolising blessings and good wishes) is also given to the *tapasvi*. The social dimensions are now emphasised more and more: they are similar to a wedding in the involvement of relatives, caste and community. Participation in these religious occasions increases social status within the caste and community. There is a great deal of talk about this. People who become rich get a forum to display their wealth through religiously legitimated mechanisms. Invitation cards are printed and sent to all members of the community, especially for the *sāngh* and *pratiṣṭhā* ceremonies.

Thus for each of these acts of *tapasya* there is a social act of non-*tapasya*. Even *dharna* and *palana* (pre- and post-fast meals) reveal interesting contradictions. In *dharna* a hearty meal, sumptuous and tasty, is eaten a day before the fast. In *palana*, there are again delicious dishes. One could logically conclude that what is gained through fasting is lost through *dharna* and *palana*. Even the *dīkṣā samaroh* (renunciation ceremony), the initiation into the *sādhu sangh*, projects utter worldliness. This ceremony consists of taking the layman or laywoman who is being initiated as a *sādhu* or *sādhvi* on a procession. This has the entire paraphernalia of a *varghoda*. Handfuls of money are thrown into the air at every few steps. The poor people and urchins who accompany the procession vie with one another to get hold of the loot. Some time ago, gold rings weighing 1 kg were thrown into the air for people to grab. Each ring was tied in a cloth so that people could easily identify the rings. The person to be initiated takes *vanola* (i.e. going round to relatives with invitations) for seven days prior to the actual ceremony, as at a marriage, and she wears her best clothes. Since she is leaving the world, she is made to taste the best of social life. *Sādhu sangh* means total renunciation for life, hence its prelude consists of high social and sensory satisfaction coupled with marked public visibility. The procession is inclusive and all castes take part. The lower castes join in the hope of getting loot. Both *pratiṣṭhā* and *dīkṣā* ceremonies institutionally involve all the castes in Sirohi, thereby enlarging the communality, albeit marginally. It gives the group a sense of power and influence, exercised through affluence and materialism.

## *VI*

At the 'institutional/secular' level (c) we shall examine the functioning of *nyat* (local sub-castes). The *nyats* are non-religious. The heads are *tilayats* who hold hereditary office. The Chaudhari and Singhi families are *tilayats* of the Bisā Oswal sub-caste, Kangtanis and Shahs are *tilayats* of the Dasā Oswals, and Bonwats and Vahiras are *tilayats* of the Porwals. The Chaudharis are the chief *tilayats*. There is a general body consisting of all the heads of families of the three *nyats*. Each *nyat* has its own *panchayat* and there is also a committee for each *kauf* (*gotra*). These caste *panchayats* have been concerned with social regulations: disputes regarding betrothal, marriage, fixing of *peramani* (dowry), observation of customs and representation of Jain castes in the functions of the royal family. During Dasera the head of a sacrificial male buffalo calf was taken to the houses of the *tilayat*s and they were required to give *neg*. At the time of any death in the royal family, *dal-roti* was sent by the *tilayat*s. The *satarwada* (ritual mourning)[7] was done by the Singhis.

Caste *panchayats* have played a significant role in social reforms. For example, the fixing of a maximum *peramani* (dowry) has been done from time to time to eliminate demand from the boy's side and curtail the exhibitionist tendencies of the richer families. Amongst Porwals this restriction is followed, but among Bisā and Dasā Oswals there is general violation of the restrictions. Bisā Oswals have traditionally taken government jobs, for example, as *diwans* (ministers), *fozdars* (officers in the army) and as cashiers to the royal family. But Porwals have been business people. Lately, Oswals have gone into business in several cities outside Rajasthan with considerable success. The desire to exhibit their wealth is uncontainable. The records of the *panchayat* reveal several other measures to seek uniformity of practice and create equality among members. There have been restrictions on the duration of meals at weddings, and also

[7] *Satarwada*: members of the Singhi *gotra* go to the palace to give company to the royal mourners. This privilege was exclusively granted to the Singhis by the royalty.

on the number of people to be invited in *vanola* (the feast before marriage).

The *panchayats* have also taken decisions in other matters, such as stopping abuses during the marriage ceremony, for example, the wearing of *chuda* (ivory bangles) which involves *hiṃsā*. These restrictions are followed for a period and then people violate them again. There are fresh directives, and new violations, and so on. There have been two major cases of excommunication by *panchayat tilayat*s. In one case a respectable and influential person was made to put the shoes of *tilayat*s on his head, for having kept a mistress. In another case a person was excommunicated for having married a woman of another caste in Bombay, despite being already married. The *panchayat* supported the deserted lady, but the 'husband' in Bombay did not care about the *panchayat* decision. In such cases the family is stigmatised, and giving or taking daughters from that family is taboo. Both of these cases occurred about 30 years ago. No excommunication has taken place in the past decade, despite the fact that in this period boys and girls have married outside the caste. These marriages have taken place outside Sirohi, and the people involved are professionals and belong to traditionally respected families.

Earlier, marriages were confined to Sirohi and nearby villages. However, with the increase in education and mobility and the taking up of careers by women, marriages have been taking place outside Sirohi. The social influence of the *panchayats* has weakened now that several families live outside Sirohi and have developed alternative linkages in the cities. In Jaipur there are caste organisations such as the Marudhar Oswal Samāj, and there are also regional associations, for example, the Sirohi Samāj. It is interesting to note that residents living outside Sirohi can maintain a link with their castes by giving *hathi*. *Hathi* (the giving of sweets for several days before marriage) is a socially legitimised indication of caste membership. '*Hathi-pati bandh*' is the usual expression for those with whom castes sever their links.

The names of household heads are listed in the register (now brought out as a book by Bisā Oswals and Porwals) maintained by the caste *panchayat*. When a family divides into two by the separation of brothers there is an addition to the list and social recognition of the separate family.

All three *panchayat*s meet on occasions when they have a common cause or interest. The Bhaipa Panchayat Samaj is the general body of all the castes in which every family head can participate. The *panchayats* own buildings, utensils, bedding and similar items which are loaned to members of all three castes as well as castes which practise vegetarianism.

Practices which involve all three castes signify the community of the Jains. These practices have been retained, despite laxity in other obligations. At the time of the first wedding in the family sweet corn (*lapsi*) is distributed to all three castes. Another *hathi* for all the three castes consists of *gur* (sweets) obligatory at all weddings.

The practice of *hajor* (greetings with folded hands) also involves all three castes. *Hajor* is undertaken at the time of a serious illness. A *pūjāri* is engaged to convey these greetings by going round all the houses and distributing coins (now 10 paise) to each family, which symbolises the announcement of a serious illness. People respond by coming for *sukh puchana* (enquiry about health and wishes for speedy recovery). The amount of *hajor* is fixed – it cannot be increased, whatever the wealth or status of the individual. The sense of equality is an important aspect of the sense of community. *Hajor* is done on behalf of the sick person both by the *susral* (in-law's house) and the *pihar* (father's house). Quite often one does *hajor* even when one's relatives are not ill. The desire to perform *hajor* is very strong lest there be criticism and gossip regarding its neglect by members of the community. In the event of an unanticipated death, *hajor* is done even after the death. In recent times, some *hajor*s have been confined to one's own *nyat* (caste).

The *lona* is a special obligation which children are required to pay after the death of the parents. Earlier it was done by giving *motichur laddus* (a type of sweet) to all three *nyats*. People now give stainless-steel utensils or cash. There is criticism of those who do not perform *lona* or *hajor*. Several families who live outside Sirohi but retain their *hathi* status (i.e. membership of the community) are often careless about their reciprocal obligations to the *nyats* in Sirohi. Their *hathi*s are taken by their relatives at home, and their children's marriages are celebrated in the cities. One often hears severe criticism of this by the locals, who say that they take *hathi*s but do not give them in return.

The Jains have a separate cremation ground and bathing-place known as *idawa*. People of all the *nyat*s participate in much of the funeral ritual, especially the funeral procession. This depends to some extent on the status of the deceased and his family: participation of the *bhaipa*[8] and close relatives has greater obligatory reciprocity than that of all the *nyat*s. During the mourning period the wife was confined in a corner for nine months, and there was joint weeping and crying (*sera varna*) observed for a year. Younger women would touch the feet of the older ones. They would put up their veils. The time for *sera varna* is from 12.0 p.m. to 2.0 p.m. During this time women from all the *nyats* and also from other castes go for *sera varna*. The widow is not allowed to go to the temple; she must wear black clothes and eat simple food. No Brahmin comes to perform the death ceremony. For three days men do not shave. Unlike the Hindus there is no *mundan* (head-shaving) ceremony, but the hair is cut. On the death of the husband, the wife's *chuda* (ivory bangles) are broken in the *samshan* (cremation ground).

The *vishi* community complex is controlled by all three *nyats*. There is a place for getting drinking water, a bathing and washing-place and rooms to stay. *Sādhus* stay in the *upāśraya* and people from the whole community worship in the temple.

## *VII*

The 'habitat/locale' level (d) is demarcated by the residential patterns of the Jains. Dwelling-areas are named after a particular *khauf* (*gotra*). People of one *khauf* live in one area, the lane being given this name, for example, Singhi Heri, Modi-Pharo Kothariyon Ki Heri, etc. The Bisā Oswals, Dasā Oswals and Porwals reside in specific locales which provide identities based on *bhaipa*, *nyat*, and collectivity. However, there are some houses of the Sonar caste in the Bisā Oswal locale, some Rajputs live in the Porwal area and some Sada Brahmins in the Dasā Oswal neighbourhood. Residential proximity provides opportunities for interaction and reciprocity. To go to a neighbour and fetch *vadi* (fire) to light one's own *chulha* (fire-place) was a common pattern prior to the introduction of gas. Cooked vegetables were exchanged between friends and butter-milk was also brought from families who

[8] *Bhaipa*: kin of a given surname, e.g. Singhi, based in Sirohi. The *bhaipa* is thus a wider concept than the *gotra* (sub-division of surname group).

stayed near by and owned cows or buffalo. Such everyday exchanges were more pronounced among *bhaipas*, despite the fact of variation in economic status. Each lane has a separate *than* (ritual place) for the deities Virji Bawasi or Bhaironji, who are considered the protectors of those areas.

The relationship of Jains with other castes was characterised by the *jajmani* system. The Bisā Oswals have always been in government service in the princely state, and only a few of their families took to business. Numerically they were in the majority and they had higher literacy than the other castes. The brighter ones among them have taken up professional and administrative work in the big cities. Women of this caste are now allowed education. There was a great deal of resistance to this from all three *nyat*s, but since the first girls came from three respectable families the opposition turned into imitation. Today, 40 or so years later, the number of girls going to school and college is very high in this caste. During the 1950s and 1960s, several Bisā Oswal families took up clerical work or school-teaching, since the princely service became government service. Some of them went to cities in South India and earned well.

The Dasā Oswals and Porwals have traditionally been in business and continue to be so with few exceptions. These castes are conservative; female literacy is low. People of these castes have their businesses in Bombay, where they have *peḍhis* (commission agents). Some of them have businesses in Madras, Bangalore or Hyderabad. As small castes with a high degree of local endogamy, everyone is related to everyone else to some degree.

The style of life of these castes, as I noted earlier, is distinctive. The Bisā Oswals have adopted modern amenities and decor in their homes. Furniture, fans and radios are part of their style of life. Bathrooms and kitchens, which were traditionally neglected, are now given more importance. The Porwals, on the other hand, spent and invested money in jewellery for women. Even the clothing of Bisā Oswals and Porwals tends to be different, as the Bisās wear modern attire.

There is a lack of group identity in the political sphere too. Jains of all three castes actively participated in the Praja Mandal movement in the pre-Independence era. These people have been in the Congress Party all along. Others who were not attracted to this movement were in the Jana Sangh. In the 1985 elections, a Bisā Oswal lady contested for the State Assembly, but the Jains were divided in their voting. Many voted and gave support on party lines rather than on caste lines.

Economic common identity is also problematic and many rivalries are involved. The economic hegemony of the Jains is due to the fact that other castes did not enter business or industry, but this created an economic culture rather than a group identity based on economic factors. A common identity beyond the self should not only give a sense of homogeneity but also a mutuality of obligations. It is true that similarity of economic status has helped in the selection of spouses from that circle. But, generally, similar economic status has led not merely to rivalries but also to the tendency towards competitive exhibitionism through *ghee boli* in religious functions.

## *VIII*

At the 'crisis management' level (e) we examine the emergence of unity and homogeneity under threat. There is a long history of anti-Jain feeling manifested through an organisation known as Anoop Mandal. It was started in 1920 by Anoop Das, who fought in Turkey in 1914 and was influenced in Europe by communism. He gave a class character to the social hierarchy in which Jains had high economic status and were able to capture administrative power as well. He came from Boli, a region near Sirohi. His movement had certain distinctive features: he used indigenous terms and language to criticise the Jains. His focus was on lower castes which were economically deprived, but excluded the Harijans. He called the Jains '*Lanka-ke Dhed*'-'untouchables from Sri Lanka'.

Folklore was created which projected Jains as outsiders, exploiters and non-Hindus (*Hindu–Muslim Bhai Bhai, Yean Jain Kaum Kahan Se Aiye* – Hindus and Muslims are brothers, but where have the Jains come from?). Harchand Soni was a comrade of Anoop Das who wrote popular verses. They were catchy and were sung, with local musical instruments, as *bhajan*s. The movement inculcated a feeling of hatred for Jains, and a number of village-dwelling Jains were raided by Anoop Mandal workers. Religion was used as a means to start a class war. The attacks on villages caused terror among the Jains. The movement spread among local tribals such as the Girasias, Bhils and Minas. The movement built huts, displayed Anoop Das' photograph, organised fairs, etc., and *bhajan*s were composed and sung by lower castes such as Kumars, Suthars, Dhobis and Rabaris.

The Jains then began to organise, and about 40 years ago the people of Deldar village resisted a raid with the help of the local Jagirdar. The Anoop Mandal was in fact popular only in the rural areas and did not find support in the towns. The royal family was against the movement. In fact, it was formally banned by the princely administration, which consisted of Jain ministers and executives. The British, however, thought that this movement could be used to curb the Praja Mandal movement of Congress which was becoming popular in the fight for Independence. The Praja Mandal was made up mainly of Jains, hence the encouragement of Anoop Mandal would lessen its power. The Anoop Mandal later was registered as a political society. Its registration was cancelled but it was renamed Sirohi Seva Samiti and reregistered. The Anoop Mandal still exists in several villages, where it has established its own huts. It becomes most active during election times and works against Jain candidates. Jains have not organised against Anoop Mandal on a continuous basis but have got together locally whenever there has been violence to sadhus.

About six years ago some Jain *sādhus* were beaten up by lower castes in Kolar, which is 6 km from Sirohi. The issue was taken up by Jains of Sirohi at the highest level. Prominent Jains at the national level then took up the case, and delegations met the Chief Minister of Rajasthan, the President of India and the press, which gave wide publicity. The culprits were arrested. The lower castes resented this and stopped the sale of milk, vegetables and other items of daily consumption to Jains. Being well off, the Jains organised themselves and arranged for milk etc., from nearby Palanpur in Gujarat. Vehicles were hired to obtain the milk and vegetables every day and distribution was done by volunteers. This went on for eleven days. The lower castes could not stand the loss, as milk and vegetables cannot be stored for long. Ultimately they relented and the normal situation was restored.

There have also been cases in Pindwara and Deldar of Jain *sādhus* being beaten up. When there are no rains in the area for a long time, famine and drought occur. Lower-caste people came to believe that the Jain *sādhus* could stop the rain by chanting *mantras*. This would help the Jains as they could then sell the grain, etc., at higher prices, hoard it and harm the economy of farmers who do not have any crop in the absence of rains. Such interpretations appear logical to lower-caste people and work as mechanisms of hatred against Jains in the area.

On such crisis occasions, Jains have united and have organised training in the use of *lathi*s, etc., to symbolise their physical power. Folklore projects Jains (Voniya in the local dialect) as physically weak and cowardly. A popular saying runs: *Posa Bhil and Pacchich Voniya, Mata Maro Bavsi Main to Leda Voniya* (Five Bhils and twenty-five Jains are face to face, oh lords, don't beat us, we are weak Jains.) The background to such stereotypes is economic. Development programmes for the poorer sections have not made villagers wealthy in this region. The Jains, on the other hand, have become richer as it is easy to achieve affluence in business. Thus economic disparities persist, although some individuals from lower castes have also achieved high economic status.

A Jain–non-Jain dichotomy does exist, but it is different from the Hindu-Muslim dichotomy. The former is viewed mainly as an economic difference, as Jains are considered as Hindus, both by Hindus and Jains. There are several similarities in the social and religious ceremonies of Hindus and Jains. Some religious functions among the Hindu lower castes are patterned on those of the Jains as far as exhibitionism is concerned. Such institution-oriented sanskritisation implies the adaptation of the practices of higher castes with a view to gaining equal status, but not membership.

Jains, through their practices of *phera chunri*, *pratiṣṭhā*, funeral processions, *vyakhans* (sermons) etc., have enveloped non-Jains in their fold. During the last *pratiṣṭhā*, Padam Sagarji Sadhu gave *vyakhans* and a large number of non-Jains came to listen to him.

On the other hand, there has been a decline in those ceremonies which involve all the three castes. Up until 1950 it was necessary to give one general meal during the wedding of a son or daughter. This has now stopped. Only for important religious ceremonies do all three *nyats* participate. Caste *panchayat*s have lost their hold: there have been no discussions and decisions on social issues for the past two decades, despite inter-caste marriages. In weddings and deaths, participation of kin and friends from other non-Jain castes has become more common.

Thus, identities are multiple. The hiatus between Jains and non-

Jains is economic and cultural. Jains have an identity which is fostered not merely by how Jains see themselves but also by how others see them. But such an identity has undergone changes. Jains have built new houses on the outskirts of the town. Identity is shared not only at the level of *bhaipa*, caste, and the three castes, but also with non-Jains of the town. This cross-cultural pattern provides a generality of harmony and unity to the locale of Sirohi – a town which has never witnessed riots between castes or religious groups.

The concept of community has to be seen in the context of some theoretical propositions.

## *IX*

At the ascetic/religious level, purely religious practice does not provide conditions for communality due to the absence of wide participation and social ceremonies.

But at the ascetic/religious social level there is considerable opportunity for all Jains to participate jointly. Since Jains do not have festivals like the Hindus, the *tapa*s practices provide the opportunity for such festivity. Simplicity of life style has led to the accumulation of wealth by Jains. There are several reasons why they spend their money on religious activity. It gives social status and also provides the opportunity for expansion of business. Although some of these ceremonies, such as *pratiṣṭhā*, involve all the *nyats* of the Jains in Sirohi, others, like *varsitapa* and *upādhyana*, are losing their area of inclusiveness. On the other hand, rituals such as *phera chunri* and *vyakhan* have led to a wider inclusiveness, drawing in some from outside the Jain community. Many practices in the social sphere are like those of Hindus. Thus, the religion provides an identity which is segmented and does not form the dominant identity.

The organisationally oriented religious institutions have brought cohesion among Jains in management, but this is confined to a small group at the top and does not provide for wider participation.

Secular institutions tend to be most effective at the level of caste. Although formal control by castes over their members has weakened and lost its legitimacy, the style of life, level of literacy, outlook and adaptability, endogamous character and pattern of exchanges create homogeneity in the *nyat*. It may be appropriate, however, to make a distinction between caste and *nyat*. The *nyat* is an endogamous group devoid of hierarchy. There are some occasions on which all the *nyats* become significant in reciprocal obligations, for example, *hathi* to all the *nyat*s at a wedding, *hajor* and *lona*. However, the area of coverage is gradually narrowing to one *nyat*. Since the Jain religion does not provide specific normative rules like Islam and Hinduism for marriage regulations, bride-price, divorce, polygamy, rate of interest, etc., caste becomes inevitable for the social regulation of the group. Theoretically there should be no castes among Jains, but operationally social life needs to be regulated. This is why the institution of *nyat* has emerged among Jains. It has some of the functions of caste, but tends to be significantly different from the Hindu caste system. It is evident that *nyat* does not have hierarchy, commensal regulations, or traditional occupations linked to it. Nevertheless, there is a *nyat panchayat* similar to a caste *panchayat* and marital regulations restrict horizontal mobility amongst the *nyats*. The *nyats* are closed endogamous categories.

The habitat/locale level signifies physical proximity. Among the Jains of Sirohi, neighbourhoods tend to be based on *bhaipa* (kin brothers) and *nyat*. This provides a continuous means of personal identity with these groups.

Crisis management encompasses all the Jains. It is intensive but shortlived, and hence cannot infuse continuous group solidarity. The quality of tolerance among Jains is determined both by the tenets of Jainism and the pragmatism of business. Relations with other communities tend to be non-antagonistic. However, the fact that a movement against Jains was able to arise among other castes, a movement that perceived Jains as economic exploiters, demonstrates the use of religious practices in creating antagonism. This should be the subject of independent analysis, in both historical and class-conflict dimensions.

If we examine the various levels at which Jains act together – and posit their identity – we can see a continuum from weak to strong. The two most significant components appear to be shared religion and differentiated *nyat* membership. Empirically, we find that there are institutions for religion: temples and *upāśras*, *pedhi* and *vishi*, which encompass all the *nyats*. Despite numerical variation in membership, their representation in management has been equal. The exclusion of any one *nyat* from control has not occurred, and conversely any attempt by a single *nyat* to dominate in the religious sphere has never succeeded. The three *nyat*s do not have any differences in religious performance/practice. This suppression of the tendency to intrude *nyat* influence into religion in order to gain greater power reveals a desire to preserve religious unity.

To what extent religion can be considered the basis of the formation of a community is an important question. Numerical strength, degree of distinctiveness, institutionalised possibilities for collective activity and influence in regulating everyday life – all of these aspects of religion can create the conditions of community formation. But, as stated earlier, Jain religion does not deal with social ethics. Social regulation in Sirohi comes from the institution of *nyat*. Religion provides only for common practice in, and joint management of, religious institutions. The *nyat*s, however, have not been able to create a cleavage in this religious sphere at the formal-institutional level. A clear distinction between religious and social institutions has thus been maintained. We therefore deduce that those religions which do not provide normative-coercive sanctions against social deviations are weak instruments for community formation.

Taken together, the *nyats* do not constitute a unified group. They continue to remain endogamous, and have become more active in religious activities as their hold on traditional social norms weakens. Nevertheless, the reference point for the *nyat* still tends to be marriage and the plethora of practices associated with it. Inside each *nyat* there is a sub-culture, and the leaders of the *nyat* act as focal points for the members. As all *nyat* members are interrelated, there is a high degree of interaction between them. The location of the people of one *bhaipa* in one street has helped to develop a sense of mutual dependence and reciprocity. In other words, relations internal to each *nyat* predominate over links between the three.

The totality of social experiences determines a dominant identity. On the criteria given in the position paper (chapter 1) it is impossible to construct the Jains as a community. Identity is contextual and normal conditions of life require *mutuality* of relationships with the surrounding population. Although Jains are perceived by non-Jains as a category, this perception is largely the result of the economic wealth of the Jains, which is not communal in expression. As we have seen, neither *nyat* nor religion has created a dominant identity at the social level. Jains do not perceive their dominant identity as Jains.

# Part 3

# Jains in the Indian world

# 10

# Jains in the Indian world

Michael Carrithers

Jains have always lived as a minority – at best, a plurality – in a rich and astoundingly varied cultural milieu in India. These three chapters concern the Jains' profound engagement with that wider world, the ways in which they have continued to mark themselves off, and the accommodations they have made.

In his chapter the Indologist Padmanabh Jaini asks whether there is a 'popular Jainism'? The sense of this question derives from a comparison with Theravada Buddhism, which in Jaini's view had gone very far towards incorporating relatively unreflective but fundamental and widespread practices and attitudes from the Indic world. Jaini shows that Jain writers in the medieval period vigorously opposed such common practices as offerings to the dead, worship of trees and mounds of earth, ritual bathing, observances connected with celestial events and the worship of deities. Jains did incorporate Indic deities into their temples, but gave them a subsidiary place, whereas Buddhists in Sri Lanka elevated similar deities to substantial positions in official Buddhist doctrine and practice.

The strong terms in which Jain writers opposed such practices gives the term 'popular' a clear meaning: those beliefs and practices which did not accord with the learned Jain interpretation of what belonged to Jainism (*jainadharma*) itself. Sri Lankan Buddhists did, on this showing, seem considerably less concerned to police their boundaries.

But Jaini's chapter also gives rise to a number of potentially fruitful questions. As Jaini shows, the institutions and texts of Jainism gave little place to *bhakti*, devotional, cults. Yet Jains do, as individuals *but not as Jains*, engage in *bhakti* in many places in India today. Did Jainism perhaps preserve itself as a set of distinct ideas and practices, and of exclusive institutions, at the price of allowing its adherents to engage personally in the wider Indian world?

And again: Jains continued to live in the cultural complexity of subcontinental India, whereas Buddhists enjoyed relative cultural hegemony on Lanka itself. Jains seldom wielded political power in a specifically Jain polity, but Buddhists did establish and maintain enduring Buddhist polities. Might these conditions not have forced the Jain intelligentsia to confront other institutions and practices in a way not required of the Buddhists?

The question of the Jain relation to Indian monarchy, monarchical ideology and the ideals of the warrior is taken up by the Indologist Paul Dundas in his chapter. He shows that metaphors of military victory and political hegemony were salient in Jainism from the very beginning. Using medieval texts, he shows how Jains developed theories of kingship, and how there was not necessarily a contradiction in practice between being a warrior and being a Jain. But he also shows that a good deal of ambiguity – between the Jain notion of *ahiṃṣā*, non-violence, and the necessary violence of kings – did attend Jain attempts to devise a distinctly Jain conception of kingship. And he discusses the perhaps irresoluble issue of whether, and in what sense, Jain kings in south India were actually Jains.

Both Jaini and Dundas deal with Jain efforts to establish conceptual boundaries with the surrounding world, whereas in her chapter the anthropologist Caroline Humphrey shows how Jains establish social boundaries. At a number of centres in Rajasthan Jain temples have become the object of a 'temple fair complex'. That is, a specifically Jain temple has become a site of worship for local non-Jains as well as the focus of a periodic fair. While on the face of it this might seem a case of Jain integration with the surrounding society, Humphrey argues clearly that these temple fairs actually dramatise the differences between Jains and others. Jains have access to the *sacra*, but others do not. Jains worship the images in the temples as Jain images, but others place their own construction on them. And the very squabbling between Digambars and Svetambars over ownership of the sites reveals an unambiguous sense of community, of common concerns and issues among Jains, which strongly excludes others.

Moreover, as managers of the temples Jains retain a sort of cultural hegemony which confirms their economic position as a tightly knit

6 A village priest (*upadhye*) directs operations at the consecration of a new image at Halondi, near Kolhapur. The wife of the chief sponsor of the ceremony bathes the images while the sponsor and another priest look on.

class of traders holding a strong position in the local economy. Their collective importance in trade is mirrored in their monopoly of some fairs and in their exclusiveness.

But this limited hegemony raised again in discussion the relation of Jains to political power. Christopher Bayly noted that the apparent elective affinity between Jainism and commerce may have been an artifact of the loss of paramount power by Jains, in the North to Muslims and in the South to Saivites. Where Jains had held power, as in medieval Karnataka, they may have indulged in downward proselytising among their subjects. Certainly Muslims in the North had gently encouraged their peasantry to take up Islamic observances. Yet in this temple fair complex Jains explicitly exclude others and refuse to proselytise. This is consistent with their struggle, as a group, for economic primacy against other groups. Bayly asked whether this might be considered a sufficient explanation of the evident inwardness

7 Digambar Jains giving *abhiseka* (anointment) of statue of Adinath during a consecration ceremony in Madhya Pradesh 1983. Photo: C. Humphrey

of Jains as a community. Could such an explanation be generalised to cover other cases where Jains are evidently inward, but do not possess such a specifically economic role?

And, finally, he and others noted that Jain festivals and processions in South India today concern only Jains and do not embrace participants from the wider society. These northern temple fair complexes seem to contradict that practice by giving a place to other communities. Does this anomaly reveal the ghostly lineaments of an earlier state of affairs? For at least one of the sites was associated with a *bhaṭṭārak*, a Jain religious leader and landowner, who would himself have been a grantee of a local king. Other fairs were instituted by kings or political leaders. May not such kings have granted to the Jains a right to exemplify in their annual ritual, if only narrowly, the symbolic form of the polity as a whole, with its different castes and communities? And might we not see in these northern cases a pale vision of what Jainism might have given us if it had achieved and maintained political hegemony?

11

# The Digambara Jain warrior

Paul Dundas

To the textual student of Jainism, it can often seem that the various elements of the Jain monastic community had a quite remarkable sense of identity. The terse statement of the doxographer Guṇaratna (1343–1418), that the Jains were originally not divided but subsequently split into the two sects of Śvetāmbara and Digambara,[1] conceals a long and diffuse history, from the initial, complex processes which resulted in 'schism',[2] to the appearance of the vast array of sub-sects and further offshoots which developed later, many having their own traditions of origin recorded by their respective followers. Accordingly, it would be easy to judge as mere pedantry the Digambara preoccupation with and affiliation according to the type of whisk used by the monk[3] or to ascribe to petty sectarian squabbling the glee with which Hemavijaya records in the *Vijayapraśasti* (10.3–11) the defeat at Ahmedabad in the sixteenth century of the members of the Kharatara Gaccha, a Śvetāmbara reforming sect, in debate with a *sūri* of the Tapā Gaccha, another Śvetāmbara reforming sect.[4] But serious issues were at stake in such situations. The Jain monastic tradition exemplifies perfectly the characteristic Indian desire to define precisely the nature of that correct behaviour by which an individual could actually be seen to be the adherent of a particular sect, and also to establish and validate descent from and channels of communication with a standard authority which, in the Jain case, was Mahāvīra and his immediate disciples. So, for the Digambaras, the whisk would establish a bond

[1] Haribhadra, *Ṣaḍdarśanasamuccaya* with the commentaries of Guṇaratna and Somatilaka, edited by Mahindra Kumar (New Delhi 1981), p. 8.

[2] For remarks on this, see Paul Dundas, Food and freedom: the Jaina sectarian debate on the nature of the kevalin, *Religion* 15 (1985), 163–94.

[3] See Dundas, *ibid.*, 188.

[4] Edited by Pt. Harvinddas and Pt. Bechardas, Benares, Vīra era 2437. The Kharatara Gaccha opposed the practice of monks living in temples, while the Tapā Gaccha placed strong emphasis on the practice of austerities.

with a particular lineage of teachers, whereas the Kharatara and Tapā Gacchas, while doubtless concerned with matters of correct behaviour, would perhaps have been more basically preoccupied with the deviation of their teacher lineage at the thirty-sixth *sūri* in descent from Mahāvīra.[5] The lists of gurus (*paṭṭāvalis*) serve to establish a history and tradition and, irrespective of whether the causes of the secessions to which they bear witness were originally questions of practice, pontifical succession or even money (the recent breakaway of a small group of monks from the Terāpanthīs may tell us something of the dynamics involved here), the cataloguing of the activities of various distinguished teachers and ascetics furnished a sense of community and achievement with which the monk could easily identify, and which elicited a feeling of loyalty from members of a monastic group. The assertion of an anonymous *ācārya* of the Kāṣṭha Saṅgha in the medieval period[6] that soul, and not sect, brought salvation probably did not strike a chord with most monastic practitioners. For another medieval Jain, Śrutasāgara, those who were not members of the Mūla Saṅgha were quite simply, not Jains.[7]

I have used the term 'community' in the sense of 'community of renouncers'[8] and, of course, the fact that I describe monastic attitudes raises the obvious objection that the classical Indologist, by employing Sanskrit and Prākrit sources, invariably describes Jainism in terms of the practice and ideology of renouncers. The accounts of lay people in the Śvetāmbara canon and the huge story literature, as well as the writers of the treatises on lay behaviour, with the possible odd exception, such as Āśādhara,[9] all reflect an idealisation based on the monastic view of the world. This might well appear an obstacle which would invalidate any attempt to discuss an aspect of early non-monastic Jain society but, rather than be totally inhibited by this, I would prefer to view the textual material I adduce as the product of a

[5] See J. Klatt, Extracts from the historical records of the Jainas, *Indian Antiquary* 11 (1882), 245–56.

[6] *Ḍhāḍhasīgāthā* 20 in *Tattvānuśāsanādisaṃgrahaḥ* edited by Pt. Manoharlal, Māṇikcandra Digambara Jain Granthamālā 13, Bombay, saṃvat 1975.

[7] *Darśanaprābhṛta* 11, with commentary, in *Ṣaṭprābhṛtādisaṃgrahaḥ* edited by Pt. Pannalal Soni, Māṇikcandra Digambara Jain Granthamālā 17, saṃvat 1977. The Mūla Saṅgha was the most influential Digambara group, the Kāṣṭha Saṅgha being an offshoot.

[8] *Saṅgha* can signify either the monastic community or the monastic *and* lay communities. See Jinendra Varṇī, *Jainendrasiddhāntakośa*, vol. IV (Delhi 1971), p. 124.

[9] See R. Williams, *Jaina Yoga* (London 1963), p. 26.

rather more broad 'learned' ideology which, until the epigraphical remains are fully exploited, is the best evidence we have for formulating some generalisations.

A useful starting-point for assessing the Jain view of society is the Digambara Prabhācandra's *Nyāyakumudacandra* (tenth century).[10] In the course of this large production, which sums up the Jain attitude towards other philosophical schools, its author attempts (pp. 757–79) to undermine two basic suppositions upon which, in his view, Hinduism was based; namely, that the Sanskrit language has immemorial and absolute authority, and that the brahman caste, which wields that language, has innate purity and, therefore, superiority.

Prabhācadra's rejection of the absolute authority of Sanskrit is an obvious effort to bolster the position of a community whose scriptural texts and liturgy were composed in dialect. He points out that the utterance of linguistic forms based on customary usage is general even amongst those who claim to be Sanskrit-speakers, and that, contrary to brahman supposition, dialect is based on an ordered system of grammar and does not, therefore, reflect a state of linguistic anarchy; indeed, through its obvious priority to Sanskrit, it can be seen to have greater prestige.[11] There can be no grounds for saying that dialect cannot be employed to describe true religion for the simple reason that dialect has to be used to explicate Sanskrit to those who do not understand that learned language. Moreover, if it were the case that only statements framed according to the traditional rules of Sanskrit grammar were capable of describing religious matters, then all sorts of appalling injunctions enjoining murder and bloodshed would become valid simply through being expressed in Sanskrit.[12]

Above all, Sanskrit does not have any special authority simply through being used by brahmans. In general terms, it is impossible to verify through any sensory or logical means the existence of a class 'brahmans' which is in some way distinguishable from the class 'men', for there would be infinite regression if it were held that membership

[10] Edited by Mahendra Kumar, Māṇikcandra Digambara Jain Granthamālā, vols. XXXVIII and XXXIX (Bombay 1938 and 1941).

[11] Prabhācandra derives Prākrit from *prakṛti*, 'primordial nature'.

[12] Note that Prabhācandra is referring not only to Vedic blood sacrifices, but also to statements in 'Thug scriptures' (*ṭhakāgama*) advising the killing of brahmans to get money. For references to the Thugs by Hindu writers, see Wilhelm Halbfass, *Studies in Kumārila and Śaṅkara* (Reinbek 1983), pp. 13 and 24.

of that caste had been handed down, from time immemorial, from father to son, and, alternatively, the claim that the father's brahmanness is established by his having engendered a brahman son, while the son's brahmanness is established through having been engendered by a brahman father is obviously circular. Prabhācadra can here poke fun at the champion of brahmanical orthopraxy, Kumārila, who naively stated that high-class families preserve precise genealogical records to prove the purity of their ancestors.[13] For the Jain, it is patently ludicrous to assume that inherited purity can be handed down from member to member of a class by means of exclusive marriage customs, since it would be at any time impossible to prove that one's ancestors were chaste and exclusive in their sexual behaviour. As Prabhācandra says, illicit amorous activity is always indulged in secretly.

Prabhācandra goes on to argue that there is no particular type of activity, such as specialised ritual practice, which serves to define a brahman because, in fact, only a few brahmans actually engage in the performance of the sacrifice. Also, merely to undergo a few rites of passage cannot alone make an individual a brahman because, theoretically, anyone could undergo these under false pretences and so himself become a brahman. As for the myth which describes the birth of the brahman caste from the mouth of the god, Brahmā, that is simply ludicrous.

Up to this point, Prabhācandra's position is not so much one of reinterpretation of the notion of the brahman, as in many of the earlier Jain texts, but rather of outright rejection of the premises on which the brahman caste is based. However, at the end of Prabhācandra's dismissal of brahman authority, his imaginary opponent asks him to explain the basis of the Jain social system (*varṇāśramavyavasthā*) and the particular practices which characterise it, such as giving to monks and the performance of austerities. The Digambara's answer is that the Jain community is based on specific and distinct individuals (*vyaktiviśeṣa*)[14] who can be recognised by their behaviour (*kriyā*) and by their wearing of the sacred thread. In other words, Prabhācandra is testifying to the existence of *Jain* brahmans.[15] The word *kriyā*, which I

[13] *Tantravārttika* 1.2.2, quoted by Mahendra Kumar.

[14] *vyakti* does not carry the same burden of meaning as the English word 'individual', signifying rather a member of a class (*jāti*).

[15] For Jain brahmans, see P. S. Jaini, *The Jaina Path of Purification* (Delhi 1979), pp. 290–1.

have translated as 'behaviour', conveys the sense both of 'proper moral behaviour' and, in particular, of 'religious rite'. The particular type of religious rituals in which Jain brahmans engaged are, although derived from Hindu life-cycle rituals, of a particularly Jain tinge and are formulated for the first time in Jinasena's *Ādipurāṇa* (eighth century, AD; = ĀP).[16] The ĀP tells us that, from the cosmological point of view, the existence of Jain brahmans and other castes can be ascribed to the bad world-age in which we live, through whose malign influence a pristine and undifferentiated human caste (*manuṣyajāti*) is transformed into a four-caste system based on social function (38.45–6). Notwithstanding the ĀP's interest in Jain brahmans and their behaviour, Williams stated[17] that Jinasena was, in fact, legislating for a warrior (*kṣatriya*) society but, unfortunately, he did not substantiate this judgement and it is, therefore, my purpose in this chapter to concentrate on the ĀP's attitude towards kings and warriors.

First, though, some general remarks need to be made about the relationship between Jainism and members of the warrior caste, for, although the religion did not draw recruits exclusively from the *kṣatriya*s, the common view that Jainism has always been followed by pacifist merchants and farmers only is incorrect, and two well-known facts need to be emphasised and considered: first, Mahāvīra himself was a *kṣatriya*[18] and, secondly, from about the fourth to the tenth century AD, Jainism seems to have received a great deal of support from aggressive and militaristic kings in South India.

The symbolism of warfare and violence is, of course, present in all the great religions of the world, often influencing the actual conduct of war itself,[19] but it is, I think, noteworthy, in the context of an examination of the Jain warrior, that martial conquest is the central image and metaphor of Jainism, giving the religion its very name. So, to take three examples from the ĀP of a theme which recurs frequently in Jain literature: Jainism is described as a weapon of war (1.4), the various ascetic practices are compared to an army which conquers the enemy, karma (4.153 etc.), and the monk is instructed to abandon his

[16] Edited by Pannālāl Jain (Kāshī 1964, 1965).
[17] Williams *Jaina Yoga*, p. xx.
[18] Compare the *Kalpasūtra*, edited by Herman Jacobi (Leipzig 1879), p. 60, line 17 which describes him as 'best of the excellent *kṣatriyas*' (*khathyavaravusabhā*).
[19] See James A. Aho, *Religious Mythology and the Art of War: Comparative Religious Symbolisms of Military Violence* (London 1981).

body like that of an enemy on the battlefield (11.98). The figure of the religious warrior conquering karma and death is a later adaptation and transformation of the old Vedic myth of the heroic figure, Indra, overcoming his foe, Vṛtra,[20] and it is possible that the concept of the monk as hero might provide part of the explanation why the *kṣatriyas* came to be associated with the earliest period of the great movements of renunciation and why their founders, Mahāvīra and the Buddha, were members of the *kṣatriya* caste. Certainly, while there was doubtless an element of anti-brahmanism involved,[21] the oft-repeated view of the *kṣatriya*s as purveyors of some kind of 'new knowledge' and of different spiritual insights from brahmanism is an exaggeration, and the frequent references in Vedic literature to kings and warriors debating and holding views on the nature of the sacrifice and the soul and attaining superiority in discussion with brahmans can best be seen in the light of the fact that such debates were held in the royal *sabhā*.[22] Although it is unlikely that any totally convincing answer can be given to the question of *kṣatriya* involvement, a fruitful line of enquiry might well be to consider the possibility that the early Jain and Buddhist monastic communities were, from the point of view of organisation and behaviour, linked with the ancient Indo-European warrior brotherhoods.[23]

Not all *kṣatriya*s in ancient India were warriors continually engaged in the performance of acts of martial violence as a profession or social obligation, but it should not, therefore, be assumed that the pivotal position which the Jain religion gives to non-violence is at variance with being patronised by 'practising' warrior adherents. In fact, Jainism has always been ambivalent about war,[24] and two examples testify to the existence of Jain practitioners of warfare at completely different periods of Jain history. The Pāli canon refers to a Jain general (*senāpati*) called Sīha, contemporary with Mahāvīra and the Buddha, who was a Jain layman (*nigaṇṭhasāvaka*)[25] while, two

[20] See W. B. Bollée, A note on evil and its conquest from Indra to Buddha, in Lewis Lancaster (ed.) *Prajñāpāramitā and Related Systems: Studies in Honour of Edward Conze* (Berkeley 1977), pp. 371–81.

[21] But note that Mahāvīra's closest disciples were originally brahmans.

[22] See H. W. Bodewitz, *Jaiminīya Brāhmaṇa I. 1–65: Translation and Commentary* (London 1973), pp. 215–17.

[23] See W. B. Bollée, The Indo-European sodalities in ancient India, *Zeitschrift der Deutschen Morgenländischen Gesellschaft* 131 (1981), 172–91.

[24] See P. S. Jaini, *The Jaina Path of Purification*, p. 313.

[25] *Vinayapiṭaka* I, pp. 233ff, and elsewhere.

thousand years later, in the sixteenth century AD and afterwards, Jains participated in what Bayly has called [26] the 'all-India military culture' and fought in the armies of the Moghul emperors. However, despite this, Indian historians of the Deccan have always been uneasy when attempting to account for the undoubtedly violent activities of the many rulers who were connected with Jainism in the medieval period, often expressing bafflement at the incongruity involved.[27] In fact, it does seem likely that total adherence to the principles of non-violence was of importance only in certain specific and precisely defined religious contexts, such as ritual or contact with a monk, and that non-violence did not inform broader issues, such as a king's obligation to expand his kingdom.[28] In the light of this, it has to be asked why kings and warriors were attracted to Jainism and wherein lay their 'Jainness'; did they actively espouse and promote Jainism or merely protect it?

Burton Stein is the only historian to have made a serious attempt to explain why Jainism was patronised by warriors in medieval South India and to elucidate the nature of the Jain king. For Stein,

> the attractiveness of Jainism was that it permitted a warrior to achieve legitimacy and 'Aryan' respectability without necessarily accepting the elements of contemporary peasant culture with which Hindu sects had become associated at the time . . . The correlation of non-peasant warrior power with Jainism compels a consideration of Jainism not so much as a heretical sect but as an ideological element in a critical period of struggle.[29]

Elsewhere,[30] Stein expands this thesis to produce a view of the Jain ruler as wielder of a 'moral' kingship opposed to the 'heroic' kingship of the early Tamils and Hindu 'ritual' kingship which was validated by brahmanical ritual and described in texts such as the Purāṇas; in these terms, the nature of the Jain king is to be morally elevated, to exemplify high ethical qualities and, moreover, to owe his position to merit rather than birth.

Stein's analysis is highly suggestive and I do not wish to take

[26] C. A. Bayly, The pre-history of 'communalism'?: religious conflict in India 1700–1860, *Modern Asian Studies* 19 (1985), 183.

[27] See, for example, S. R. Sharma, *Jainism and Karnataka Culture* (Dharwar 1940), p. 148.

[28] Compare the attitudes of Jains in present-day Jaipur described by James Laidlaw, Profit, salvation and profitable saints, *Cambridge Anthropology* 9, no. 3 (1985), 54.

[29] Burton Stain, *Peasant State and Society in Medieval South India* (Delhi 1980), pp. 79–80.

[30] Burton Stein, All the kings' mana: perspectives on kingship in medieval South India, in J. F. Richards (ed.) *Kingship and Authority in South Asia* (Madison 1981), 115–67.

serious issue with it here. However, it must be said that, while it is difficult to deny the existence of rulers who manifested a strong commitment to Jainism, such as, for example, the last Rāṣṭrakūṭa who apparently died by religious suicide,[31] in general terms, it is probably more appropriate to view South Indian kingship as an institution which transcended conceptual boundaries such as Jainism or Hinduism and, instead, we might surmise that kings and their feudatories incorporated elements of Jainism into their cosmology not only to achieve 'Aryan' respectability, as Stein suggests, but also because the presence of sizeable Jain communities possessing considerable economic power made it expedient to do so. We cannot totally discount inner, spiritual conviction as a serious, determining factor, but more important would have been the necessity for the king to preserve, if not guarantee, the Jain community's position as an integral component of society as a whole. Moreover, it must also be said that the textual material on which Stein's analysis is based is somewhat thin. The *Tiṟukkuṟaḷ*, for all its fame, is little more than a collection of gnomic sententiae, while the numerous inscriptions of a Jain character, although providing much valuable information, have to be handled with caution, since their contents were governed both by the pan-Indian rules of royal panegyric and also by the fact that an inscription made at a Jain holy spot would obviously stress the fact that its patron was exclusively Jain. In particular, the tenth-century textbook of political theory, Somadeva's *Nītivākyāmṛta*, to which Stein ascribes great importance, barely shows any Jain traits at all.[32] As all the textual material is, in any event, highly idealised, I would contend that a far richer source for the understanding of the Jain perception of kingship is, in fact, the ĀP. Its particular relevance can be seen more specifically in that Jinasena, the author, was probably addressing it to his patron, the powerful monarch, Amoghavarṣa I Rāṣṭrakūṭa, and also because it was, according to legend, the inspiration for that most conspicuous exemplification of the Jain warrior, the statue of Bāhubali at Śravaṇa Belgoḷa, the focal point of South Indian Jainism.[33]

Jinasena was a member of the Pañcastūpānvaya, later called the

[31] See J. F. Fleet, *Indian Antiquary* 20 (1891), 35.
[32] Compare K. K. Handiqui, *Yaśastilaka and Indian Culture* (Sholapur 1949), p. 115.
[33] See Saryu Doshi (ed.), *Homage to Shravana Belgola* (Bombay 1981), p. 47.

Sena Gaṇa, a monastic group which probably came originally from Benares and was subsequently to develop connections with Śravaṇa Belgoḷa.[34] By his own testimony (ĀP, chapter 1), he is the final participant in a process of lore-making going back to Ṛṣabha himself, the first *tīrthaṅkara*, who recited the ĀP to his son Bharata. Ṛṣabha's chief disciple hears it and moulds it into a literary work which is handed down by all the *gaṇadharas* until Gautama, Mahāvīra's chief disciple. It is to be noted that according to Jinasena, Gautama recites the ĀP at the behest of Śreṇika, the king of Magadha, who listens to it as an act of expiation, for he had previously delighted in acts of violence and the breaking of lay vows (2.21–5).[35] The point is implicit: as Gautama instructs Śreṇika in the behaviour of a Jain king, so does Jinasena instruct Amoghavarṣa. The provenance of the ĀP which has been handed down to Jinasena by a succession of teachers, and subjected to the vicissitudes of the Kali Age (2.135–6), ensures that it is no ordinary literary work: it is the first and only *purāṇa*, to be distinguished from the false Hindu texts which teach violence. Anything which exists outside it is a sham. It is to be believed, studied and meditated upon (1.204, 2.115, 2.154); it leads to heaven and fame (1.205), and its very name purifies (2.155).

Viewed more dispassionately, the ĀP can be seen to be, with its completion by Jinasena's pupil, Guṇabhadra, the most important Digambara example of the Jain literary genre known as Universal History or, more accurately, the Deeds of the Sixty Three Illustrious Men, as the ĀP is called in its chapter colopha, and, as such, is a means of synthesising a vast amount of heterogeneous themes and legends, some of non-Jain origin, into a specifically Jain mythological context. Much of the raw material of the Universal History can be found scattered round the various strata of the Śvetāmbara canon, but it is difficult to say anything specific about its development.[36] The ĀP, while being influenced by the Hindu epics,[37] and incorporating the occasional Buddhist motif such as the *gandhakūṭī*, the perfumed

[34] See A. N. Upadhye, Jinasena and his works, in *Mélanges d'indianisme à la mémoire de Louis Renou* (Paris 1968), pp. 727–32 and: Pañcastūpānvaya, reprinted in *Upadhye: Papers* (Dharwar 1983), pp. 279–83.

[35] Śreṇika accumulated *karman* which led to rebirth in hell; however, he will eventually become the first *tīrthaṅkara* of the next world-age.

[36] See Klaus Bruhn, Repetition in Jaina narrative literature, *Indologica Tavrinensia* 11 (1983), 38.

[37] See S. Jha, *Aspects of Brahmanical Influence on the Jaina Mythology* (Delhi 1978), pp. 2–3.

chamber of the *tīrthaṅkara*,[38] is essentially a huge expansion of chapters 2 and 3 of the Śvetāmbara text, the *Jamvuddīvapannatti*, which juxtapose Ṛṣabha and Bharata to exemplify two different types of kingship, Ṛṣabha being the 'emperor of the excellent dharma' (*dhammavaracakkavaṭṭī*), while Bharata is the 'emperor of the four directions of India' (*cauraṃtacakkavaṭṭī*). The ĀP, in common with later tradition, views the two as father and son, and binds their respective careers together more tightly by stating that three crucial events occurred simultaneously: Ṛṣabha's attainment of enlightenment, the arising of the wheel (*cakra*) in Bharata's armoury which proclaims him to be a *cakravartin*, an emperor,[39] and the birth of a son to Bharata who will ensure the continuation of the Ikṣvāku dynasty of which Ṛṣabha is the founder (24.2). While the early part of the ĀP describes their rebirths in the 'world of enjoyment' (*bhogabhūmi*) where salvation cannot be gained, the true beginning of the ĀP can be held to be the transition (12.3) to the 'world of '*karman*' (*karmabhūmi*) where the law of retribution takes full effect and human beings follow various occupations (*karman*). It is here that Ṛṣabha created the *kṣatriya*, *vaiśya* and *śūdra* castes (16.184), the brahmans being created afterwards by Bharata,[40] and appointed the kings of the earth (16.257). In chapter 42, the ĀP does give a model of normative Jain kingship which I will summarise later, but I would suggest that, in the more strictly narrative passages, it views, often obliquely, kingship as ambiguous, and, as in the famous Buddhist legend of Aśoka the Fierce,[41] as something both valuable and dangerous and open to corruption by flawed men.

The central activity by which a *cakravartin* legitimises himself is the *digvijaya*, the 'total conquest' which is an extension of the *pradakṣiṇā*, the ritual circling of an object of devotion, and which involves the encompassment of the four cardinal points of India by the *cakravartin* in the role of a conquering king (*jigīṣu*) who imposes

[38] See John S. Strong, Gandhakūṭī: the perfumed chamber of the Buddha, *History of Religions* 16 (1976–7), 390–406. Note also the use of the term *prajñāpāramitā* (2.45, 2.55 etc.) and the reference to Jainism as 'the middle way' (20.8).

[39] See Jan Gonda, *Ancient Indian Kingship from the Religious Point of View* (Leiden 1969), pp. 123–8.

[40] See Pannālāl Jain's Hindi introduction to the ĀP, (1964, p. 43) for a discussion of why Ṛṣabha did not create the brahmans.

[41] See John S. Strong, *The Legend of King Aśoka: a Study and Translation of the Aśokāvadāna* (Princeton 1983).

order and prevents anarchy (16.251–3).[42] Before starting out on each stage of the conquest, Bharata, the first and prototypical *cakravartin*, solemnises the event by fasting and meditation (28.54) and the performance of *pūjā* and then follows the wheel, the symbol of his kingship, round the various parts of India, pausing to perform a *pradakṣiṇā* in Saurāṣṭra, the future abode of the *tīrthaṅkara* Nemi (30.102), and, circling all the while, his capital of Ayodhyā,[43] the central point of the land of the Āryans. The gradual progression around India by which the Bharata subjects rival kings (28.24–7), punishing, for example, those who tax their subjects excessively (29.26), is done without violence, but rather through innate capability (*śakti*; 28.30), the prime qualities of the *cakravartin* being calmness and energy (29.36). The barbarians outside the land of the Āryans, who are not subject to *karman* and *dharma*, are also brought under Bharata's sway (31.136ff). On completion of the conquest, Bharata returns to his capital, the whole process having been the result of his merit (*puṇya*) won in previous lives (30.125, 129; 31.155; 37.190–201), for merit is the cause of all beneficial results and Jain doctrine is the cause of merit (17.21–2; 28.210–20 and 32.199).

However, Bharata's conquest is firmly rooted in *saṃsāra*, transmigration, and, despite its ostensibly beneficial nature, it is totally inferior to Ṛṣabha's achievement. The ĀP here utilises the theme of ascetic conquest, frequently found in Indian hagiographical literature,[44] by stating that it is the *tīrthaṅkara* who, by setting out on his mendicant wanderings, performs the true world conquest; it is Ṛṣabha who has fought the real battle and won the true victory on the battlefield of meditation (20.247–8). Although he does not possess any royal insignia or have any recourse to arms, Ṛṣabha has still conquered his enemies (25.15–21). He is the real victorious king (20.241,260), who has overcome not simply India but the three worlds

42 See Ludwig Alsdorf, Zur Geschichte der Jaina – Kosmographie und – Mythologie, *Kleine Schriften* (Weisbaden 1974), pp. 78–80.

43 See Hans Bakker, The rise of Ayodhyā as a place of pilgrimage, *Indo-Iranian Journal* 24 (1982), 103.

44 See Richard Burghart, Renunciation in the religious traditions of South Asia, *Man* 18 (1983), 641, and Phyllis Granoff, Holy Warriors: a preliminary study of some saints and kings in the classical Indian tradition, *Journal of Indian Philosophy* 12 (1984), 291–303. From the Jain point of view, a fully worked out version of this theme is Meghaviyaya's account of some of the celebrated *sūris* of the Tapā Gaccha, the *Digvijayamahākāvya*, edited by A. P. Shah, Singhi Jain Series 14 (Bombay 1945).

(22.237; 25.3,7) and the god of death (25.70), while Bharata's conquest has only taken place at the pleasure of the *tīrthaṅkara* (28.61). As the ĀP signalled at its outset (1.1,5,16–17) the *tīrthaṅkaras*, who have rejected worldly kingship, are the rulers of the kingdom of omniscience and their chief disciples are its crown princes.[45]

The inferiority of Bharata's achievement and the imperfect nature of his kingship are highlighted in chapters 34–36 of the ĀP, which describe his attempts to absorb the kingdoms, bestowed by Ṛṣabha, of his brothers and, in particular, of his half-brother Bāhubali. When the brothers complain to their father that, despite the *digvijaya*, they are in no way beholden to Bharata, Ṛṣabha replies that the *cakravartin* will enjoy kingship as his merit dictates and that, in the end, he must inevitably abandon it (34.120); only when he has achieved release will he be fully successful. Worldly kingship is transitory and inferior to the true kingship of austerities of the monk (17.80,263; 34.114–24,132). So the brothers, 'embraced by the royal prosperity of austerities (*tapolakṣmī*), intent on the achievement of omniscience, forgot the royal prosperity of kings (*rājalakṣmī*)' (34.132), and renounced. Bāhubali, in Digambara tradition the first being of this world-age to achieve liberation, does not occur in the Śvetāmbara canonical version of the story of Bharata and Ṛṣabha, being mentioned for probably the first time in the *Vasudevahiṇḍi* (approximately fourth century AD),[46] and I would tentatively suggest that his introduction into the old story reflects the growing Jain awareness of the potential dangers of kingship. Later versions of the story describe Bāhubali as an example of pride, owing to his initial inability to achieve enlightenment, but this motif does not occur in the ĀP and, although there are passing references to his being proud (35.8–10), he is depicted as an essentially heroic figure, the true personification of the Jain warrior. In rejecting Bharata's command to hand over his kingdom, Bāhubali also rejects the validity of the *cakravartin*'s world conquest, criticising it on the grounds that it was prompted by sheer greed and rapacity, and thus implicitly compares it with the Hindu

[45] That three of the *tīrthaṅkaras*, Śānti, Kunthu and Ara, were also *cakravartins* I ascribe to the exigencies of the scheme of sixty-three figures of the Universal History.

[46] See Dalsukhbhai D. Malvania, The story of Bharata and Bāhubalī, *Sambodhi* 6 (1977–8), 1–11, and Prem Suman Jain, Bāhubali in Prakrit literature, in T. G. Kalghatgi (ed.), *Gommateshvara Commemoration Volume (A.D. 981–1981)* (Shravanabelgola 1981), pp. 76–81.

*digvijaya* described at *Mahābhārata* 2.33, where Arjuna instructs the Pāṇḍavas to perform a world conquest to swell their coffers. Bāhubali refuses to be forced into paying homage to his brother simply on the grounds that he is older (36.105–7), and his description of Bharata's treating the kings of India as a potter does clay (34.126) is a pointed reference to the fact that it is, in reality, Ṛṣabha alone who is the creator and organiser of the social world; it is to Ṛṣabha that Bāhubali owes his kingdom and position. Bharata is enraged, thus manifesting the worst possible flaw for a king, and the two half-brothers resolve to fight. In the preliminaries to the battle, the onlookers express grave reservations about violent war and especially about Bharata's role in provoking it (36.26–33), and the two agree to single combat with no weapons, in which Bharata is eventually worsted (36.36–63). Again falling prey to anger, Bharata breaks his word and hurls his wheel at Bāhubali, but it does not strike and instead performs a *pradakṣiṇā* around him (36.63–6). Rather than kill Bharata, Bāhubali realises the transience of kingship and renounces. On the path to enlightenment (36.104–85), Bāhubali becomes a conquering king (36.138): 'refulgent through his victories over the pains and torments of the renouncer's life (*parīṣaha*), having conquered the internal enemies, he destroyed his foes, the passions, and enjoyed the kingship of austerities' (36.143). 'Anybody who, with inner senses quieted, meditates upon Bāhubali, will win the same, glorious Jain victory' (36.212).

The ĀP's description of Bharata's anger and his cheating in combat, the criticism of the *digvijaya* expressed by various figures, and the frequent statement of the superiority of the kingship of austerities point to a Jain interpretation of kingship as an imperfect and potentially dangerous institution which, for all its beneficial qualities, is worthy of only partial admiration, and which requires the guiding and controlling presence of ministers imbued not only with the values of Jainism but also with a strong degree of pragmatism.[47] The ambivalent nature of kingship as expressed in the ĀP can best be seen at 15.100–25 where Bharata's mother, before his birth, has a dream in

[47] For example, Mahābala, one of Ṛṣabha's earlier incarnations, is instructed in Jainism by his minister, Svayaṃbuddha, who also refutes three heretical ministers (5.1–86); the King of Magadha is prevented from rashly attacking Bharata by divine advisers (28.124–57); Bharata is advised by a minister not to give way to wrath (34.72–9), and ministers prevent a bloody battle between Bharata and Bāhubali (36.38–40).

which the Earth, Mt Meru, the sun, heavens and oceans are devoured. Although Ṛṣabha interprets this to mean that she will have a son who will protect the earth, the image is also very much one of destruction. The ĀP makes it clear that the true warrior, the true king, is the one who, like Bāhubali, abstains from violence and, instead, conquers the spiritual enemies. The continual invocation of Bāhubali's name and the emphasis on his heroism in the literature which can, loosely, be called 'tantric', which describes the means to attain magic powers and a short cut to enlightenment, testify to the resonance of this legend in the later tradition.[48]

A more general account of kingship and warrior behaviour occurs in chapter 42 of the ĀP where Bharata instructs an assembly of *kṣatriyas* in the *kṣātra dharma*, the duties of the warrior and king. The specifically Jain nature of the warrior is shown by the assertion that he is not born from his mother's body but rather from the Three Jewels, namely, right knowledge, right faith and right conduct (42.15), and so, those who are not warriors can become so by taking monastic ordination (42.28): in other words, 'warrior' can mean not only the individual who participates in the world of warfare and kingship, but also the ordinary monk. In the following account, however, it is clearly the warrior as temporal ruler who is being described. According to the ĀP (42.3–4) the *kṣatriyas* were enjoined by Ṛṣabha to protect and the objects of their protection are five: religious community (*kula*) (literally 'family',[49]) doctrine, self, subjects and equality. I give a brief summary here.

Protection of the religious community is first described in general, essentially pan-Indian terms: the king must obtain material prosperity without transgressing *dharma* and must safeguard it, increase it and bestow it upon worthy people (42.13). The manner in which the actual integrity of the religious community can be safeguarded is conveyed by using an idiom of Hindu sacrifice. The Jain warrior cannot take the *śeṣa*, literally, the 'sacrificial leftovers',[50] of members of other sects, only the *śeṣa* of those who serve the *tīrthaṅkaras*

[48] Muni Jambūvijaya (ed.), *Sūrimantrakalpasamuccayaḥ anekapūrvācāryapraṇītaḥ*, 2 vol (Bombay 1969 and 1977): vol. I p. 21, p. 93, p. 94 etc., and vol. II p. 199 and p. 344.

[49] *Kula*, specifically, means those who are suitable for monastic ordination (*dīkṣā*). See Jinendra Varṇī, *Jainendrasiddhāntakośa*, vol. II (Delhi 1971), p. 130.

[50] For observations on *śeṣa*, see David L. Shulman, *Tamil Temple Myths: Sacrifice and Divine Marriage in the South Indian Śaiva Tradition* (Princeton 1980), pp. 90–1.

(42.18–22). Although, as a rule *śeṣa*, in later Hinduism, signifies offerings such as flowers and fruit which are made to an image and are then redistributed amongst the participants in the ritual, here it seems to be used metaphorically to convey the sense of 'doctrine'. 'When *śeṣa* is taken from a member of another sect, then one's soul is diminished. If an inimical heretic should deposit poison-flowers upon a king's head, then surely that king will experience disaster' (42.20–1). Jinasena stresses that, as warriors are descended from the very first *kṣatriya*, Ṛṣabha, who is the personification of the Three Jewels, the essence of the Jain religion, warriors are, accordingly, related (*sajātīya*) to monks and can, therefore, receive *śeṣa* from them. Any contact of whatever sort with members of other sects is wrong, and, if kings do not energetically protect the spiritual community from them, then people will be deceived by the teachings of false *purāṇas* (42.30).

Doctrine is defined as knowledge of what is right and wrong with regard to this world and the next (42.31) and the king is instructed to cultivate and protect this. Kingly science (*rājavidyā*) does give an understanding of worldly affairs, but only Jainism can provide knowledge of the two worlds of *saṃsāra* and liberation (42.34). To this end, Jain kings must firmly hold that there are no spiritual leaders other than the *tīrthaṅkaras* who are unique (42.41–7). The *kṣatriya* should turn his mind, when it is awakened, away from other doctrines and establish it in the true path of Jainism (42.112).

Protection of the self, or soul, should be performed with particular reference to the next world, and the best way to do this is through *dharma* (42.115–17) which is defined as 'abandonment' (*tyāga*; 42.124). So, kingship should be abandoned and austerities practised (42.121), thus contradicting the Hindu injunction that kings should never renounce,[51] and, finally, life should be abandoned by the religious death so that heaven and, ultimately, liberation can be attained (42.129–33). It is only the Three Jewels which pertain directly to the self, nothing else has any connection at all (42.129). The *kṣatriya*, who does not know the self and does not protect the self, will have a bad death from poison or arrows and there will be evil consequences in his next birth (42.134–5).

[51] See Greg Bailey, *The Mythology of Brahmā* (Delhi 1983), p. 210. Chapter 18 of the *Uttarajjhayanasutta* is the *locus classicus* for an account of legendary Jain kings who renounced.

The means of protecting subjects is conveyed by comparing the king to a cowherd (42.238ff). Amongst other considerations, a Jain ruler should make sure that he has loyal servants and a loyal army. Although it is inevitable that a king will fight his neighbours in order to expand his kingdom, if he is attacked by a more powerful neighbour, then the enemy should be conciliated because war is bad for the people (42.195–6). But, above all, the Jain king should safeguard his kingdom from 'scripture barbarians' (*akṣaramleccha*), that is, Hindu brahmans, who live off the Veda, delude people by reciting words of unrighteousness and take pride in their false scriptural knowledge, delighting in violence and meat-eating. They should not be given any special privileges, but be made to pay their taxes in the same way as farmers. It is only Jain brahmans who, because their excellence stems from their good qualities rather than their birth, are worthy of honour (42.181–92).

Finally, and rather blandly, protection of equality means evenhandedness towards one's subjects. The evil, that is, those who perform acts of violence, should be punished, and the good, who gain their livelihood in the proper manner, that is, the Jains, should be protected (42.200–3).

The ĀP, then, gives both a specific and a general idealised account of the Jain warrior and king. The former account is based on a mythical prototype according to which kingship, for all its many virtues, is demonstrated to be imperfect and transient. The true, Jain, warrior is the individual who fights the spiritual battle and attains the permanent kingdom of liberation. Temporal, profane conflict is thus contrasted with and shown to be inferior to religious war. The latter account provides a model for a Jain kingdom which, in adhering to Jain principles, takes care to vest social authority in members of the Jain religious community.

In discussing Prabhācandra's and Jinasena's writings, I have been taking it for granted that there exists a phenomenon which can, for the sake of argument, be designated as 'Jain identity'; the grandiose edifice of the Universal History and, elsewhere, the vast corpus of pious exemplification which is the story literature give substance to this assumption. But what is it that underpins this identity? For the teacher lineages I referred to at the outset are perhaps of immediate relevance only to the monk. In fact, one does not need to read very far in the literature or to know a great deal about the practice of the religion to suggest that it is the principle of non-violence, *ahiṃsā*, which is the central concern of Jainism. As the medieval compendia make clear,[52] any activity, no matter how meritorious, is utterly fruitless if the individual does not practise non-violence. According to the ĀP (39.20–30), Jainism possesses all the significant components of Hinduism: the Veda, the *purāṇas*, the law books, correct social behaviour, ritual, *mantras*, deities, ascetic accoutrements (*linga*) and rules about proper types of food, but the main difference is that Ṛṣabha has promulgated all these elements in accordance with the principle of non-violence. The true Veda, for example, is the Jain scriptures which proclaim *ahiṃsā*, while the Hindu Veda is no more than the voice of death; the real *mantras* are those employed at Jain ceremonies, not at animal sacrifices; the true deities are the benign *tīrthaṅkaras*, not the bloodthirsty Hindu deities, and so on. Unfortunately and significantly, this assertion of moral superiority seems to have been lost on the authors of the Hindu *purāṇas* who tended to be more impressed by the disagreeable demeanour of Jain ascetics than by the lofty ethics of the religion they practised; indeed, Jainism is more often than not conflated with Buddhism by these writers, and the principle of non-violence ascribed to the Jains' great intellectual opponents.[53]

In short, non-violence did not serve to confer a unique identity in the Indian world at large, for it was also a component of Buddhism and much of Hinduism, and the conclusion must be that any attempt by the textual student to define Jainism as a distinct and self-contained entity will end in frustration. Jainism, which accepts the existence of the soul, differentiates itself from Buddhism which denies the soul, but, at the same time, shares with Buddhism a strong anti-brahmanical stance and conviction about the efficacy of individual self-improvement. On the other hand, Jainism, which forcibly rejects Hindu customs such as animal sacrifice and making offerings to one's ancestors, articulates its views about the key metaphysical question of the soul in a language and idiom often identical with brahman texts.[54]

52 Śubhacandra, *Jñānārṇava* 8.19; Hemacandra, *Yogaśāstra*, 2.31.

53 See W. D. O'Flaherty, *The Origins of Evil in Hindu Mythology* (University of California Press 1976), p. 186.

54 See Colette Caillat, Expressions de la quête spirituelle dans le Dohapāhuḍa (anthologie Jaina en apabhraṃśa) et dans quelques textes brahmaniques, *Indologica Tavrinensia* 3–4 (1975–6), 125–38.

The situation seems confusing but, in fact, need not cause despair. If we heed Staal's advice,[55] and succeed in escaping the constrictions and restraints of our textual labellings and orderings, we may discover that, on closer examination, categories and reifications such as 'Jainism' and 'Hinduism' melt away and, in the end, we find ourselves confronting a socio-religious continuum which can only be described as 'South Asian'.

[55] Frits Staal, 'The Himalayas and the fall of religion' in Deborah E. Klimburg-Salter (ed.), *The Silk Route and the Diamond Path* (UCLA Art Council 1982), pp. 38–51.

# 12

# Is there a popular Jainism?

Padmanabh S. Jaini

In asking the question, 'Is there a popular Jainism?', we are looking for practices within Jaina society that can be considered inconsistent with the main teachings of the religion, but so thoroughly assimilated with them now that they are no longer perceived as alien. In sociology, this study has taken the form of an examination of the 'great' and 'little' traditions within a culture, and we are familiar with the notable research done in this field by such pioneers as M. Srinivasan and Louis Dumont, which has dealt with various creeds within Hinduism. Considerable advance has been made in applying this method to the study of the Theravada Buddhists of Sri Lanka, and to a lesser extent of Burma, by such younger scholars as H. Bechert, G. Obeyesekere, and R. F. Gombrich. In the latter's *Precept and Practice*,[1] a study of traditional Buddhism in the rural highlands of Sri Lanka, published nearly two decades ago, Gombrich has ably dealt with the kind of questions which we are asking here, with reference to Jainism. There is certainly a great deal of similarity between the Theravadins and Jainas, both due to the large number of mendicants within their respective communities as well as to the many practices engaged in by lay people that can be traced to brahmanical elements introduced in ancient times. A critical study of Jaina society following the leads of Gombrich's study of the Theravadins would yield very similar results, but the gap between Jaina 'precepts' and 'practices' would probably be much smaller.

Jainism, like Theravada Buddhism, is a *Śramaṇa* religion, and its primary teachings concern the path to nirvana that is to be followed by those who are able to renounce the world. However, it also claims to

[1] R. F. Gombrich, *Precept and Practice* (Oxford, 1971).

teach a lesser but nevertheless honorable path of 'merit-making' for those who choose to remain in the household life. While the two paths are not truly complementary, they must still accommodate each other, if only because the mendicants are dependent upon the beneficence of the lay community for their support. The Jaina mendicants have opted for the exclusively 'supermundane' (*lokottara*) path, which is flexible enough to allow a certain amount of pastoral activity through which to guide the laity. The latter lead a sort of amphibious life, with one foot on the worldly path of making money and merit, and the other, rather hesitantly, on the path of nirvana. As a result, they are constantly forced to seek a balance between the two paths. The mendicant Jaina lawgivers, unlike their brahman counterparts, did not claim the prerogative of laying down laws for the lay people, yet they hoped to persuade them by a process of education to adopt only those worldly ways which were conducive to the path of nirvana. This is clear from the declaration of a tenth-century Jaina mendicant, Somadeva:[2]

> There are only two duties of the layman:
> The mundane (*laukika*) and the supermundane (*pāralaukika*).
> The former depends on the world and the customs thereof (*lokāśraya*);
> The latter is what one learns from the words of the Jina.

Somadeva was not, however, permitting the Jaina laymen to follow 'worldly custom' indiscriminately: this had to be judged by the one standard that invariably applied:

> All worldly practices are valid (*pramāṇa*) for the Jainas,
> As long as there is no loss of 'pure insight',
> Nor violation of the 'precepts'.

A wide variety of Hindu religious practices came under the scrutiny of Somadeva, who proposed to determine which of these 'worldly practices' were permissible to the Jaina layman.[3] The Jaina list of

[2] 'dvau hi dharmau gṛhasthānāṃ laukikaḥ pāralaukikaḥ / lokāśrayo bhaved ādyaḥ paraḥ syād āgamāśrayaḥ / . . . / sarva eva hi Jainānāṃ pramāṇaṃ laukiko vidhiḥ / yatra samyaktvahānir na yatra na vratadūṣaṇam, *Upāsakādhyayana*, kārikā 477, Bharatiya Jnanapitha, 1964.

[3] sūryārgho grahaṇasnānaṃ saṃkrāntau draviṇavyayaḥ / saṃdhyā sevāgnisatkāro gehadehārcano vidhiḥ // nadīnadasamudreṣu majjanaṃ dharmacetasā / tarustūpāgrabhaktānāṃ vandanaṃ bhṛgusaṃśrayaḥ // gopṛṣṭhāntakanamaskāras tanmūtrasya niṣevaṇam / ratnavāhanabhūyakṣaśastraśailādisevanam // samayāntarapākhaṇḍavedalokasamāśrayam / evam

proscribed practices included almost all rituals of the Hindus, most of which would be regarded today as belonging to the 'little tradition'. Somadeva declared that a Jaina must not indulge in the worship of the sun or fire, of trees or mounds of earth, since there was nothing sacred about these objects (*mahābhūtas*).[4] Nor should he bathe in the river or the ocean in hopes of gaining merit, nor spend money in connection with an eclipse (*grahaṇa*) or the passage of the sun into the summer and winter solstices (*saṃkrānti*). As for the 'holy' cow, no more inherent sacredness was attached to it than to other animals; hence the practice of touching its tail or drinking its urine was nothing but superstition (*loka-mūḍhatā*). He even considered the performance of *sandhyā* (a Vedic ritual) as wrong, since it involved sipping water at twilight hours, a practice not worthy of a devout Jaina. But the strongest words of condemnation were aimed at the practice of offering *śrāddha*, the funeral service to the manes.[5] *Śrāddha* presupposes the existence of a world of manes (*pitṛloka*). Since the Jainas maintain that the soul must be reborn instantaneously in either heaven, hell, human or animal/vegetable existence, they therefore deny any *pitṛ-loka*, and adoption of this practice would undermine their very cosmology. Moreover, feeding the brahmans in order to help the deceased to pass from a ghost-life into the *pitṛ-loka* would make a mockery of the doctrine of karma, the efficacy of individual action, a cardinal tenet of all Śramaṇa religions. It should be observed in this connection that the Theravadins also held views similar to these of the Jainas, but were unable to prevent their laity from falling prey to these customs. On the contrary, Buddhist monks in Sri Lanka participated in ceremonies like *matak-bhoj* (meal for the dead), and developed new doctrines like *patti-dāna* (merit transference) and *patti-anumodana* (rejoicing in the transference of merit), in their attempt to incorporate a clearly heterodox practice into Buddhism, giving rise in the process to what may be termed 'popular' Buddhism.

The second area in which the Jaina laity needed education was with

ādivimūḍhānāṃ jñeyaṃ mūḍham anekadhā // varārthaṃ lokavārtārtham uparodhārtham eva vā / upāsanam amīṣām syāt samyagdarśanahānaye // (*Upāsakādhyayana*, kārikā 136–140.

4 na svato 'gneḥ pavitraṭvaṃ devatārūpam eva vā / . . . vyavahāranāyapekṣā tasyeṣṭā pujyatā dvijaiḥ // Jinasena's *Ādipurāṇa*, xl, 8, Bharatiya Jnanapitha.

5 See P. S. Jaini, Karma and the problem of rebirth in Jainism, in *Karma and Rebirth in Classical Indian Traditions*, ed. W. D. O'Flaherty (California 1980).

[ref]erence to the nature of the deity. One became a Jaina by taking [ref]uge in a Jina (spiritual victor), a mendicant who had completely [ov]ercome all forms of attachment (*rāga*), aversion (*dveṣa*), and delusion (*moha*), and was therefore worthy of worship. But the Jainas were surrounded by a vast majority of people whose deities, although armed with weapons and surrounded by spouses, nevertheless promised their devotees both salvation as well as daily bread and butter (*yogakṣemaṃ vahāmy aham*, as Kṛṣṇa says in the *Gītā*). Combating the influence of these Vedic and Purāṇic deities became an urgent preoccupation with the Jaina mendicants of medieval times. Somadeva typifies the missionary zeal with which Jaina teachers undertook the task of exposing the alleged divinity of the Hindu trinity:[6]

> Brahmā has his mind obsessed with Tilottamā, the nymph,
> And Hari, the Lord of Lakṣmī, is attached to her;
> Śambhu is half-man and half-woman,
> Look at these authorities on salvation!
> Vasudeva is his father, and Devakī his mother,
> He himself engaged in royal duties;
> Yet Hari is called a god!
> He dances naked and kills brahmans at will,
> Destruction of the three worlds is his sport!
> Yet Śiva is said to be a god!
> One whose conduct is no better than that of a householder,
> One whose conduct is inferior even to that of an ordinary mendicant,
> If such a one be a god,
> Surely, there would be no dearth of gods!

Somadeva's comparison between Hindu gods and Jaina mendicants must have had a telling effect upon the Jaina psyche. Despite the tremendous social and emotional pressures that the medieval *bhakti* movements must have exerted, no cult of Śiva or Viṣṇu ever developed within Jainism. Nevertheless, Jaina teachers rejected only Śiva's ability to lead people to salvation; they accepted his existence as a minor god, and, according to one account, even used him to promote their own religion. Ācārya Hemacandra is reported by his Jaina

[6] Brahmā Tilottāmacittaḥ Śrīpatiḥ Śrīhariḥ smṛtaḥ / ardhanārīśvaro Śambhus tathā 'py eṣāṃ kilāptatā // gehinā samavṛttasya yater apy adharasthiteḥ / yadi devasya devatvaṃ na devo durlabho bhavet // *Upāsakādhyayana*, kārikā 62–93.

biographers to have converted the Śaivite King Kumārapāla (1143–72) by showing him a vision of Lord Śiva and obtaining from the latter a declaration that the religion of the Jina was superior to all. The king is said to have assumed at that very moment a life-long vow of vegetarianism, the hallmark of Jainism.[7] As for Rāma and Kṛṣṇa, the two most prominent avataras of Viṣṇu, it is well known that the Jainas composed new Rāmāyaṇas and Harivaṃśa-purāṇas in which they elevated Rāma to the status of a Jaina saint by attributing the murder of Rāvaṇa to Rāma's brother, Laksmaṇa, and punished Kṛṣṇa for his war-mongering and sexual exploits by consigning him to purgatory.[8]

The Jaina success in resisting the intrusion of brahmanical gods into their faith can be contrasted with the Sinhalese Theravadin attempt to maintain the purity of the Buddhist tradition. The two most powerful gods in the modern Sinhalese pantheon are not Buddhist but Hindu, one being Viṣṇu, and the other being Kataragama, a local variant of Kumāra Kārtikeya, a son of Śiva. It is true that neither was allowed to usurp the paramount position of the Buddha; nevertheless, without any valid reason Viṣṇu has been elevated to the status of a Bodhisattva, and Kataragama, although not a Buddhist either, has been accorded the position of protector of both Buddhism and the island. By making such concessions to the popular belief that Hindu gods were efficacious in worldly affairs, the Buddhist Sangha allowed a form of popular Buddhism to arise. The fact that shrines to these gods were erected on temple grounds proves that the Sangha officially supported 'Buddhist' cults that worshipped Hindu gods.

In this context, mention may be made of a purely Buddhist divinity of Sri Lanka, known by the name of Nātha. He is identified with the Bodhisattva Avalokiteśvara, a remnant of the Mahayana cult that has survived from ancient times. The popular Buddhism of modern times, probably influenced by western-educated Theravadins, has sought to

[7] . . . śrīHemācāryaḥ kiñcid dhiyā nidhyāya nṛpam āha: alaṃ purāṇadarśanoktibhiḥ śrīSomeśvaram eva tava pratyakṣīkaromi, yathā tanmukhena muktimārgam avaiṣi iti . . . / atha . . . garbhagrhe . . . nṛpo . . . apratimarūpam asambhāvyasvarūpaṃ tapasvinam adrākṣīt/ . . . divyā gīrāvirāsīt: 'rājan, ayaṃ maharṣiḥ sarvadevatāvatāraḥ / . . . etadupạdiṣṭa evāsaṃdigdho muktimārgaḥ' ity ādiśya tirobhūte . . . / atha taraiva nṛpater yāvajjīvaṃ piśita-prasannayor niyamaṃ datvā tataḥ pratyāvṛttau kṣamāpatī śrīmadAṇahillapuraṃ prāpatuḥ / Merutuṅga's *Prabandhacintāmaṇi*, p. 85. Singhi Jaina Granthamālā, vol. I, 1933. See also G. Buhler, *The Life of Hemacandrācārya* translated by M. Patel, Singhi Jaina Series 11 (1931).

[8] See P. S. Jaini, *The Jaina Path of Purification*, ch.9 (California 1979).

identify Nātha with the Bodhisattva Maitreya, the future Buddha. Jainism also believes in a future line of twenty-four Jinas, and it is assumed that King Śreṇika, a contemporary of Mahāvīra (and the father of the Buddhist King Ajātaśatru) will be the first Jina of the new era. But the Jainas have never permitted the cult of a future Jina to develop, as it would be inconsistent with their doctrine that one may worship only a *tīrthaṅkara* in order to obtain salvation. Maitreya, enjoying heavenly pleasures while he awaits his descent to earth, might be holy to the Buddhists, but to the Jainas he would still be unworthy of the same honour that one accords to a mendicant. The fact that King Śreṇika's soul is consigned not to heaven but to hell, as a consequence of committing suicide, is an additional indication that the Jainas have adhered to their doctrine far more scrupulously than the Buddhists. By not allowing an opening for excessive worship of the future Jina, the Jainas have eliminated one more possible source for the formation of a 'popular cult'. Similarly, Jainas have never worshipped the remains of the Jinas, and consequently have never developed anything parallel to the worship of the relics of the Buddha, the most popular practice in Sri Lanka.

I am not suggesting that the Jainas were impervious to every form of outside influence. The conspicuous presence of *yakṣa* images in almost all major medieval Jaina temples must belie any such claim; moreover, their continued worship by Jaina laymen even to this day parallels the Theravadin cults of *devas* and *yakkhas*. Even so, a look at the Jaina *yakṣa* cult, particularly as it was legitimised within the original tradition, would show that the Jainas were probably less supportive of these cults than the Theravadins, and hence more successful in arresting the growth of a 'popular' form of Jainism based on them.

It is well known that supernatural beings, variously referred to as *devas*, *nāgas*, *gandharva*s and *yakṣa*s, were worshipped by the pre-Buddhistic people of the Gangetic valley as 'guardian deities' who had specific protective functions. Buddhist and Jaina canonical texts abound in descriptions of their abodes, called *caitya* or *devāyatana*, which were situated outside major cities like Campā, Rājagraha and Vārāṇasī. The *caitya*s were inhabited by *yakṣa* chiefs, such as Pūrṇabhadra and Maṇībhadra, who were also the tutelary gods of certain tribes and clans. Festivities were held in their honour on days sacred to them, and offerings of various kinds were made. Such *caitya*s became the resting-places of many ascetics, including the Buddha and Mahāvīra, during their visit to these cities. Unlike ordinary people, the Buddha and Mahāvīra were not afraid to challenge the *yakṣa*s' occupation of these grounds; hence they were able to subdue and convert them to their respective faiths, and enlist them as protectors of their lay followers. Several Buddhist *suttas*, notably the Maṅgalasutta, the Ratanasutta and the Āṭānāṭiyassutta, mention by name these converted demigods, who were promised a share in the merit earned by the laity in exchange for their protection.

One would expect the Jainas to have followed the example of the Buddhists and grant a similar status to their *yakṣa*s. But the ancient Jaina texts are conspicuously silent on the status of the *yakṣa*s within their religious fraternity; no Jaina *sutta* similar to the Buddhist *suttas* just mentioned has been found, nor have I come across statements that advocate the desirability of pleasing the *yakṣa*s. Even the early Jaina images at Patna and Mathura are devoid of their company, except for those of the Jina Pārśva which are hooded by a cobra in a fashion similar to that of the Mucalindanāga Buddha. The subsequent development of a Jaina *yakṣa* cult can probably be traced to this hooded image of Pārśva.

By contrast, in the post-Gupta period, we begin to find images of the Jinas flanked by figures of guardian deities. No one knows for certain when this innovation took place. It is unlikely, however, that during their migration from Bihar in the Śunga period, the Jainas would not have taken with them cults of their own city-guardian deities, including those of Maṇibhadra and Pūrṇabhadra, which are repeatedly referred to in their sacred texts. It would seem probable that they would have even picked up a few more such deities on their way to Mathura, and thence, via Rajasthan and Gujarat, to the Deccan. A migrant community can be expected to adopt the deities of host communities as a means of integrating themselves with the local inhabitants. These new gods, being non-Jaina by nature, would inevitably have been looked upon by the Jaina teachers as unwelcome accretions to the original faith. It appears quite certain that the Jaina teachers of the early medieval period undertook the task of purging these non-Jaina admixtures from the lives of the Jaina laymen. It is possible that they could have devised a new set of guardian deities to replace the local, non-Jaina ones, thus giving the Jaina laymen the kind of protection that they had come to expect from the local gods. Only a stray reference in the work of Jinasena, an eighth-century Digambara teacher, has survived to show that the Jaina *ācārya*s had been active in educating their laity in this manner. Jinasena, who is credited with formulating a large number of Jaina house-holder rites, stipulates that a person upholding the true Jaina faith should remove images of the 'false gods' (*mithyā-devatā*) from his residence. 'He should in a public manner (*prakāśaṃ*) take them away somewhere else', says Jinasena, 'and abandon them, saying "Until now, out of ignorance, you have been worshipped by us with respect. However, now the time has come for us to worship our own guardian deities (*asmat samaya-devatāḥ*). Pray, do not be angry. You may go wherever you please."'[9] Such a statement would seem to indicate that the laity of Jinasena's time were prone to worship non-Jaina gods, and that a movement to re-convert these Jainas gained strength under the leadership of the Jaina monks.

The reference to Jaina guardian deities in Jinasena's quotation above also suggests that it was during this time that Jaina teachers decided to institute a cult of guardian deities closely associated with that of the Jinas. Although there is no formal concept of an *iṣṭa-devatā* (favourite deity) among the Jainas, because the Jinas are above granting boons, for some reason or other, certain Jinas have enjoyed greater popularity among the Jaina laity than others. One would expect that Mahāvīra, being the last Jina and the closest historically to the Jaina community, would be most worshipped. But such is not the case. The shrines dedicated to his predecessor Pārśva, who preceded him by 250 years, are far more numerous in fact. The next two Jinas, in order of popularity, are Ṛṣabha, the first Jina, and Nemi, the twenty-second Jina and a cousin of Vāsudeva Kṛṣṇa. As for the rest of the Jinas, few independent images of them have been found, apart from their portrayal in a stereotyped row of twenty-four Jinas.

Pārśva's popularity over the other Jinas is probably due to his association with his guardian deities, the snake god Dharaṇendra with

[9] nirdiṣṭasthānalābhasya punar asya gaṇagrahaḥ / syān mithyādevatāḥ svasmād viniḥsārayato gṛhāt // iyantaṃ kālam ajñānāt pūjitāḥ sma kṛtādaram / pūjyās tv idānīm asmābhir asmatsamayadevatāḥ // tato 'pamṛṣṭitenālaṃ anyatra svairam āsyatām / iti prakāśam evaitān nītvā 'nyatra kvacit tyajet // *Ādipurāṇa*, xxxix, 45–47.

his consort Padmāvatī. The Jaina Purāṇas maintain that Pārśva, while still a young prince of Varanasi, had saved a pair of snakes hidden in a piece of firewood, which was being kindled by a non-Jaina ascetic for a sacrifice. Pārśva stopped him from burning the log and showed him the dying pair of snakes. He uttered the holy Jaina litany (*pañca-namaskāra-mantra*) in the presence of the snakes, and as a consequence they were immediately reborn as the *yakṣa*s Dharaṇendra and Padmāvatī. The haughty ascetic fiercely hated Pārśva, and was reborn as a demon (*vyantara*) named Śambara. When Pārśva subsequently renounced the world and sat in meditation, Śambara, remembering his past enmity, showered a hailstorm over him. And it was at this time that the pair of *yakṣa*s, Dharaṇendra and Padmāvatī, remembering the good deed done to them, came down to protect their saviour Pārśva. Dharaṇendra spread his hood over the seated Pārśva, while his consort, who could not be permitted to touch an ascetic since she was female, stood by his side raising a parasol over him. This scene appears in the Ajanta caves (*c.* ninth century) and is probably the earliest iconographic representation of the cult of these two *yakṣa*s in association with Pārśva.[10] The primary purpose of the legend was no doubt to stress the great potency of the Jaina *mantra* and the power it had to lead a dying person to heaven. But the fact that these two 'snake gods' helped Pārśva in his time of calamity also contributed to the establishment of a cult in which they were worshipped as intercessors by the laity. Since Jaina doctrine does not allow worship of the laity, the category to which *yakṣas* belong, these two 'snake gods' could be invoked as guardian deities only in connection with the worship of the Jina Pārśva, whose attendants they had chosen to become.

Once the worship of such exalted householders had been legitimised, the establishment of a popular cult of guardian deities opened the way for further assimilation of non-Jaina elements. Thus, certain well-known Hindu gods and goddesses, who were already associated with sacred places adjacent to the sites of Jaina temples, could be incorporated into the Jaina fold.

The Girnar Hills in Saurashtra, famous for the inscriptions of Aśoka and Rudradāman, are sacred to Jainas and non-Jainas alike. The highest peak of this mount is dedicated to a Hindu mother-

[10] See U. P. Shah, Evolution of Jaina inconography & symbolism in *Aspects of Jaina Art & Architecture*, ed. U. P. Shah and M. A. Dhaky (Ahmedabad 1975).

goddess named Ambikā, and a nearby peak is sacred to the Jainas who believe it was the site at which Nemi, the twenty-second Jina, attained *nirvāṇa*. Although there is no story connecting Ambikā with Nemi in the way that Padmāvatī was linked with Pārśva, it was only natural for the Jainas to associate them by making Ambikā (also called Kūṣmāṇḍinī) into Nemi's guardian deity. Similarly, other *yakṣas*, especially Kālī, Jvālāmālinī, Mahākālī and Gaurī, whose names definitely suggest connections with the Śaivite deity, Durgā, may have been brought into the Jaina pantheon as guardian deities of the Jinas and Suvidhi, Śītala, Śreyāṃsa, Vāsupūjya (nos. 9–12) respectively.[11] Jaina laymen could then worship them as their own deities, without abandoning the Jaina faith.

Such legitimisation of *yakṣa*-worship within the Jaina faith may have helped to prevent the influence of Vaiṣṇava and Śaiva *bhakti* movements on the Jaina laity. All doctrinal compromises have their price, and Jaina lay-people, who previously had only worshipped the Jinas, were increasingly attracted to the worldly benefits available from the *yakṣa*s, while the mendicants busied themselves with the task of devising new rites, litanies, and tantric practices to placate the *yakṣa*s. This resulted in a new class of clerics, called Yatis and Bhaṭṭārakas, hitherto unknown to Jaina society, who claimed for themselves a special status similar to that of the '*mahant*s' of Hindu religious establishments. Several centres, called Maṭhas, of such administrative clerics, came into existence all over western India, and from these the clerics conducted an extraordinary number of business transactions, such as building temples and erecting images, both of the Jinas and of *yakṣa*s. They also instituted various new rites and rituals to be employed in their worship, and managed large endowments offered by devout laymen for the perpetuation of their cults. Initially, the *yakṣa*s could not be worshipped independently of Jina images, but gradually special annexes housing them were built adjacent to the main shrines, thereby increasing the importance of *yakṣa*s in the Jaina ritual. Eventually they were granted a status nearly equal to that of the Jinas themselves.

[11] See 'Tīrthaṅkara' in Jinendra Varni, *Jainendra-siddhānta-kośa* (Bharatiya Jnanapitha, Delhi, 1970–3). It should be noted that the names of the *yakṣa*/*yakṣis* are not mentioned by Jinasena and Gunabhadra in their *Ādipurāṇa*/*Uttarapurāṇa*, the main biography of the Jinas in the Digambara tradition.

Several admonitions of leading Jaina *ācārya*s of the twelfth and thirteenth centuries show that this must have caused a great deal of alarm to some monks. Once again we may quote Somadeva, who was cognizant of the fact that the *yakṣa*s had ceased to be mere complements to the Jina, and had nearly usurped the Jina's role as objects of worship. He sternly warned the Jaina laity against such gross heresy: 'Whoever treats as equals to the Jina, the Lord of the three worlds, and these demi-gods of the lower worlds, and worships them equally, surely is heading downward (toward purgatory). These deities were conceived in the holy scripture purely for the sake of guarding the teachings of the Jina. Therefore, these demi-gods should not be honoured beyond their proper share in oblations by Jainas who hold the right view.'[12]

Another layman of the thirteenth century, Pandit Āśādhara (the author of the *Sāgāradharmāmṛta*) did not proscribe the worship of the *yakṣa*s, but did decry it. He proclaimed that while weak-minded and ignorant people might stoop to *yakṣa* worship, the person of true insight would never do so, even when beset by great calamities. Such weak-minded people, he said, should be instructed and reaffirmed in their devotion to the Jina. We do not know what impact, if any, these admonitions may have had on contemporary Jaina society. There is no doubt, however, that the corruptions produced by the excessive adoration of *yakṣa*s engendered protests against those monks who had been branded as *caitya-vāsīs* (temple-dwellers), who were looked upon as apostates from the true mendicant path. The Jaina reform movement of the fifteenth century declared idol-worship (*mūrti-pūjā*) itself to be a form of heresy unsupported by the ancient scripture, and its leader, Lonka Shah (*c.* 1450), formed a school which called itself *Sthānaka-vāsīs* (i.e. 'dwellers-in-halls' in contrast to the 'temple-dwellers'). This school sought to purge all temple-oriented rituals from Jaina practice, and to reintroduce the laity to the meditational practices which were exemplified by the images of the Jina. The emergence of this reformist sect within Jainism has no parallel in Theravada Buddhism, and its success can only be compared to that of Lutheran Protestantism within Christianity. The Sthānakavāsis have flourished in the Punjab and Rajasthan, and form a very important

[12] devaṃ jagattrayinetraṃ vyantarādyāś ca devatāḥ / samaṃ pūjāvidhāneṣu paśyan dūraṃ vrajed adhaḥ // *Upāsakādhyayana*, k. 697.

group today, claiming as many as 1,000 monks and 1,400 nuns within their community. They are the true forerunners of Indian iconoclastic movements, even preceding the beginnings of Sikhism, which was founded by Guru Nanak (1469–1538). They might also be considered to have been a significant force behind the creation in 1875 of the Aryasamaj, a socio-religious movement founded in the Punjab by Swāmī Dayānand Sarasvatī (1824–83), a Hindu ascetic who not only shunned all image worship, but even rejected the cults of the *purāṇic* gods.

I began this chapter by exploring the characteristics of a popular form of Jainism, by comparing them with certain practices prevalent in the Buddhism of Sri Lanka. The comparison showed that the Jainas, unlike the Theravadins, were able to preserve the purity of their tradition by preventing the rise of popular cults based on worship of relics and of a future teacher. This study showed also that, while Buddhist monks became willing participants in popular rituals associated with offerings to the dead, the Jaina mendicants vigorously condemned them and effectively educated their laity to shun all such forms of superstitious behaviour. Both *Śramaṇa* traditions were greatly successful in resisting the Hindu theistic devotionalism that threatened to assimilate them. But both succumbed to strong popular demands for the worship of demigods, and had finally to legitimise some form of a cult of 'guardian deities'. In this respect, popular Jainism paralleled popular Theravada Buddhism, and both went through an identical phase in which brahmanical accretions to their original pantheon hastened the degeneration of their monastic institutions.

In subsequent periods, however, the Jainas, unlike the Theravadins, initiated strong reforms to check the corruption resulting from excessive *yakṣa* worship. But one should not exaggerate the impact of the reformists. After initial successes, the iconoclastic Sthānakavāsīs, like many other reformists in India, formed a sect of their own, effectively removing themselves from the mainstream of the religion. Moreover, lay devotees of the Sthānakavāsī sect did not cease to worship at all temples, but only at the Jaina shrines. Many of the Rajasthan and Gujarat adherents were converted from Śaivism centuries ago,[13] and they continued clandestinely to worship their

[13] For a list of the Rajasthani communities converted to Jainism, see A. C. and B. Nahta, *Kharatara gacchake pratibodhita gotra aur jātiyāṃ* (Hindi) (Calcutta n.d.).

'family deities' (*kula-devatās*), such as Cāmuṇḍā and Durgā. As for the Digambaras and Śvetāmbaras, their reformed religiosity found expression in such ritualistic activities as building new temples and consecrating more and more Jina images, thus seeking to gain merit in a legitimate manner. Indeed, the popular Jainism of our time is little more than indulgence in the most expensive and spectacular forms of image-worship. This was illustrated in 1981 at the celebration of the head-anointing (*mastakābhiṣeka*) ceremony of the 1,000-year-old monumental image of Lord Bāhubali at Sravaṇa-belgola.[14] The devotional ecstasies aroused in the hearts of Jainas by the dramatic scenes of that ceremony affirm the enduring presence of a popular form of Jainism, markedly different from the rigorous asceticism of its great tradition.

[14] See Saryu Doshi, *Homage to Shravana Belgola* (Marg Publications, Bombay, 1981).

13

# Fairs and miracles: at the boundaries of the Jain community in Rajasthan

Caroline Humphrey

If you ask a Jain which are the main centres of active Jain worship in Rajasthan, he is likely to reply with the local names for three important 'temple complexes':[1] Kesaria-ji in Udaipur District, Mahāvīr-ji in Sawai Madhopur District, and Nākoḍā-ji in Barmer District. We could add to this list Padampura, near Jaipur, which is, as it were, a temple complex in the making. But in terms of the general pattern of Jain religious organisation these are all highly unusual places. They are not situated where there is a concentration of Jain population, but rather in the rural hinterland. They are attended by people of all Jain sects; indeed they are open to scheduled castes and tribes, people who normally never pass the austere portals of Jain temples. Each of them has as its focus a celebrated *mūrti*, the image of a Tīrthaṅkar, which is attributed with miraculous powers, foreign to the proper Jain understanding of the nature of the Tīrthaṅkar. All of these temples are strongly linked by virtually identical myths to particular territories. And at each of these sites we find that there is an annual fair (*mela*) of enormous popularity and regional economic importance.

Non-Jains are attracted to the *mela* for religious as well as economic reasons: the opportunity to take *darshan* of the miraculous image, to make requests for miraculous boons, and participate in its ritual procession (*jatra*) with which the fair culminates.

Religious fairs are a significant interface of Jain relations with other communities. The Jains define themselves by their adherence to a *separate* religion. But, as a predominantly trading group, they are concerned to establish a religious attraction and a legitimation for their economic position *vis-à-vis* other communities. However, the

[1] By 'temple complex' I mean a cluster of religious buildings and service facilities round one main temple.

8 Śvetāmbar Jain family worshipping Nākoḍā Bheru-ji at the pilgrimage centre of Nākoḍā, south Rajasthan. Photo: J. Laidlaw

problem is more complex than this. There is a contradiction between religious and economic motives. Essentially, Jainism as a religion is not exclusive: anyone more or less[2] can become a Jain by adopting Jain beliefs and life styles. Indeed, many Jain *munis* (ascetics) are of non-Jain origin by birth.[3] But in present-day rural Rajasthan the economic interests of the group which carries the religion are against expansion.

I shall argue that popular elements of Indian religion, the cult of *yakṣas*, long since absorbed into popular Jainism, are used to attract non-Jains, and that, besides this, Jains allow an accretion of regionally current symbols and concepts of the supernatural to be 'mapped on' to

[2] Certain Jain sects are currently more inclined towards conversion than others (e.g. the Kanji Swami movement in Gujarat and Madhya Pradesh), but even so converts are only really encouraged within castes where there are already Jains.

[3] Arvind Aggarwal, personal communication.

9 Ghantakaran, a protector deity in a Śvetāmbar Jain temple in Jaipur, 1983.
Photo: C. Humphrey

the Jain *sacra*. But the Jain community manages nevertheless to hold itself aloof by not revealing 'Jainism' itself. Rather, they permit a multiplicity of meanings to ritual acts, 'Jain meanings' and those held by non-Jains. The fair is the occasion for this flowering of communal religious activity, in which, nevertheless, the various communities mark themselves off as different. This is the only occasion on which Jains interact on a *religious* level with other groups, and, perhaps for this reason, it is these huge fairs which 'draw out' the Jains as a community, despite their internal sectarian divisions. Paradoxically, it is perhaps the unfettered celebration on these occasions of popular cults, the possibility of miracles, which Jains as it were 'share' with other communites, which allows all Jain temple-going sects to claim a stake in these holy sites.

As traders and moneylenders in rural areas, Jains operate a series of tightly-knit family businesses which depend on a certain amount of mutual help, while being in competition with newer trading arrivals. The position of traders as middle-men between the towns and the rural hinterland is one which rests on difference, the division of labour between producers, and between producers and entrepreneurs. They convey manufactured goods from the world of the city and agricultural products from the populations of the countryside. The Jains as traders need to maintain supra-local and even supra-regional links in order to perform this middle-man role (Cottam 1980). But if the Jains were to attempt by religion either totally to exclude or totally to convert the rural peoples their structural position would be entirely changed.

For this reason I think we can see parallels to the story I am about to describe among other trading groups in rural western India. Muslim merchants of South Rajasthan and northern Madhya Pradesh also promote their own fairs (*mela*s) in the annual cycle (Agrawal 1980). In the Hindu Pushtimarg faith, centred on the temple complex at Nathdwara, we can see an even closer parallel. Patronised largely by Oswal trading people from Gujarat and southern Rajasthan, Nathdwara again brings together the miraculous statue,[4] the supernatural link with a specific territory, and the popular annual fair (Jindel 1976).

[4] The Pushtimarg followers of Vallabhacharya do not in fact allow the sacred image to be called '*mūrti*', as this term implies a separation of the divinity from the physical representation. The concept of '*swarup*' unites the divine with the image, which *is* the deity.

Although the patterns of inclusion and exclusion in these two examples are in detail different from the Jain case, they can be seen as variations in the management of a similar structural situation.

Let us look more closely at our four Jain temples with their fairs. Normally, Jain temples are situated in centres of Jain population, usually cities or towns, and temples are attended regularly by Jains living near by. They are owned or managed by distinct Jain sects or by sections of castes subsumed within sects (Banks 1985). Non-Jains very rarely visit these temples. But all of the four '*mela*-temples' are located in country districts where there are unusually high proportions of scheduled castes and tribes but very few Jains (Mathur 1976). The cult has created, alongside the main temple, other subsidiary temples, *dharmśālā*s where visitors can stay, sometimes a medical centre, a small bazaar, and a settlement of artisans, servants and others connected with service at the temple. Special transport and other facilities are laid on at the time of the fair only.

To take Kesaria-ji as an example, we find that the surrounding district is populated by 90 per cent Bhil tribals with around 10 per cent of Hindus/Jains.[5] The small temple town of Rishabhdeo, named after the first Tīrthaṇkar Ṛṣabha (or Ādināth after his enlightenment), locally called Kesaria-ji, has a population of about 5,000, of which 50 per cent are Jains, the rest being Hindus (mostly Brahmins) and a very few Bhils. Of the Rishabhdeo Jains, 95 per cent belong to the Digambar Bispanthi sect and the Nārsinghpura and Dasa Humada sub-castes (S. L. Doshi 1978). A small group of Śvetāmbar Jains arrived in the town about 100 years ago and has been in more or less continuous competition with the Digambars for control of the temple. At present the main temple, though apparently owned by the Digambars, is open for worship by both sects, Digambars in the morning and Śwetāmbars in the afternoon. The temple contains Hindu and Bhil deities[6] as well as the central Jain image, and people

[5] I am indebted to Matthew Jones for this information about Rishabhdeo. The figures given are those locally supposed to be the case and perhaps exaggerate the proportions of Bhils in this area. Mathur (1976) gives scheduled tribes as 33.66% of the population of Udaipur District as a whole, 63.64% in Dungarpur, and 72.93% in Banswara, while the average in Rajasthan is 12.13%.

[6] There is a pair of silver-clad deities in the temple which apparently depict Bhil gods (these may be *bhomia*s). When in the temple, the Bhils ignore all Jain *mūrti*s except for the one found in the ground. Sometimes, on the way out, they pay respects to the large stone elephants on either side of the main doorway. Matthew Jones, personal communication.

from these communities regularly worship there. On the occasion of the annual fair tens of thousands of people of all groups worship at the temple. In contrast to the normal Jain pattern, we see here (a) the temple-complex as an outpost among aliens, and (b) a mixed caste and sectarian pattern of management among the Jains, together with a supra-community pattern of worship.

Mahāvīr-ji, to take another example, has historically been the seat of a Bhaṭṭārak, a Jain semi-religious semi-secular official whose kingly demeanour, settled residence (*maṭh*), and rule over landed property (*adhikā kṣetra*) is in sharp distinction with the detachment from property and wandering existence of the Jain ascetic. At Mahāvīr-ji several prominent trading familes from different castes and sects have competed to construct and restore the temples and images. The lists of lesser donors, whose names are inscribed on the temple walls, include a wide range of Jain and non-Jain surnames: Aggarwal, Saraf, Bakhliwal, Saraogi, Sogani, Jaswal, Chabra, Gujar, Singhi, Kasliwal, Porwal, and Gupta. Here we see the institutionalisation of attachment to territory, together with supra-*jāti* patronage of the temple.

Although our 'fair temple-complexes' are the foci for pilgrimages, they cannot be identified simply as Jain *tīrth*s (sacred pilgrimage sites). Sangave notes that Jains divide their *tīrth*s into two categories, *siddhakṣetra*s from where the ascetics realised their liberation, and *atiśayakṣetra*s which are sacred for other reasons, including the presence of *mūrti*s which bestow favours on their devotees (1980: 254). Our temples fall into the latter category. But economically important fairs do not exist at all *tīrth*s. Visitors at most Jain *tīrth*s are either Jain pilgrims or tourists interested in the architecture, but they do not on any large scale include devotees from other non-Jain communities. Hence, though the 'fair temples' have much in common with *tīrth*s, and Nākoḍā-ji is sometimes called a *tīrth*, I would separate them out as having distinct characteristics in the socio-economic structure.

Fairs in western India are based on *jatra*s (religious processions), *ur*s (Muslim festivals), *pradakṣina* (circumambulations of holy sites) and other religious occasions. They vary in size from small ones which attract only the people of a given locality to larger ones of zonal and ultimately regional significance.

We can suggest a parallel between, on the one hand, Agrawal's local, zonal and regional fairs and on the other the 'levels', in Eschmann's typology, of temple influence: local or tribal, subregional, regional, and all-India levels (Eschmann 1978: 84). Our three main 'fair temple complexes' would appear to have regional status. Jains travel to Mahāvīr-ji, for example, for religious purposes throughout the year from all over Rajasthan and from neighbouring parts of Madhya Pradesh and Gujarat. Some people even come from Assam and Bihar. At the fair itself virtually the entire population of the village hinterland turns up. Traders of regional status (Agrawal 1980: 136–40), conveying goods from cities as far away as Bharatpur, Mathura, Agra and Delhi appear at the Mahāvīr-ji *mela*.

### *The religious significance of the Jain fair*

The annual fair at the temple complex is the occasion for the procession (*jatra*) of the *mūrti* (image of the deity) and its most intensive worship. In order to understand the religious attraction of this event for non-Jains we must look at the mythical history of the cult of these images. I shall describe the example of Mahāvīr-ji. The other temple complexes have very similar myths.[7]

Local informants told me the following story. In a village called Chandangaon, inhabited entirely by non-Jains, a dairy farmer called Krapa Ram of the Jat caste[8] found that one of his cows was coming back every evening dry of milk. He decided to follow it to see what was happening. To his astonishment he saw the cow go to a spot in the fields and voluntarily give forth its milk to the ground. In curiosity he

[7] (a) The *mūrti* of Pārśvanāth was discovered underground at Nākoḍā village when a Jain layman had a dream. Everyone went to the indicated place, but dig as they might they could not discover the statue. Then in another dream, the Bheru-ji pointed out the spot. The idol was found, but it could not be raised from the ground. Only after the Nokar Mantra was said would it be moved. Two villages disputed over which should have it. They then put the *mūrti* on a cart, but without an ox to pull it. When the cart was pulled towards Nākoḍā village it would not move, but when it was drawn towards Virampur, it moved easily. Although the temple is now at Virampur, the image is known as Śri Nākoḍā Pārśvanāth.

(b) At Kesaria-ji, a long time ago, a Bhil farmer had a cow which did not give milk in the evenings. He followed it to see who was stealing his milk. He found that the cow was standing under a tree and giving its milk of its own accord. The Bhil dug there and found a black statue of Pārśvanāth in the ground. The spot where the statue was found is called Paglia-ji, and is located just outside the present temple complex. It is at Paglia-ji that the annual *mela* is held.

[8] In C. S. Gupta (1966: 69) this is given as Kripa Das of the Chamar caste.

dug at the place and discovered a buried statue. The villagers decided to build a small hut over the *mūrti* where it was found. This place is now called '*devata-ka Tila*'. The deity miraculously fulfilled their desires and soon became very popular and a focus for intense worship.

After a while a rich Jain *seth* (merchant), Amar Chand Bilala, got to hear about the god, and when he went there he realised that it was a Jain deity. It was a Digambar Jain idol and he had to have it. The god miraculously saved a Jain *diwan* from an execution which the Maharaja tried to carry out. The merchant built a huge temple for it at his village, called Baswa. The *mūrti* was bathed with milk and holy water and a chariot prepared for its journey.

Krapa Ram felt very sad that it was to go. 'Are you going to desert the poor people for the rich people? Do you prefer almonds and rich dried fruits to our humble drop of milk?' he asked. His wife told Krapa Ram that it served him right for neglecting family life for the god. The *mūrti* was placed on the chariot, with the *seth* in the driving seat, but try as he might the cart would not move. The *seth* prayed to the god and asked, 'Why does the chariot not move?' The deity replied, 'Until Krapa Ram pushes the wheel and sees me off without complaint, I will not budge.' Then Krapa Ram touched the wheel, and the chariot moved.

In this story we see several key features of the 'fair temple complex'. The idea of the deity is identified with a specific *mūrti* of a Jain Tīrthaṇkar which has miraculous powers. The image is located territorially by the site of its finding in the earth, and subsequently, even though rich temples may be built for it, this original spot remains sacred. The non-Jain finder of the *mūrti* always retains some rights over it. At the Mahāvīr-ji *mela* the parading of the image re-enacts the myth: starting in its chariot at the site of finding, a descendant of Krapa Ram must touch the chariot before it goes on its ritual journey to the main temple. Although the story suggests that two different villages were involved, in fact the site of finding is today located in the temple complex, a few hundred yards from the main temple. A small shrine (*charan chhatri*) with a representation of the footprints of the deity is erected there. People of the Jat caste control this site and make a small charge for people to worship there (something which is resented by the Jains, who sometimes try to refuse to pay).

At Padampura near Jaipur, the 'fair temple complex' in the making, we find a similar sacred geography. In the centre of a humble village is the shrine with footprints, where the cow gave her milk and the image was discovered. Near to it is the wooden shed-like 'temple' constructed by the villagers for its worship. Some quarter of a mile away there looms the immense marble temple, still unfinished, in which the miraculous Jain *mūrti* is now housed. Every year at the *mela* the image is taken out by chariot, going round the boundaries of the village, into the shrine, and then back to the main temple.

At the Padampura fair, which lasts for several days, the streets of the village are filled with shops and booths. Thousands of devotees and fairgoers throng the village, cramming the huge *dharmśālā*s, and spilling over into tented encampments. Before the main day of the fair there is a great auction for the right to bathe the idol, to place garlands round its neck and silver canopies over its head, the rights to leading places in the procession, or to make offerings at the *pūjā*. It is Jains who take part in the bidding and win these prestigious roles. People from many other communities surge into the temple to worship the god. However, they are only allowed to take *darshan* (holy sight of and from the deity), not to perform *pūjā*, which is reserved for Jains alone. At Mahāvīr-ji, people of the Mina and Gujar tribes come in great numbers. However, because of a fight which took place between them some years ago, they are allotted different days for ritual participation. The Minas accompany the chariot with the *mūrti* to the river, where it is given a ritual bath. They then disperse. On the following day, the procession returns to the temple, now accompanied by the Gujars. At this temple also, *pūjā* is reserved for Jains alone.

But the tribal people believe in the efficacy of the *darshan* of the miraculous Tīrthaṅkar image. Orthodox Jains would say that the sacred gaze brings spiritual calm. They might even agree with the notion that the beauty (*abha*) of the image varies with the time of day, in the morning, during the day, and after sunset. But, on the whole, Jains do not agree that the Tīrthaṅkar image can itself grant this-wordly boons to the faithful. This function they would reserve, if they agree with it at all, for the protector deities of the Tīrthaṅkara. But non-Jains are oblivious to this distinction. Once in the temple (for further discussion, see p. 219), they make requests for safe birth of children, for luck in business, for relief from illness, for success in examinations or new jobs. Often people make vows: if the god will grant them what they wish, they will make a gift to the temple. At Mahāvīr-ji women wishing for children make swastika signs in red paint all round the white outside wall of the temple. At Rishabhdeo there is a story that a wealthy man with no heir went to the statue and promised to give a baby's weight in saffron (*kesar*) if a son were to be granted to him.

His wishes came true and he was as good as his word. This is the origin of the name Kesaria-ji for this *mūrti* of the Tīrthaṅkar Adinath, for whom an offering of saffron is thought still to be particularly appropriate. On another occasion, when a Brahmin impudently threw a 1 rupee coin at the image, saying 'If you have any strength you will show it to me', the coin immediately flew back and hit the Brahmin on the head. At Padampura, all castes go to the temple for relief from spirit-possession. This takes place at the evening *ārtī*, not the morning *pūjā* (which only Jains in a state of ritual purity are allowed to perform). People possessed by spirits because of some sin they have committed go night after night to the temple. The process of finding out which spirits are present and what they want in order to be appeased and go away is called 'the god's court' (*bhagwan-ka darbar*, the term *bhagwan* being reserved normally for the Tīrthaṇkar). The exorcism of spirits seems to be shared by the Tīrthaṇkar image and the protector deity (see also p. 222). None of these activities are specific to the Jain religion, and indeed they are considered by some devout Jains as inferior, non-religious, or even inimical, concerns.

We see that at the fair, and in a less intense fashion throughout the year, the Jains, albeit with restrictions, open these temples and lend their 'gods', for the benefit of other communities. In order to see why this happens we must look more closely at the position of Jain fairs in the rural economy.

### *Fairs in the regional economy*

We turn now to the status of these large temple-based *mela*s in relation to other fairs. Agrawal's study of fairs in northern Madhya Pradesh (Agrawal 1980) shows clearly that religious fairs (*mela*) must be distinguished from periodic markets (*hat*) which have no religious significance. Religious fairs are held on auspicious days (*tithi*) in a series of luni-solar calendars which are used for religious purposes but also by traders and others in daily life. *Mela*s occur in traders' cycles, commonly a winter cycle and a summer cycle, in districts defined by administrative and geographical boundaries. It so happens that the three religiously inauspicious months (roughly May–August) coincide with the three months of heat, when farmers are busy. Because they use a different calendar, Muslim fairs sometimes come into conflict with the Hindu ones, that is, they sometimes occur on the same dates in the same district, but the Jains adjust to the Hindu cycles and fit their fairs to take spaces, both geographical and in time, in the regional series.

The 'fair temples' are located in rural districts, surrounded by populations of isolated villages or scattered settlements. Permanent bazaars are a long way away. Many villages do not have made-up roads or regular transport to towns. Seasonal fairs are the main economic outlet, and it is for this reason that their location and timing is so closely tied to the agricultural cycle. As T. B. Naik wrote about the Bhils, 'These fairs are, as it were, instantaneous cities, where the Bhils can buy all their needs. The towns are difficult to get to. But the fairs are held quite frequently, almost every month in their very midst. It is easy for them to purchase what they want, and they can also sell goods, grains, a horse or cow that is in excess in the family' (Naik 1956: 200). We can indeed see that the agricultural economy is one reason for having fairs at all. To maintain a permanent bazaar it is necessary to have constant flows of products for sale, and a population with money to buy at all times. But farmers have products to sell primarily at harvest times, and these of course are also the times when they have money to buy. Thus Agrawal found that the upland Malwa plateau, which has double-cropping, has two series of short fairs in spring and autumn, while the lowland Nimar district, with its single crop, has fewer and longer fairs during the winter alone (1980: 64, 127). From the fair cycles he cites, we can see that simultaneous fairs occur when there are many crops, which are difficult to transport, to be bought up all over a district. Traders go to any fairs in their cycle, but they give preference to those of their own religion. Attendance at fairs is high, from both traders and the public, when the flow of economic goods coincides with the religious importance of a locale.

But, as Braudel has pointed out, the fair is more than an instance in the usual trade cycle (1979:82). We can gain some insights from his magisterial survey of commerce in Europe in the early modern period. The tight circle of exchanges between the countryside and the local town is represented by the regular market. The function of the fair is to interrupt and expand these links. Big fairs can mobilise the economy of an entire region. Braudel continues, 'The fair is envisaged as a pyramid. The base consists of many minor transactions in local goods, usually perishable and cheap, and then one moves up towards the luxury goods, expensive and transported from far away. At the very top of the pyramid came the active money market, without which business could not be done at all – or at any rate not at the same pace. . . . It does seem that the fairs were developing in such a way as, on the whole, to concentrate on credit rather than commodities, on the tip of the pyramid rather than the base' (1979: 91). In Europe, 'fairs were not so much "natural markets" arising from the presence of commodities and buyers and sellers seeking one another out, but rather artificial constructs of patrons, the result of privileges and franchises granted to trade at certain places and times, whereas it is laden down elsewhere by dues and taxes' (1979: 93). Fairs thus began to decline with the rise of capitalism and free trade.

It is not clear to what extent we can extend this analysis to contemporary rural India. Such is their religious importance that the authors of the *Census of India 1961* reports on Fairs and Festivals disagreed even on their economic significance, some seeing them as basically religious occasions (Trivedi 1965) and others as economic events held only 'in the name of religion' (ibid). However, the contrast between the fair and the regular market or bazaar does seem to hold: the one flourishes in the absence of the other. Fairs occur where regular, efficient markets are not present.[9] In the eighteenth century, fairs used to spring up outside cities, to avoid the *octroi* and other taxes, the 'dispersed market', as Bayly terms it (Bayly 1980). In the British period, when taxes were charged on trade across administrative boundaries, fairs appeared on the frontiers. Agrawal notes the gradual decline of one such fair, at Multan on the boundaries of Ratlam, Dhar and Gwalior States, after Independance, when such frontier taxes were abolished. Earlier, Multan had been given special facilities to promote trade by the rulers (Agrawal 1980: 47, 120–1).

[9] Jains are 1.8% of the population, but hold 10% of the fairs in Dhar District (Agrawal 1980: 111).

Another type of fair in India grew up in response to through trade, as opposed to local trade (Bayly's 'entrepôt markets' 1980: 21). Rapid growth was determined by administrative boundaries, or by particular trades, for example, at points suitable for cotton bulking, rather than by local demand. A further type was the 'regional entrepôt' which emerged at geographical borders. Here, characteristic products of one region were exchanged for those of another (*ibid.*).

Amongst the various Jain temple fairs we can probably find all of these economic types. Certainly, Nākoḍā-ji and Kesaria-ji were sited on important and ancient through-trade routes, and the latter also seems to have a 'regional entrepôt' function in trade between forest and agricultural regions.

### *Jains in the structure of economic and political relations*

S. L. Doshi's study of the Bhil tribals of south Rajasthan in the region of the Kesaria-ji temple complex (1978), and Agrawal's work on the adjacent parts of Madhya Pradesh (1980) both make clear that Jains have a large share in rural trade[10] and that much of this is conducted at fairs. Secondary trading groups in the region are Shia Muslims (Bohras) and Kalaks (distillers). The Jaina are also the main moneylenders (*sankar* or *sahukar*), now being superseded in some places by cooperatives and banks. People of all communities take loans, but the borrowers *par excellence* are the tribals. Bonded labourers (*sagari*) would often work for the *sahukar*s in lieu of payment (S. L. Doshi 1978: 35). The ties between the moneylender and his borrowers (*asami*) were often set up at fairs. The district being divided up into the various *sahukar*s' territories, moneylenders did not compete with one another. Despite laws against moneylending and debt-bondage, and the expansion of Jains into the grain trade, selling of merchandise, medicines and management of cotton factories, moneylending still remains the traditional Jain occupation in these districts (Agrawal 1980: 100–50). Muslims do not engage in moneylending, perhaps because of prohibitions against taking interest. Now, whether the

[10] Braudel points out that a hierarchy of markets worked well in China when there was a stable government, but when wars arose between dynasties, fairs sprung up for trade between the people of the different states. When things became peaceful again, fairs disappeared from the interior, and remained only at the external frontiers for trade with non-Chinese populations (1979: 131).

Jains are involved primarily in trade or in moneylending, the economic relations are 'vertical', cross-caste and cross-community.

But it is not only, or even primarily, traders, merchants and moneylenders who benefit economically from fairs. The income from the fair itself, taken from traders' rents for stalls, taxes on bullock carts, and other charges, goes to the organisers. The expenditure, on allowances for officials, and provision of water, light and sanitation, is invariably less than the income, according to Agrawal (1980: 173). In the case of Jain fairs the profits today go to fair management trusts usually associated with the temple. At Mahāvīr-ji, for example, the Bhaṭṭārak used to manage both the temple and the fair until he was accused of corruption in 1923, when the fair was handed over by the Digambar Jain Panchayat of Jaipur to the Court of Wards. In 1930, the Panchayat took over from the court and has kept control ever since. The Digambar Jain Panachayat also now manages the temple. Fairs, of course, produce thousands of donations from the public to the temple (for a detailed study see Agrawal 1980: 167–81). Temple income from all sources (from the land, from donations by individuals, from government grants, and from charities) goes not only on the daily services, but also to create the splendour of buildings and public ritual which demonstrate Jain status *vis-à-vis* other communities. One of the most visible of these shows is the *rathayātra* at the fair itself. This is a 'ritual space' in which a hierarchy becomes manifest (by means of the auctions among Jains and by the customary restrictions observed by other communities mentioned above).

'Vertical' relations are the basis also for Jain political support. Jains are spread throughout western India in small numbers (an average of 1.9 per cent of the population in the districts of Rajasthan: Mathur 1976). K. A. Gupta's study of politics in a small town in agricultural north-west India shows a faction led by Rajasthani Jains opposed to one led by Hindus (1976). The issue was control of the town council, which could exert considerable influence on local trade and business. Over time, allegiance to either of these factions was highly variable, but the author makes the interesting observation that the Jain faction recruited its support among other communities exclusively by economic ties (i.e. with groups either trading with or working for the Jains), while the Hindu faction gained support from a range of ties including kinship, caste, and political patronage as well as economic links.

These studies do not describe our 'fair temple complexes' themselves, but the available ethnography seems to present a sufficiently consistent picture. Jains in the rural districts, at the frontiers of their operations, have a need to establish and maintain 'vertical' ties. This does not just apply to groups 'below' them in the hierarchy of esteem. If we look at the history of the Rishabhdeo temple, we see that links with Hindu state power are also important. The temple seems to have been founded in the eighth century by Digambar Jains. On an important trade route from the coast to the state of Mewar, the temple attracted rich donations from travelling merchants. From the fourteenth to the twentieth centuries it was the subject of disputed ownership between Digambar Jains, Hindus, and latterly Śvetāmbar Jains, the outcome depending on each group's relationship with the Rajput rulers of Mewar.[11] As in other parts of India, patronage of outlying temples and *tīrth*s, especially where a kingdom was dependent on the loyalty of tribes, was an essential presupposition for consolidation of royal power (Kulke 1978: 129).

Jains were, however, careful to keep a certain autonomy in relation to such political patronage. A tax-free land grant of the village of Jaisinghpura from the Maharaja of Jaipur was accepted for the upkeep of Mahāvīr-ji in 1782, a time when a Jain held the office of Diwan in the State (C. S. Gupta 1966: 69). But when the Jaipur Maharaja proposed rebuilding the temple the Bhaṭṭārak objected, saying that the original Jain family of *seth* Amarchand Bilala should keep the right to reconstruction. Only when the king replied that he wanted to build a temple from religious feeling, and not in order to claim rights over it, did the Bhaṭṭārak agree that the Maharaja and others should be allowed to contribute.

Besides these 'vertical' links, we can discern also 'horizontal' relations of competition between various Jain groups for control over these extremely lucrative and prestigious temples. The case of Kesaria-ji has already been mentioned. In Jaipur, Śvetāmbar Jains claim that Mahāvīr-ji was first controlled by Jodh Raj Paliwal, a Diwan at court, and a Śvetāmbar Jain from the small and comparatively poor Paliwal caste. Subsequently, the Digambars, wishing to establish a pilgrimage site of their own in the north when they gained power at the Jaipur court, first managed to convert most of the

[11] The period of Śvetāmbar ascendancy at this temple is attributed to their power for a time at the court of Mewar.

Paliwals and then took control of the temple. The remaining Paliwals then appealed to their co-sectarians, the rich Oswal Śvetāmbars, for help. But the Oswals, not wishing to offend the powerful Digambars, remained inactive. To this day the temple remains in Digambar hands, although a court case brought by the Paliwals is still enmeshed in an endless legal process. From this we see that, despite deep sectarian divisions, sacred sites are able to evoke aspirations for control across the spectrum of temple-going Jain groups.

At these temple complexes, income is also spent on a network of religious and charitable institutions for the benefit of all. Of course, some institutions exist primarily for Jains (teaching halls, places for the preparation of special Jain foods, *dharmśālās* where only a Jain way of life is acceptable, etc.). But the hospitals, orphanages, dispensaries and schools, which operate under the title 'Jain', are commonly open to all, and therefore not sectarian. These institutions present a locus of 'horizontal' Jain integration. We may cite the several large public *dharmśālās*, hospital, library, higher secondary school, girls' school, roads, water-works, and the electric power station constructed at Mahāvīr-ji as an example (C. S. Gupta 1966: 71).

## *Popular beliefs and religious misunderstanding*

How is religious legitimation given to an institution, such as the temple fair, which is by definition cross-caste, cross-religion, and even cross-sect?

In Rajasthan, there is no love lost between social groups which mark themselves out by occupation, life style, and religious practices as different from one another. S. L. Doshi remarks on the hostility which exists between the Bhils and the Sunni Muslims (who run the police), and between the Bhils and the trading groups (Banias) who are mostly Jain (1978: 145). In Rishabhdeo town, Jains are quick to point out that Bhils are untrustworthy rogues, prone to stealing, even killing, consumers of alcohol and meat, with no respect for the sanctity of marriage. Bhils are despised for their spendthrift attitude to money. Bhils, on the other hand, tend to see Jains as miserly and likely to cheat them over loans and trade. Although worship of the Jain Tīrthankar at Kesaria-ji Temple represents some acknowledgement of

Jain spiritual power, Bhils take a pride in visiting the temple without the humble demeanour of caste Hindus. In the *rathayātra* at the fair they dance wildly in front of the procession, as it were defying it to move forward.[12] We see these attitudes duplicated at Mahāvīr-ji where it is Gujar and Mina tribals who go to the Jain fair. I have heard city Jains from Jaipur complain that Gujars are so wild that they would fight Minas for access to the deity, and that they storm into the temple without removing their shoes. There is no foundation at least for the latter rumour, but its existence demonstrates the latent hostility between social groups.

This chapter is not the place to explore the various markers by which different social groups distinguish themselves in Rajasthan. We could note only the major divisions, between the so-called tribal peoples 'who are content to be called "the sons of the earth" (*Bhomaputra*) or "the sons of the forest" (*Venaputra*), while Rajputs attribute celestial descent to themselves' (Tod 1829: 445), between vegetarian groups, such as the trading castes, and meat-eating groups, such as the Rajputs, or between those who wear the sacred thread and those who do not. A vast number of sometimes cross-cutting, but above all public, markers set groups apart.

But there exists nevertheless a common pool of ideas at the sub-religious level of 'popular belief'. Some of these concepts and attitudes are extremely widespread. We find, for example, the myth of the cow which offers its milk to the buried deity in many Hindu cults, some as far away as Nepal (Miller 1979: 106). The theme of the interred statue is probably linked in Rajasthan to the magical powers attributed to wandering holy men who, among both Hindus and Muslims, are believed to 'take *samadhi*', concentrating all spiritual power in the head, where it attains a last moment of self-surrender which will join it with the universal spirit. At this moment of death the disciples lower the holy man, seated in the lotus position, into a pit and bury him with earth. They then build a *chaitri* to mark the spot (Carstairs 1957: 101), a shrine which has the same form as the *charan chhatra* erected over the spot of our buried Jain statues, or erect a *samadhi* shrine in the Muslim idiom. Famous *samadhi* shrines are the sites of Hindu and Muslim fairs (e.g. the Jambheswar Fair in Bikaner District organised by the Bishnoi sect: C. S. Gupta 1966: 49–54).

[12] Matthew Jones, personal communication; Howard Jones, personal communication.

We could perhaps link this theme also, at the psychological level, with the phantasy of suddenly acquiring wealth. Carstairs noted as a widespread phenomenon the daydream or actual dream of the god-like stranger who gives instructions to go to some spot, dig there, and treasure would be found. Rumours were rife that this had actually happened. Carstairs found all his village informants to believe that this might happen to them, any day (Carstairs 1957: 90).

Another motif, which it is not possible to investigate here in detail, is the relation between milk and the snake which lives underground. At the Teja-ji *mela* near Kishangarh, the foundation myth cites the cow which offers her milk to a spot in the ground, here a hole inhabited by a snake. Teja-ji is the most popular deity of the Jats in Rajasthan, and supposed to offer cures for snake-bites (Prabhakar 1972: 49). At the Baneshwar Fair the myth gives the cow offering her milk to a Śiva lingam found in the ground. The cow struck the lingam with her hoof, causing the top of it to break into five parts. This lingam is called Swayambhū Lingam, that is, self-born (Prabhakar 1972: 57). That similar ideas penetrate into Jain popular practices is seen from the Jain shrine outside Jaisalmer, where devotees offer milk to a cobra living in a hole in the ground. If the cobra accepts the offering this brings the devotee great good luck.[13] The popularity of the cobra-hooded Pārśvanāth, the only Tīrthaṅkar to be widely recognised by non-Jains outside the fair context, can also be related to the snake theme (see Jaini this volume). The association in their different ways of the cow and the lingam/snake with metaphors of fertility is surely not irrelevant to the preoccupation with bearing children which is found among the devotees at the temple-complexes.

Indeed it seems clear, as already mentioned, that the image of the Jain Tīrthaṅkar is attributed, by its non-Jain worshippers, with popular symbolic values which have nothing to do with Jainism. The statue of Tīrthaṅkar Ādināth, at the Ṛṣabhdeo temple complex near Udaipur, is, as we have seen, popularly known as Kesaria-ji. There may be an association of ideas with Kesaria Kanwar, a name for Gogadev, worshipped near Udaipur as a snake-god. In this case, saffron was again brought as an offering to the deity by a merchant wishing for an heir (Kothari 1982: 18). It is noteworthy that Gogadev

[13] Josephine Reynell, personal communication.

is both the subject of a *bhakti* cult among pastoral tribes for his rescuing of cows from Muslims, and worshipped by Muslims as Goga Pir on the grounds that he converted to Islam (Sharma 1968: 226; C. S. Gupta 1966: 45). The Rishabhdeo statue mentioned above is also known by Bhils as Kala-ji or Karia-baba, and it seems probable that they have their own mythology associated with the deity in this form.[14] At both Kesaria-ji and Mahāvīr-ji the tribal peoples sing devotional songs which have nothing at all to do with Tīrthaṅkars or with any aspect of Jainism. At any rate, Jains in Jaipur suggested to me that popular worship at the temple-complexes of Mahāvīr-ji and Padampura has its own rationale, though they were vague and possibly incorrect as to what it consists of. They associated it with the idea of the earth-deity, Bhomia. Bhomia is a generic name for minor territorial deities, widely worshipped in the form of stones. 'The Jats who come to our Jain festival,' said my Jain friends, 'must think of our Mahāvīr statue as a *bhomia* of their people, because the statue was taken out of the ground.'

Here it must be made clear that what is being suggested is that it is the statue of the Tīrthaṅkar which is perhaps regarded as a *bhomia* by non-Jains. This, if it is true, represents a denial by the tribal people of distinctions rigorously upheld by the Jains in most religious contexts. In religious discussion Jains hold the Tīrthaṅkar to be simply a prophet in a non-theistic religion. Popular beliefs intrude into the carefully maintained categories of a major religion. It is this which is allowed at the temple fairs, whereas it would be inadmissible at a normal Jain temple. Tribal people, it is acknowledged, can believe what they like. Not only is this not resented by Jains, but the ritual acknowledges, as we have seen, the necessary role of the non-Jain finders of the *mūrti*.

Whatever may happen at *jatra*s when the ordinary people briefly assert their mastery and defiance in the Jain world, the distinctions between ritual categories which allow such mastery to be represented continue to be upheld. They are not absolute, however, but seem to exist in overlapping agglomerations of ideas. Thus, what must be experientially separate because it is material, for example, the structured space of the temple or the different iconographic forms of the

[14] N. K. Singhi, personal communication.

deities, is often conceptually ambiguous. This means that possibilities exist for Jains to see as exclusive ('not theirs') what another group may regard as inclusive ('ours').

Virtually all Jain temples have *bhomia* images, formless stone-shaped heads, which are regarded by Jains as the local protectors of the temple. Such *bhomia*s are found at the shrines of all deities in Rajasthan, such as those to Mata-ji, Dev Narayan, Teja-ji and Goga-ji. An unclear similarity exists between *bhomia*s and other protector spirits called Bhairon, Bhairav, Bheron, and Bheru-ji, these being minor incarnations of Shiva. Although the Bhairon is iconographically distinct from the formless *bhomia*, being in the shape of a martial bust with weapons and moustaches, the functions of the two are not distinguished, and many people in my experience use the terms interchangeably. What is significant for us is that these essentially earthly territorial protectors are attributed with similar functions to yet other protector deities, the Jain *śāsan-devtā*s (themselves identifiable with the ancient Indian *yakṡa*s) which guard the Tīrthaṅkars. From at least the eighth century AD, according to iconographic materials, each Tīrthaṅkar has been associated with a male and a female *yakṡa/śāsan-devtā*. The names of these deities differ from region to region, and they are commonly thought to be a Jain concession to Hindu popular cults of place (Misra 1981). If we look in detail at the pattern of worship at our 'fair temple complexes', we find that protective gods of one kind or another are given unusual prominence.

Usually at a Jain *pūjā* in a town temple, the protector deities (*śāsan-devtā*s, *bheru*s and *bhomia*s) will be given only a rather perfunctory offering after the main worship of the Tīrthaṅkars and their disciples is completed. But at temple complexes such as the Nākoḍā Pārśvanāth or Padampura, the seekers after boons will usually only take *darshan* at the main shrine and then proceed to lengthy prayers and *ārati* in front of the protectors. At Nākoḍā village it is clearly the protector, known as Nākoḍā Bheron Dev, who has the most popular appeal. Located on an ancient long-distance caravan route, Jain activity was known at this place, under different names, from the third century AD onwards. The present main temple at the complex was initially dedicated to the Tīrthaṅkar Mahāvīr, and then subsequently to Pārśvanāth when this idol was found underground. But what endured through all changes was (a) the site, and (b) its territorial protector Bheron Dev. According to legend, it was Bheron Dev who indicated the presence of the Pārśvanāth *mūrti* in the ground. A shrine to Bheron Dev is located just outside the sanctum of Pārśvanāth. The guidebook to the temple says that it was since the image of Bheron Dev was restored that the *tīrth* has gained such enormous popularity.[15]

At Padampura there is a similar distinction between the main temple, dedicated to the Tīrthaṅkar Padamprabhu, and the shrine of the guardian deity Kṣetrapal which is located in the temple wall beside the main entrance. Kṣetrapal is represented as a figure, so thickly layered with vermilion that one cannot distinguish his shape, bearing a tiny Tīrthaṅkar image on his head. Māhavīr-ji also has an important Kṣetrapal shrine, here understood to be a form of Bhairav.

Some clues to this duality can perhaps be found if we look at shrines associated with multi-community religious fairs in other parts of the Hindu world. We can cite here a series of *jatra*s in Nepal, where the shrine to the main deity, offered only milk and vegetable produce, is separated from the site where animal sacrifices are made to a territorial protector spirit, Bhairung. At one of these *jatra*s, Thami tribal people perform ritual 'blood drinking' after the sacrifice, thus saving the life of the high goddess, according to the myth, and allowing the high-caste Newar Hindus to hold the festival without defiling themselves. 'The Newars cannot hold their annual ritual without us', the Thamis say (Miller 1979: 56–7). At another *jatra*, associated with a large *mela* in the remote hills, Tamang tribal people do a similar service for Hindu Chhetris, and the site of the sacrifice is again distinct from its associated 'pure' shrine (*ibid.*: 105–15). In both of these cases, the *mela* is frequently the occasion for outbursts of hostility between the autochthonous tribal people and the incoming high castes.

In Rajasthan, although animal sacrifices do not of course take place at Jain festivals, Jains sometimes exaggerate the 'uncleanness' of the tribal and low-caste participants in the myths. 'It was a shoemaker who found the statue', they say about Padampura, but the man is still alive today and he is a Jat farmer. What all of this indicates is that the Jain *jatra*, while uniting society in common celebration, has

[15] Another popular Jain explanation is the following: the *mūrti* when it stops is choosing a protector. The magic of stopping the chariot is the *mūrti*'s, while the miracles for people are the *bhomiya*'s. James Laidlaw, personal communication.

means of creating distinctions: between the humble site of finding the statue and its magnificent temple residence, between the Jain Tīrthaṅkar and the warrior-protector, between *pūjā* and *darshan*, between the pure Jain worship and the sinful aura of spirit-possession. What is not clear, however, is that non-Jains recognise these distinctions according to the same values as Jains.

Thus we find, as mentioned above, that the Tīrthaṅkar, contrary to Jain ideas, is not really distinguished from other deities. At Mahāvīr-ji the term 'Devata-ka Tila' is used by ordinary people for the spot where the statue was found, though Jains normally distinguish clearly between deities '*deva*' and the Tīrthaṅkars '*bhagwan*'. Both here and at Padampura, the miraculous *mūrti* is also called 'baba' by the common people, a term which is also employed for Bhairavs and Bhomias. At Padampura it is supposed to be the Kṣetrapal who rids people of evil spirits. But fact, those possessed go first into the temple, where in a state of unconscious hysteria they writhe on the floor in front of the miraculous *mūrti* of the Tīrthaṅkar, the women's hair flying in the air, in complete disregard for conventionally correct temple demeanour. Excited by the rhythmic clapping and chanting of the *āratī* ritual, the possessed finally rush out of the temple to the Kṣetrapal shrine, where the protector god may, or may not, exorcise the spirits – 'on the order of the Tīrthaṅkar', as I was told.

In some ways, in this situation of 'vertical' patronage, we are reminded of the process of 'Hinduisation' of autochthonous gods as tutelary deities by royal kingdoms, described by Kulke in relation to the cult of Jagannath (Eschmann, Kulke and Tripathi 1978). But here we have, if anything, the opposite: the penetration of popular religion into Jainism. The possessed at Padampura are comprised of both Jains and non-Jains. There is no doubt that many Jains will acquiesce in these practices, but I never met any Jain who did not simultaneously distinguish them from 'real Jainism'. Jains will always, for example, make a radical distinction between the Tīrthaṅkar and the protector deities. What distinguishes this situation from the Hindu case is the holding back by the Jains of 'Jainism' itself, and it is this, I shall argue, which is one of the features by which we can identify the Jains as a community.

It seems clear, given the deep sectarian divisions between Jains, that what 'real Jainism' is must differ according to the religious and philosophical concepts of the various groups. This is not to say, however, that there are no underlying values which distinguish Jains from other communities. It is not possible to tackle this enormous question here. But what we can do is to look at the contexts in which Jain (as opposed to non-Jain) values for distinctive ritual categories *are* acknowledged.

This is the case in the competition between different Jain sects over what are commonly acknowledged to be Jain *sacra*. It is one of the relatively unusual features of the 'fair temple complexes' of Māhavīr-ji and Kesaria-ji that Śvetāmbars and Digambars are in dispute over their ownership.[16] As great wealth is at stake this is not perhaps surprising. It is clear that, irrespective of the legal rights and historical antecedants, the most politically powerful Jain caste in the region tends to gain control, and Jain castes do not cross-cut the Śvetāmbar–Digambar divide. But what is perhaps more remarkable is the fact that whichever sect has control of the fair temples, people of the other nevertheless go there as devotees.

In the cases of Padampura (Digambar), Nākoḍā (Śvetāmbar), and Mahāvīr-ji (Digambar), control is clear and the pattern of worship is settled. Devotees of the other sect must simply accept what they find. But at Kesaria-ji, the main temple accommodates both forms of worship. The rivalry here led to fighting in 1927 in which four Digambars were killed and forty-four were injured. Subsequently, a police presence was established and it was generally acknowledged that people of all religions could worship there. The Śvetāmbars and Digambars agreed to divide the day between them; not a simple matter but an operation involving a different form of *pūjā* and the complete redecoration every day of all of the Jain *mūrti*s. Though non-Jains are hardly ever knowledgeable enough to tell the difference, it is impossible for a *mūrti* to be at the same time Digambar and Śwetāmbar (in disputed cases, see note 16, the image is thickly covered with paint, which covers up the crucial features). This very fact makes the point that there is a frame of reference within which ritual distinctions are acknowledged by all Jains. Individual people or groups may have their own 'meanings' for particular sets of marks

[16] Other examples are known from Madhya Pradesh, for example at Shripuj, where there has been a long-standing dispute over ownership of the temple, again focussed on the sectarian attributes of the main *mūrti*.

within this symbolism, but the understanding that there are differences between Digambar and Śwetāmbar rituals is universal among Jains. Such distinctions are not merely empty formalities but have their roots in deep philosophical disagreements between the sects. What is clear is that they are commonly accepted *by Jains* to be indicators pertaining to 'Jainism' itself. These matters are not brought to the attention of non-Jain devotees. The Bhils are allowed to continue with their idea of 'Kala-ji' for Tīrthaṅkar Ādināth, and Jains neither know nor care what this tribal concept might be.

The Jain fair with its religious festival provides a legitimation for Jain presence in regions where they are in a minority. Fairs are, it seems, often created 'from above' by patrons who can benefit from having a fair at that site. By giving the autochthonous population rights in their ritual, the Jains acknowledge the supernatural power of the place and the people of that place. This is in some ways analogous to the high-caste–tribal relations in rural Nepal, and even to the symbolic ascetic purity attributed to the tribal hunters and gatherers of Central India by caste Hindus (Gardner 1982). At the same time, the Jains draw 'the sons of the earth' into their sphere of hierarchical religious patronage. In this situation the lower castes and tribes accept Jain conditions (restrictions on which days they can enter the temple, being allowed to do *darshan* but not *pūjā*, etc.) in return for the miraculous beneficence of the merchants' god. The economic conditions which tie poor farmers to moneylending Jains reinforce the actual hierarchy hidden behind the access to the deity. Though it is not only the poor who throng to Jain *jatra*s, hostilities of occupation and life styles prevent the Jains from encouraging converts and non-Jains to accept Jain values. As a religion Jainism is theoretically open to all who accept its principles and beliefs. Indeed, some farming people at Padampura village call themselves Jains. But there is a chasm of upbringing and understanding between people brought up as Jains and those who merely desire benefits from Jain deities. Popular regional beliefs and practices tend to bridge this gap, and some Jains do undoubtedly take part in popular religious practice, but even so it seems apparent that Jains can hedge themselves off by hierarchising these practices within their own religious system. In 'vertical' relations Jains lend their gods as well as their money, but just as the Tīrthaṅkar can be worshipped simultaneously as a miraculous *baba* and reserved for devotion as a pure and ascetic prophet, so the wealth engendered by the fairs can be used for status-making display and also for internal charitable purposes within the group.

The 'vertical' articulation of social relations at the 'fair temple complex' thus serves in fact to allow Jains to appear as a distinct community while opening their *sacra* to all. At the same time, we can only say that these are 'Jains', as opposed to some distinct sub-section of Jains, because all Jain groups acknowledge the paramouncy of these sacred places. If this acknowledgement is actually manifest in 'horizontal' rivalry for public acknowledgement of one set of sectarian ritual markers over another, it is nevertheless true that it is these religious fairs, at which non-Jains suddenly irrupt into the circle, that more than almost any other institution evoke a common Jain enthusiasm. Because popular religious cults are thought of by Jains as 'not Jain' they do not have sectarian attributes, and it is this which allows *all* Jains to take part in them if they wish. The 'mapping' of popular enthusiasms onto the austere Jain Tīrthaṅkar has the effect of raising religious emotions. That doctrinal differences are then frequently called into play in relation to the essential Jain *sacra* is a corollary of the fact that the Jains know the importance *as a community* of the triumphant festivities of the fair.

# Part 4

# New Jain institutions in India and beyond

14

# New Jain institutions in India and beyond

Caroline Humphrey

These chapters discuss recent Jain institutions, particularly in the context of the modernising movements which swept through India in the late nineteenth and twentieth centuries. The issues raised by all three chapters are: the extent to which the leadership in such institutions is founded on purely Jain criteria, the importance of the institutions, and the degree to which they depart from strictly Jain values. Do they indeed question the validity of the notion of 'strictly Jain values' in the present day?

In order to answer such questions we must have some notion of what Jain values are and what constitutes 'primaeval' Jain institutions. M. Carrithers chapter is the only one in this section to address these questions directly and in relation to a specific sociological reality. Readers should note that the level at which Carrithers is analysing the notion of community is twofold: (1) the experienced local community, as discussed also in J. Reynell, Howard Jones, C. Cottam Ellis and N. K. Singhi, and (2) the imagined sense of the larger community, a concept which is also mentioned by M. Banks. As M. Carrithers' chapter is also the only one to discuss the sociology of the southern Jains, we should sketch its critical features, as distinct from the north and west, here.

Southern Jains are not divided into sects, but all belong to the Digambar group. Even the distinctions within the Digambars found in the north (mainly the division between the *muni*-led traditions on the one hand and the modernising Kanji Panth on the other) seem to be absent. Southern Digambars do have castes, but as V. Sangave points out these are now commensal, which is not always the case in the north. The largest number of southern Jains are farmers, which also differentiates them from Jains in the north, who see farming as an occupation harmful to living creatures, that is, involving *himṣā*.

Moreover, although the southern Jains are a minority, as in the north, they have a strong rural base with sufficient numbers and economic clout to figure significantly in the local political scene.

M. Carrithers argues strongly for the continuity of essential Jain institutions over the centuries. The 'primaeval' Jain institutions are local endogamous communities, temples with their priests, the function of women in rearing the next generation, the *muni*s with their transmission of religious traditions, and the *bhaṭṭārak*s who both managed the 'religious' wealth of the community and promulgated Jain doctrinal literature. Despite the decline of certain of these elements in various periods – the *muni*s before the revival of Santisagar at the beginning of this century and the *bhaṭṭārak*s in the last few decades – Carrithers maintains the essential structure has continued in the *longue durée*. In the past, those Jain institutions which were tied into this structure were thereby enabled to prevail in conflicts with new movements, despite the general trend in Jain as well as Indian society as a whole to modernisation. Carrithers suggests that the Southern Indian Jain Association (Daksin Bharat Jain Sabha), the foremost of the modernising institutions, has managed to attain its present powerful position by virtue of the fact that it has taken over much of the functional space previously held by the *bhaṭṭārak*s, that is, the promulgation of doctrine.

The modern Sabha does not have the managerial function of the *bhaṭṭāraks* in relation to property, nor their role in mediating between the lay people and the ascetics. Indeed, some members of the Sabha are, if anything, opposed to what they see as 'backward' and 'ill-educated' practices. If the Sabha (and similar organisations) has gained its force at the expense of the *bhaṭṭārak*s, it would be interesting to speculate whether the *bhaṭṭārak*s' managerial and mediating functions are now felt as a lack. Among the Śvetāmbar Sthānakvāsi Jains of Jaipur, who of course do not have temples, prominent Jains openly regretted the gulf between ascetics and lay people, and the absence of any more mundane religious figure to draw together the various groups of worshippers.

Readers will note that in the Jain context the word 'modernise' has a particular reference. Both Carrithers' and Sangave's chapters make clear that 'modernising' essentially implies an emphasis on Jainism as a moral force applicable in principle to Indian society as a whole, as opposed to the 'traditionalist' focus on ritual and worship. 'Modernising' to Jains, as Banks and Carrithers point out, may mean in part the rediscovery of ideas which were 'always there'. But many of the ideas so prominent in the early twentieth century clearly came from outside the religious context. Issues such as brideprice, dowry, age of marriage, child initiation, admission of Harijans to temples, and so forth, divided Jains into conflicting groups. Indeed, into warring groups – despite *ahiṃsā* – such were the passions raised. Have such conflicts seriously threatened to dissolve a Jain sense of community? These chapters suggest that they have not, for a variety of reasons.

First, as Banks and Carrithers indirectly suggest, such conflicts are not new (e.g. the rise of the Sthānakvāsis in the fifteenth to sixteenth centuries) and nor are they likely to cease. It might be imagined, however, that the recent reform movements are different from those in earlier times in that their leadership is largely lay. In Carrithers' Sabha, the leadership is made up of laymen and may be characterised as follows: it is (1) capable of making informed judgements by virtue of education; (2) it is in touch with a wider world through the English language; (3) it achieved status through criteria external to Jainism, and (4) it was devoted to a natural constituency, that is, an implicit community. Only the second of these is a new phenomenon. Mukund Lath pointed out at the conference (1985) that the Adhyatma movement arose from within Jainism, though its leaders too were premodern, educated lay people. Jaini, in chapter 3, this volume, gives the further example of the lay Pandit Asadhara who in the thirteenth century led a reform against the popular worship of *yaksha*s (guardian deities of non-Jain origin).

Secondly, as Carrithers points out in his chapter the Jains were among the first in India to start such reform associations at the end of the nineteenth century. The reforms often brought the growing English-literate professional middle classes into conflict with more conservative elements, but the effect was not to homogenise Jains with other Indians. Indeed, the intention and the effect were frequently to emphasise the difference between Jains and others, especially Hindus. The moral superiority assumed by Jains over the 'laxity' of Hinduism had spin-off effects, as we see in Sangave (e.g. the purging of Hindu elements from the Jain marriage ritual). It is significant that the very surnames Jain and Jaini were a product of the reforming era, at the turn of the century, as Padmanabh Jaini has remarked at the conference, 1985.

Thirdly, both Carrithers and Sangave show that the very fecundity of reform movements among Jains, and the energy and passion with which they were/are promoted, implies that they have increased the sense of a distinct Jain identity. The disagreements between Jains over some of the reforms argue as much for the intensity of this sense as they do for divisiveness. This is a point which appears in the chapters by Reynell, Humphrey and Cottam Ellis.

Sangave's example of the conflict between Jains on the issue of worship in temples by the Dasa (lower status) caste groups is highly instructive. Dasas were excluded from temples by the higher status Bisa (Visa) groups in a range of castes divided in this way. Readers may note that in Sirohi, according to Singhi, Dasas and Bisas now worship together. But in Meerut, United Provinces, in 1910 the judge's decision went against joint worship, and what did many Dasas do but abandon the Digambar and join the Śvetāmbar sect. Structurally similar is the case of Kanji Swami in the 1930s. Originally a Sthānakvāsi *muni*, he came into conflict with his colleagues over his radically new interpretation of doctrine (and perhaps over some other matters too) and ended up by embracing the Digambar scriptures, but not their monks or rituals. Kanji Swami was influenced by Srīmad Rājchandra, the Gujarati Jain reformer mentioned in Banks' paper. Both examples, the Dasas and Kanji Swami, suggest that there does exist a vision of a total Jain community within which disagreements and realignments can be accommodated. Some people might grumble that Kanji Swami was 'not a real Digambar', but most of his now very large following has come from Digambars, not from the original, disaffected Sthānakvāsis.

An important point to emerge from both Banks and Carrithers is that the reform teachings themselves, even in England, usually refer to very early Jain doctrine. To use Banks' term, they are 'neo-orthodox'. Chitrabhanu's movement in America, mentioned by Banks, shows the extent to which 'Jain doctrine' is flexible when it makes converts. But the vast majority of Jain reform movements do not seriously aim to convert non-Jains. The aim and the idiom are to remind Jains of their own principles.

15

# Reform movements among Jains in modern India

Vilas Sangave

Unsurprisingly, in view of the close social affinities between the Jains and the Hindus, we find the development and prevalence of very similar social conditions and problems among both. Due to the deep impact of new forms of thought and culture, the spread of education, the application of new technology, and the acceptance of new social values in the late nineteenth and twentieth centuries there developed a strong awareness among the Jains, as among Hindus, of the necessity for reforming social and religious practices. Jains reacted to this awareness along the same lines as the Hindus, but on behalf of their own community and in the light of its special identity. As a result we find that several reform movements were initiated and carried out by and for Jains during the twentieth century in the fields of religious and social practices.

## *Socio-religious reforms*

As regards religious practices we find that leaders of different sects among the Jains launched several reform movements pertaining to the social dimension of religious matters.

Among reform movements of the Digambar sect the *Dasā Pūjādhikāra Āndolana*, that is, the *Dasā*'s Right to Worship Movement, occupied a prominent position. *Dasā*s are those belonging to the *dasā* division found in a number of Jain castes, such as Agaravāla, Osavāla, Hummaḍa, and Porvāḍa in Northern and Western India. While the term *visā* signifies 'twenty in the score' or pure blood, *dasā* signifies 'ten in the score' or half-pure blood. In each caste social respectability declines from the *visā* to the *dasā* division, and hypergamy is practised, so that a *dasā* family can offer its daughters up the hierarchy to a *visā* family. Restrictions were also placed on *dasā*s' access to interdining with *visā*s. Along with these restrictions religious disabilities were also imposed on *dasā* persons, so that they could not worship in temples at all, even though *dasā*s constituted a substantial part of the membership of the relevant castes.

This unfair discrimination became the target of leading intellectuals and especially *dasā* persons among the Digambar Jains. The reform movement was spearheaded by the learned and venerated teacher Gopāladāsaji Baraiyya of Banaras. He declared unambiguously that 'in accordance with the liberal principles of Jainism the *dasā*s have the equal right to worship like the non-*dasā* persons'. The stand taken by the intellectuals was opposed by rich persons of the *visā* division. After a protracted controversy the matter was referred to a court of law in Meerut, United Provinces, in 1910. The plaintiff, a *dasā*, issued the summons against twenty-two persons of the *visā* division in respect of a local temple.

The judge found in favour of the defendants on the grounds that there was no established custom of allowing *dasā* persons to worship in such a temple. This gave rise to widespread disturbances between the *visā* and *dasā* sections. The *visā* persons remained adamant, and consequently many *dasā* persons left the Digambara sect and joined the Śvetāmbara sect.

In the second decade of the twentieth century the Akhil Bhāratiya Jain Pariṣad of Delhi revived the movement and, due to its strenuous efforts, conditions changed. *Dasā* persons began to enjoy in full measure their right to worship in Jain temples and even built temples from their own funds for common use. In this case the spread of a liberal ideology through education, coupled with the egalitarian ethic of the Jain scriptures, allowed Jain leaders to reform a widespread discriminatory practice.

A second movement of a socio-religious nature also arose among Digambara Jains. In response to the spread of literacy and the use of printing-presses, a number of leading intellectuals began publishing Jain periodicals. These included Babu Suraj Bhānaji (1868–1945), a pleader of Saharanpur U.P., who published the monthly *Jainhitopadeśaka* and the *Jain Gazette*; Babu Jyotiprasādaji Jain (1882–1937) of Devaband U.P., who published the Urdu monthly *Jain Pracāraka* and the Hindi monthly *Jain Pradīpa*; and Seth Hirachand Nemchand

10 Jain laymen, active in the South Indian Jain Association (*Dakṣin Bhārat Jain Sabhā*), address a public meeting of Digambars in Kolhapur.

Doshi (1856–1938) of Solapur, Bombay State, who published the Marathi monthly *Jain Bodhak*; and Pandit Chandrasen Vaidya. These figures, led by Babu Suraj Bhanaji, also began to advocate the printing and translation into vernacular languages of Jain holy scriptures, which up till then existed only in manuscript form and were not to be touched by laymen. Publishing institutions, such as *Jain Siddhānta Prakāśini Saṃsthā*, were founded to publish such series as the *Jain Āgama Grantha Mālā*.

In reaction against this modernising current traditional Jain pandits, mostly in M.P. and U.P., began to agitate, and the main organisation of the northern Digambara Jains, called the Digambar Jain Mahasabha, of Mathura, U.P., began to support the traditional point of view. This anti-printing movement came to be known as the *Śāstra-mudraṇa Virodhi Āndolana*, or Anti-Scripture-Printing Movement. The orthodox Jains considered it a sin to touch a sacred printed book, and imposed a ban on keeping such books in temples. Murder threats were made against those involved in printing, and printing-shops were blown up.

But in conditions in which Hindus and others were also printing

11 The *bhaṭṭārak* Laxmisen of Kolhapur has specialised in the dissemination of vernacular Digambar Jain literature.

their scriptures such a reactionary movement could not stand against the tide. Slowly the opposition fizzled out, the printing of ritual literature and sacred texts gathered strength, and a number of publishing concerns flourished and printed series of sacred literature. The availability of such knowledge helped Jains in many parts of India to understand the tenets of their own religion and engage in many sorts of reform with greater confidence.

As among the Digambaras, so among the Śvetāmbara sect important movements of a socio-religious nature took place. In the first two decades of the twentieth century prominent intellectuals and other leaders of the *mūrtipūjaka* Śvetāmbara Jains in Bombay City and Gujarat started the *Bāla-dīkṣā pratibandha āndolana*, the Prevention of Child Initiation Movement. The movement was directed against the widespread practice of initiating young people and even children below the age of ten years into the ascetic order of the sect. It was felt that such minors are not at all in a position to take an independent decision concerning the adoption of asceticism as a life goal.

The issue was taken up by writers in many Jain journals of the time, and was pursued with especial vigour by the Jain Yūvak Saṅgh of Bombay, an organisation of youth concerned with social matters. The campaign dragged on for many years, and general public opinion moved slowly toward putting a virtual ban on such child initiations and of prescribing an age limit for entry into the ascetic order. As a result of this agitation the old princely State of Baroda passed legislation prohibiting child initiation within the state. Though the practice was a deep-seated one which even today carries on, the impact of the campaign, and of such legislation, seems to have been noteworthy.

Another movement was spearheaded by intellectuals and leaders of the Sthānakavāsī Śvetāmbara sect. This was the *Ek Ācārya Āndolana*, the One Religious Head Movement, started with a view to establishing the authority of one pontiff over the entire ascetic order of the Sthānakavāsī sect. Among Śthānakavāsī Jains the laity is completely attached to the ascetics for the performance of religious rites and ceremonies as a consequence of the total absence of idol-worship in temples. Sectarianism among the ascetics was therefore felt to be very divisive of the lay community as well.

After long agitation the movement succeeded in establishing the control of one *ācārya*, pontiff, which also brought unity to the laity, up till today. Such unity is not enjoyed among the Digambara Jains and the *mūrtipūjaka* Śvetāmbara Jains.

## *Social reforms*

In addition to the above movements of a socio-religious nature, purely social reform movements were launched by Jain intellectuals at the beginning of the twentieth century in different parts of India. As among Hindus, among Jains these were responses to a consciousness of new values among the educated, but were specifically directed to the Jain community. Age of marriage, preliminaries to marriage, selection of marriage partners, the form of the marriage ceremony, widow remarriage, and certain other social practices were subjected to the attention of the reformers.

Though there is evidence that adult marriage was the order of the day among Jains in ancient times, in the medieval period the practice of child marriage became prevalent among Jains, as among Hindus. The practice became so deep-rooted that it was felt by the common people to be sanctioned by religion to marry their children at an early age. Even children below five years of age were married.

Among Jains, opposition to this practice originated in southern Maharashtra at the very first meeting of the Dakṣin Mahārāṣtra Jain Sabhā in 1899. In journals and public meetings the leaders of this representative organisation campaigned for years against the practice. This reform movement was opposed by Jains from North India, who wished to continue the practice. Such organisations as the Akhil Bhāratiya Digambara Jain Saṅgh of Mathura, U.P., and the Bambāi Prāntik, Digambara Jain Sabhā of Bombay represented this reactionary point of view. In time, the practice of child marriage faded away, and now it is difficult to find a single case of child marriage among the Jains of any sect.

Bride-price and dowry were similarly the subject of concerted campaigns. As early as 1904 the Dakṣin Mahāraṣtra Jain Sabhā actively opposed the irreligious custom of bride-sale. It was thought that bride purchase was practised chiefly by low-class Jains in the South, and that this was an improper and antisocial practice. It was found that ancient Jain writers on law did not approve this as a proper observance among the people. The practice has by now disappeared, but has also declined among many other communities as well.

Similarly, dowry was found to be an excessive practice, especially in the north and west, where it could lead to the ruin of families. From the beginning of the twentieth century several Jain organisations in these areas passed resolutions against giving dowry. Yet, even though legislation has been passed against the practice, the dowry system is still in operation in one form or another. In this respect Jain marriage customs perhaps reflect customs found among other persons of a similar socio-economic status in India.

Intellectuals and leaders also found that in ancient Jain scriptures full freedom was given to people in the choice of their marriage partners from the very beginning, so that the prohibition of intercaste marriage was not an original trait of the Jain community. But the notions of the *varṇa* system of social organisation, and later the medieval practice of caste and *sajātiya* marriage with members of one's own caste or sub-caste came to prevail among Jains. By the end of the nineteenth century a large number of such sub-castes had come into being in the small Jain community throughout India. These practices increased caste sentiments and loyalties, created a cultural gulf between the castes, and raised the number of unmarried people.

The intellectuals and social workers therefore launched the Antarjātiya Vivāha Āndolana, the Inter-caste Marriage Movement, which gathered strength through the first two decades of the century and was still very active in the third decade. Various learned treatises were published in support of the movement and several national and regional associations of Jains forcefully championed the cause of the movement through different means of propaganda. The vocal opposition of orthodox parties slowly dwindled and the system of intercaste marriage was approved by different sections of the Jain communities. Even ascetics began to accept meal offerings from families which had contracted intercaste marriages. Yet the ultimate object of the campaign was not attained, for intercaste marriage has not become common practice.

Though intercaste marriage movements existed among Hindus as well, Jains identified caste as a Hindu practice from which they were purifying themselves. And a similar attitude was taken to other social practices.

Thus, even though marriage was a religious sacrament and the detailed rites of the marriage ceremony were laid down in Jain scriptures, Jains habitually performed the marriage ceremony according to Hindu ritual and with the help of Hindu priests. Due to the spread of religious knowledge among the Jains and to the rise of consciousness about the independence of Jain religion, the Jains slowly began to feel that they should celebrate the marriage ceremony, the most important event in their lives, in accordance with the sacred Jain ritual laid down for the purpose. Jain associations in many parts of India took up this cause and succeeded in wiping out the Hindu elements in marriage ceremonies among the Jains. At the same time they attacked another objectionable practice which they saw as being Hindu, that of arranging dances of prostitutes at the time of the marriage ceremony. They succeeded in putting a stop to this, too.

A similar attitude was taken by reformers toward other practices. Due to their efforts we see that the worship of Hindu gods has diminished, the observance of Hindu festivals like Holi and Sitala-saptami has been discontinued, the performance of the *śraddhā* ceremony for the ancestors is declining and bad social practices such as bride-price, child marriage, excessive expenditure on ceremonies connected with pregnancy and death, and beating the breast over someone's death are all going out of vogue.

In many parts of India, Jain associations, newspapers, and publishing ventures were begun in the late nineteenth and early twentieth centuries. These were led by educated persons who took an interest in their own community and who were concerned to eradicate what they regarded as bad or irreligious practices which had crept into Jainism in the medieval period, due to the influence of other religions, both Hindu and Muslim. Further, such persons and associations have created a new interest in Jain religion, history, literature and culture. Generally Jains now marry only Jains, Jains perform their marriages according to Jain rites, Jains have taken to religious education, and the observance of Jain daily practices has increased. But if these associations and publications have created a heightened awareness of the distinctive nature of the Jain community, they have not created a sense of oneness among all Jains irrespective of the differences of sect, caste, region, language, occupation, etc. On the contrary they have fostered sectarian and separatist tendencies.

# 16

# Orthodoxy and dissent: varieties of religious belief among immigrant Gujarati Jains in Britain

Marcus J. Banks

## *Introduction*

In seeking to bound and define the subject-matter of this volume, M. Carrithers and C. Humphrey have isolated five criteria by which the term 'community' can have analytical significance for any study of the Jains. These criteria represent both actors' and analysts' viewpoints and together present 'community' as a complex of features, rather than as a single analytical tool. In this chapter I wish to concentrate on two of the criteria – the sharing of a common culture, belief and practice and the consciousness of an identity as Jains – and the examine these within the context of an immigrant Jain community I studied in England.[1]

The study of belief, especially religious belief, is fraught with difficulties, whether they be those that arise from trying to determine the specific content of a belief system, or those that surround the question of what it means 'to believe' at all (see Gombrich 1971, for example). Indeed, the problems attendant upon trying to define 'belief system' are analogous to those encountered in trying to define 'community'. In this chapter I try to show that just as Jains themselves may be fragmented and divided, so the religion permits various interpretations which match divisions in a Jain 'community'. Yet, just as Jain communities may, in fact, be 'potential and imagined but by no means unreal' (chapter 1, p. 12), so Jainism itself can exhibit a fiction of cohesion and inclusiveness which can serve to bind a fragmented community.

[1] Throughout the chapter I shall continue to use the word 'community' in its generally accepted sense and will offer some assessment of this in the conclusion. Fieldwork was conducted as part of my doctoral research from June 1982 to January 1983, with shorter subsequent visits. I am grateful to the SSRC (now ESRC) for supporting my research.

## *Jains in Britain*

Of the 20–25,000 Jains resident in Britain today, almost all are Gujarati.[2] Of these, a large majority (I estimate some 75–80 per cent although there are no figures to support this conclusively) have come from the three East African countries (Uganda, Tanzania and Kenya) within the last fifteen years, or are the offspring of migrants from these countries. With a few minor exceptions, these Jains all belong to two castes or *jāt*s: the Halari Visā Oswal and the Visā Srimali.[3]

While the Halari Visā Oswals constitute a regionally specific *jāt* in India, in that all Halari Oswals in the world trace their origin to fifty-six villages around the city of Jamnagar in Saurashtra (Gujarat), and have a strong corporate identity (as a *jāt*, but not necessarily as Jains), the Visā Srimalis in Britain have more diverse origins, although most trace their descent to some part of Saurashtra. The Halari Visā Oswals have been an endogamous *jāt* for at least a century, and whilst most are Deravasi (the local term for *mūrti pūjaka* or idol-worshipping) Jains by religion, a few follow the Hindu Swaminarayan sect, although this is no bar to marriage. Various alliances have been formed between territorially specific Visā Srimali groups in Saurashtra over the past 200 years, and today Visā Srimalis in England are free to intermarry, although there is some resistance to marriage between Visā Srimalis from Saurashtra (peninsula Gujarat) and those who originate from central and southern Gujarat (the Gujarat 'mainland'). The Visā Srimalis are exclusively Jain but are divided by sect into Deravasi and Sthānakavāsi. Visā Srimalis and Halari Visā Oswals do not intermarry, either in India or overseas. Although the majority of Halari Visā Oswals and about half the Visā Srimalis live in the London area, there are significant numbers elsewhere in the country, especially in the Midlands. They have settled in areas that maintain a large number of Asian immigrants and, as in Gujarat, it is not possible to distinguish the Jains from Gujarati Hindus by language, dress or any other visible markers. For some, Jainism is one of the least important aspects of their social identity (both corporate and individual) and is outweighed

[2] Technically of course, they are all British. I use 'Gujarati' as an ethnic and not a legal identification.

[3] The Halari Visā Oswals in Britain have received some attention from academics (see, for example, Michaelson 1983; Shah 1979). To my knowledge, nothing has been written about Visā Srimalis in Britain.

by their received status as 'immigrants' and their self-perception as Gujaratis. Nevertheless, attempts have been made by the two *jāt*s (or, more accurately, by individuals within the two) to cultivate a specifically Jain identity, and it is with one of these attempts that the remainder of this chapter is concerned.

## *The Jain Samāj*

My work in Leicester focussed on a group of Srimali Jains who had organised themselves into a 'Jain Samāj' and who had bought a large building in the town centre to serve as a meeting-place and temple.[4]

Initially the Samāj had included both Oswals and Srimalis (about 100 families in each case) but the two *jāt*s had fallen out, largely over issues of status, and the building was purchased by the Srimalis alone. However, the Leicester Srimali community is by no means wealthy enough or large enough to support such a project unaided. After the split with the Oswals (which, as a *jāt*, is wealthier) the Srimali leadership campaigned hard to attract finance from other sources, both Jain and non-Jain, Asian and non-Asian. For example, donations were made by local non-Jain Asian shopkeepers, as well as by wealthy Jain diamond merchants in Holland. Successful grant applications were made to various local and central government agencies for the newly purchased Jain centre to act as a community centre with facilities for the unemployed, a creche and so on. This backing was attracted by advertising the Jain centre as a centre for the propagation and study of Jainism: a religious criterion, in other words.

However, such a strategy, while successful in the acquisition and fitting-out of the building, was not universally welcomed by all the Srimalis in Leicester, for it rested on a very particular interpretation of Jainism. I have discussed elsewhere (Banks 1985) how the Leicester Srimalis were troubled by an ambiguous identity which lay half way between the religious identities of immigrant Muslim and Sikh groups in Leicester and the regional or *jāt* identity of immigrant Hindus. Some Srimalis felt that their religious identity was a minor thing, similar to the weak sectarian affiliation of Gujarati Hindus, and that their *jāt* identity (as Srimalis) was far more important. A similar

[4] Although about half the Srimalis under discussion are nominally Sthānakavāsi, they had adopted elements of idol-worship, either in East Africa or in Britain. There are some important differences between Sthānakavāsi and Deravasi attitudes and behaviour but I shall treat them as one for the purposes of this discussion.

observation was made by Morris in Uganda, where he observed that while Asian Muslims were divided along sectarian lines, Hindus were divided by *jāt*, forming groups that they (and Morris) called 'communities' (Morris 1968). Morris felt that this was due to an inherent weakness in Hindu sectarian recruitment. For such Srimalis in Leicester, Jainism was merely an adjunct to their *jāt* identity, shared only by one other *jāt* in Britain (the Halari Visā Oswal). However, other Leicester Srimalis saw Jainism in a far more 'Westernised' light, as a world or great-tradition religion, which existed independently of any elected group and which contained issues of relevance to all humanity. It is these two approaches to Jainism that I examine in the next section.

## *Orthodoxy, neo-orthodoxy, heterodoxy*

As in any community, no matter how small, there are perceivable and quantifiable differences between individuals, in terms of occupation, education, income and so forth. There are also divisions engendered by the particular structure of the community, most noticeably between the leaders and the led. For example, one night during the festival of Paryushan at the Leicester Jain centre when the bidding for the lamp-waving ceremonies of *ārtī* and *maṅgaldīvo* was slow, the *ārtī* was finally awarded to the Jain Samāj.[5]

It was performed, however, by members of the committee. This led later to an argument, with some of the Srimalis feeling that the (elected) committee was not necessarily synonymous with the Samāj, and that 'ordinary' (i.e. non-committee) members of the Samāj should have performed the ceremony. In part, the argument was simply the outcome of a personality clash, but it was also an expression of more deep-seated resentment on the part of those who felt they were losing control of 'their' Samāj and centre. Although I accept Morris's proposition that the progress and organisation of *jāt* (and other) associations rest largely on the aspirations of self-motivated leader-figures (Morris 1968:40), I do not believe that the other members are necessarily indifferent or apathetic.

How does the practice of Jainism in Leicester differ from that in

[5] Although bidding may happen nightly at Jain temples in India, in Leicester it occurs only during Paryushan.

India? The most obvious point of divergence is the absence of ascetics (*sādhus* and *sādhvīs*) in the Leicester community. Jain ascetics may travel only by foot, and are therefore unable to travel outside India. In East Africa – where the same absence of ascetics also prevailed – there had probably been greater contact with India, at least initially, but still the essentially ascetic system of *gaccha*s had been transmuted into the two sectarian nodes (Deravasi and Sthānakavāsi). In Leicester, the leaders of the Samāj (the elected committee and unofficial 'elders' – retired men who had become wealthy in East Africa and who now live with their children in Leicester), act as authority figures and decision-makers – roles that ascetics as well as laity play in India, particularly in religious matters. While ascetics in India are responsible only to themselves and their *ācārya*s (such as in allocating money raised by the laity during Paryushan) the leaders of the Jain Samāj are theoretically responsible to their members and, in the case of the committee, can be refused re-election after their two-year term of office. In fact, however, the membership of the executive committee has stayed stable for the last eight years or so. The committee consists of a president, an honorary vice-president, a general secretary, an assistant general secretary, a treasurer and assistant treasurer and a woman (the nominee of the Bhagini Kendra, the 'ladies' circle'). Routine committee meetings are generally attended by the president, the two secretaries and the treasurer. Members of the committee, except for the woman, are all professionals: two doctors, a dentist, a lawyer and an accountant, while the sixth is a successful businessman. While these professions are not representative of the rest of the Leicester membership, which largely consists of shopkeepers, factory workers and unemployed, they are important in maintaining the credibility of the Samāj to the non-Leicester membership (many of whom are businessmen). This is a source of tension in the Jain Samāj: the aims and expectations of the Leicester membership are potentially at odds with those of the greater membership. While the leadership must cultivate its patrons it must not alienate its local supporters. The Leicester Jains made substantial financial contributions to the centre and make up the bulk of the numbers at any function, simply by virtue of their residence in Leicester. The patrons themselves may expect different things of the Samāj: the city council and other official bodies that have given grants expect some kind of community centre (in the standard English urban sense) to emerge; Jains in India, who are donating a marble temple, wish to glorify their religion and earn themselves merit (*puṇya*). My concern is, however, essentially a study of the Leicester Srimalis, and hence only the Leicester part of the Samāj (which does not have regional branches, though it does now have a London office).[6] But the differences in aims and expectations that I note on the wider scale are also to be found within the Leicester community, and it is to this level that I wish to devote the rest of this chapter. Divisions in Leicester arose as a result of perceptions of the present and the future – how much, and in what way, should one adapt to life in Britain and, more importantly, what was to be the role of Jainism in this adaptation? The way I choose to identify these differences is in terms of beliefs about Jainism. In India, differences in belief are articulated through the framework of sect and *gaccha*, perhaps leading to the creation of new sects, such as the Kanji Panth. I am not trying to say that differences in belief cause sectarian division, though that is often how such divisions are perceived, especially by those who are partisan. However, sectarian differences of this kind can really only be articulated within, or in the presence of, the ascetic community. In Leicester, without ascetics to control or guide, a wide variety of religious beliefs could thrive in the Srimali community.

Before going any further I should outline the characteristics of these differences, or 'tendencies' as I shall call them – the varieties of religious belief. I have isolated three major foci, but together they form a continuum, or more accurately, three points of a triangle, rather than discrete groups. For convenience I have labelled them: orthodoxy, heterodoxy and neo-orthodoxy.

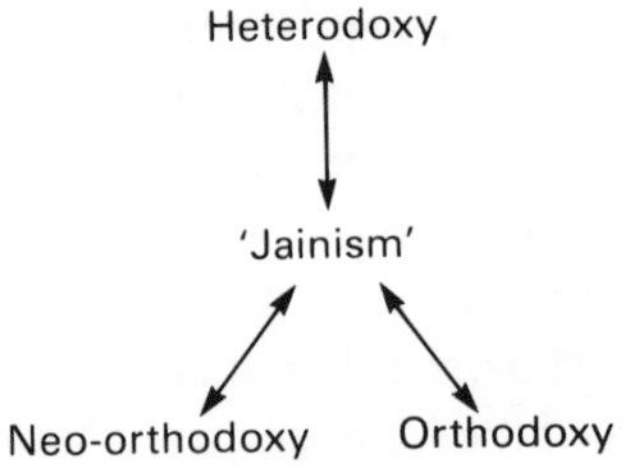


[6] I discuss the aims and expectations of this wider membership in Banks, forthcoming.

It should be stressed that these are categories of belief, not believers; an individual may at any one time espouse one or more of the viewpoints, but this is not fixed or binding. I have deliberately left the categories and their definitions vague, partly because there is not a fixed, dedicated group devoted to each of the belief types, and partly because it is my opinion that some individuals at least, who do distinguish between categories of belief (and go on to make identification with particular individuals), do not articulate their identification for fear of causing clear, opposed groups to emerge. In 1982 (when I conducted fieldwork) the status quo, if fragile, was maintained despite the tensions. Arguments, such as that described above over the *ārtī* ceremony, did break out from time to time, but did not lead to a major cleavage of the community, from which both sides would stand to lose. The model is also largely abstract, given that the orthodox tendency does not really have any base in Leicester though it is thought to be the prevailing type of belief in India, and as such individuals gauge their viewpoint against it. That is to say, if I were to identify the tendencies with specific groups of people, there would only be two – heterodox and neo-orthodox. But because I identify them with categories of belief, and hold that an individual may shift between these categories, it is necessary to discuss orthodoxy. Of the other two, neo-orthodoxy is largely a self-applied label, while heterodoxy is an attitude seen in others, or noticed with regret in oneself, if it is noticed at all. The terms are of course of my own coining. The Jains themselves used terms such as 'modern', 'forward-looking', 'broad-minded' and, especially, 'scientific' to describe the neo-orthodox position, and 'traditional' 'old fashioned' and 'narrow minded' to describe the orthodox position. Heterodoxy was less easily identifiable, but was the position adopted by those who were (in their own eyes and the eyes of others) 'simple' and 'uneducated', who had no knowledge of 'deep philosophy' and who lacked time to follow 'real' Jainism, which was thought to be very demanding and difficult. (As I conducted my interviews in Leicester mostly in English, I give the English terms my informants used. Doubtless similar, non-specialised, vocabulary would be used in Gujarati.) I discuss the interrelationship of the tendencies in more detail below, while here I outline the characteristics of each of the tendencies.

*Orthodoxy*

Orthodoxy may be considered as traditional Jainism, rooted in sectarianism and ritual. It is exemplified by the ascetics who hold knowledge and hence power. From the orthodox viewpoint Jainism is a fully revealed religion. Mahāvīr and the rest of the *tīrthaṅkar*s have outlined the path to salvation and no further elaboration is necessary. Ascetics guide one along this path but do not propose new routes. Orthodoxy flourishes best in parochial undisturbed situations. Many of the ordinary Jains that I later encountered on fieldwork in Gujarat, especially women, may be considered to be orthodox (and are thought so by heterodox Leicester Srimalis): unquestioningly they continue their daily round of temple visiting, *pūjā*s, consultation with ascetics and observation of all the dietary restrictions. While stress is laid on knowledge, comprehension of that knowledge is not really necessary for lay Jains, who can be guided by the ascetics. The performance of ritual is necessary, but it is not thought to please or pacify any transcendent deity. Rather, it is thought to foster in one the discipline and conscientiousness which earn *puṇya* (merit) or shed *karma*s, as well as reaffirming the religious economy of the community.

When an individual in Leicester did adopt an orthodox position (usually when bemoaning the lack of religious commitment in his own children) he usually ascribed it to his own upbringing: that his parents or grandparents had forced him as a child to go to the temple or *upāśraya*, to learn Jain recitations and mantras, and to pay homage to the ascetics. That is, religious commitment is not something which comes naturally or which is given by God, but something which one, and others on one's behalf, must toil over. Orthodoxy was generally thought to be the province of women and the elderly, partly because they had more time for all the rituals, and partly because they were less subject to external influences and disruptions. Many of the parental generation told me that while they had to make do as best they could in England, their parents (in East Africa or India) had been 'true' Jains, if a little narrow-minded. In some respects it might be more accurate to refer to this tendency as 'orthopraxy' as it is identified with largely unquestioned adherence to a round of actions. But I retain the term orthodoxy because I am concerned with the belief about (and underlying) these actions rather than the actions themselves.

*Heterodoxy*

This was the position adopted by most of the Srimalis in Leicester for most of the time. One of the key features of the heterodox outlook is belief in a supreme God.

Many modern works on Jainism, especially those written in the early twentieth century, sought to distinguish it as a valid religious system *vis-à-vis* Hinduism and Christianity (see for example, C. R. Jain 1919). Such works often refer to Jain 'atheism'. The Jains do acknowledge and worship a whole variety of deities who inhabit the sixteen heavens (*ūrdhva loka*), the earth and even the first hell (P. S. Jaini 1979: 129–30). These gods play a large part in Jain mythology; for example, Indra, the king of the gods, who ordained that the embryonic Mahāvīr should be transferred from his Brahman mother's womb to Trisala's. Yet particular aspects of Jain philosophy, most notably the doctrine of *karma* and the strict and absolute rules by which *karma* is supposed to operate, mean that there is no place in the Jain system for a transcendent deity who created the universe and ordains its affairs. The *tīrthaṅkar*s and other *siddha*s in *īśat-prāgbhāb-hūmi* (the final resting place of emancipated souls) are of course omniscient and omnipotent, living in perfect bliss. But they cannot interfere with the affairs of the world (nor in the affairs of gods and demons in other parts of the universe). All the *tīrthaṅkar*s, however, have a pair of 'guardian' deities (*śāsana devatā*s) – one male, one female – who are usually associated in popular mythology with helping the potential *tīrthaṅkar* to achieve omniscience. Some guardian and other deities have achieved a prominent place in Jain orthopraxy: idols of Cakeshwari and Padmāvatī – female deities associated with Rishabha and Pārśvanāth respectively – are found in many Jain temples[7] and deities of the directions feature prominently in the rituals for consecrating idols and new temples. Although most Srimalis in Leicester were aware of these deities, few men at least had any specific knowledge of them. Several of the *śāsana devatā*s were known (an embroidered backdrop behind the idol in the temple room at the Jain Centre depicted Padmāvatī and Dharendra attending Pārśvanāth), but no one I questioned had incorporated them into their

[7] Because these gods and goddesses figure largely in iconography, temple ornamentation and elaborate *pūjā*s, they seem to hold far less importance for Sthanakavasi Jains in India.

personal cosmology, or directed prayers or requests to them specifically.[8] Instead I found a widespread belief in the power of the *tīrthaṅkar*s to aid.

With reference to the medieval conflict between Jains and Virasaivites in the Deccan, K. K. Handiqui states:

> ' The Saivas contended that the Jain conception of the Arhat [*tīrthaṅkar*] was wholly inadequate: if he was an omniscient teacher, we must ask who his teacher was, and if he was a saint devoted to austerity, there must be someone to vouchsafe the result of his efforts. In either case, it was necessary to postulate a superior Being, self-existent and without a beginning, and He was no other than Mahesvara or Siva'.
>
> (1949: 347)

No matter how much emphasis the Jains place on the inexorable and automatic functioning of the laws of *karma* there is always the opening available for one to insert a first cause, as in the example above. The involvement of gods and goddesses, many bearing the same names as, or in fact actually being, Hindu gods and goddesses, not only in the orthopraxy but also in the mythology of Jainism, only serves to weaken the paramountcy of *karma* as an explanation of man's experience of the universe. Many of the Leicester Srimalis therefore had no difficulty in adopting a theistic outlook: some believed that the *tīrthaṅkar*s were the paramount divinity, expressing itself through a series of *avatāra*s, others, such as the 'elders' who met at the Jain Centre each morning for worship, during which they sang '*oṁ jaya jagadīśa hare*' (the hymn to the lord of the universe – a Hindu *bhajan* or devotional song) felt that the paramount deity lay behind the *tīrthaṅkar*s.

The work of R. F. Gombrich (1971) and others has raised the question: what do people mean when they say 'I believe in so-and-so'? a question that is, to my mind anyway, ultimately unanswerable. Short of reducing all such beliefs and expressions of belief to the realm of personal psychology, I think the best way to approach such an issue is through a system of analogy. I, as an analyst, can use analogy by saying that certain Jains believed in a controlling, creating deity

[8] When I was discussing deities with an ascetic in India, I was told that prayers and requests made to particular *tirthaṅkars* were 'intercepted' by the relevant *śāsana devatā*s, who, pleased that 'their' *tīrthankar* was being singled out, did what they could to grant the request.

beyond the *tīrthaṅkar*s in the way that certain Hindus believe in a controlling, creating deity beyond the named deities in the Hindu pantheon. Similarly, the Jains themselves can use analogy: one Leicester Srimali likened Mahāvīr to Jesus (because I, as an Englishman, was automatically thought to be a Christian). Like Mahāvīr, Jesus was a good man who expounded a moral code and was prepared to suffer for his beliefs (Jesus of course died, while Mahāvir merely had wooden spikes driven into his ears). Jesus prayed to God the Father for strength and guidance; as Mahāvīr also needed strength and guidance, he too must have prayed to his 'father' – *ergo*, there is a presence beyond the *tīrthaṅkar*s. Of course, the fact that according to what we know of Mahāvīr's life he did not pray to anyone (in the Christian sense) is irrelevant. My informant's belief in divine immanence was such that the analogy could be drawn. Belief in an interventive God brought with it a shift in focus in terms of the aims of religious practice and belief: no longer does one practise the religion to achieve liberation, but instead to please God – thus introducing the idea of *bhakti*. In consequence heterodoxy is open to all forms of religious expression where *bhakti* may be found, and most of the Jains in Leicester visited the town's Hindu temples occasionally, or even frequently, and had Hindu deities in their home shrines. One or two people I spoke to had visited a Sikh *gurudwara* or a Christian church also. (No one admitted to having ever visited a mosque, either in this country or abroad.) Attitudes to heterodoxy were mixed: some individuals were closely involved with Hindu groups in the city, yet perceived no conflict between this and their membership of the samāj, even when challenged, whilst others spontaneously admitted that the Hindu beliefs and practices they followed were at variance with Jain teachings, but said either that there was no proof that the Jain path itself was correct, or that while the Jain *dharma* probably was correct it was so austere and unrewarding that they preferred to derive at least part of their religious satisfaction from other sources.

Like orthodoxy, heterodoxy is concerned with knowledge. Jainism is conceived of as a religion of learning, and hence inaccessible to those with little education and no free time.[9] Most people when adopting the

[9] Britain was often characterised as a busy country where everyone works long hours, is always in a hurry and never has any free time. Even if the informant was himself unemployed or retired, he would still consider this busy-ness to constrain him.

heterodox viewpoint bemoaned their ignorance of 'deep philosophy' but felt that if sufficient knowledge were acquired, a devotion to 'true' (orthodox) Jainism was bound to result. I myself was considered to be a case in point. I was a vegetarian, had studied Jainism through books and was due to go to India where I would meet ascetics, visit famous pilgrimage places and perform rituals. Several people asked me if I was intending to become an ascetic (there are cases known of Europeans taking *dīkṣā*). However, although the religious aspect of Jain identity was ignored or considered unimportant by those adopting a heterodox viewpoint, the social aspect certainly wasn't. People who espoused the heterodox viewpoint generally considered that their religious affiliation was just one more aspect of their *jāt* identity. One Srimali informant tried to convey this to me by telling me that the Halari Visā Oswals were a 'different kind' of Jain, that beyond considerations of sect and *gaccha* the fact that they were Oswals made them different as Jains.

*Neo-orthodoxy*

While orthodoxy and heterodoxy are categories of religious belief, neo-orthodoxy claims for itself the status of a science. As found in Leicester, neo-orthodox Jainism is not so much a system for achieving salvation, but a science for the individual in his present situation: the strict dietary restrictions are essential for a healthy body; the meditations and other austerities bring about a healthy and peaceful mind. It is also a science for society: I was told on many occasions that if everyone (Jain and non-Jain) were to adopt Mahāvīr's principle of non-violence (*ahiṃsā*) all mankind's troubles would cease. On one occasion I was told that Mahāvīr was the first communist. Mahāvīr was similarly credited with making many scientific discoveries centuries before Western scientists did, including the existence of bacteria, the nature of the atom and the theory of relativity.[10]

Neo-orthodoxy for the most part ignores the Jain ascetics, considering them to be narrow-minded and ritualistic: with sufficient

[10] One of the important principles of Jain philosophy – *anekāntavāda*, the theory or doctrine of many aspects, which states that while a thing is permanent in its substance, its qualities and attributes constantly change – is often translated as the 'theory of relativity' by Jain authors (e.g. J. Jain 1975: 68) and hence the confusion with Einstein's theory. One GCE 'A'-level schoolboy went so far as to tell me that Einstein had taken his famous equation, $e = mc^2$, from an ancient Jain text.

knowledge and discipline the individual has no need of ascetic guidance. Moreover, with this knowledge and discipline anyone can be a Jain, and those who are born into Jain families do not have a statutory right to salvation; the Jains in Leicester who most consistently held a neo-orthodox position often claimed to have had some kind of 'conversion' experience, or to have changed their way of thinking and come to a deeper appreciation of Jain teachings. A case in point was that of the Samāj's president. A solicitor from India (he had not been to East Africa) he claimed to have had little interest in the religion of his birth until about 1975. Prior to this he had tried to achieve personal status aggrandisement through several organisational channels: the Rotary Club, the local Conservative Party, the Indian National Club. In each case he had failed, usually because of some personality clash, and accusations (on his part) of racism in the non-Asian organisations. Then he had turned to his own culture, begun to read books on Jainism, realised the truth of what they were saying, and became president of the Samāj (of which he had always been a member). If such experiences were possible for people like the president (a Jain 'by birth') then it was possible for anyone, Indian or European. Hence neo-orthodoxy is a proselytising faith, unlike orthodoxy which is exclusive or heterodoxy which is eclectically inclusive (that it, it seeks truth in other religious systems and at the same time welcomes the adherents of those systems but does not seek to convert them to a new path).

Neo-orthodoxy in Leicester draws its inspiration, directly or indirectly, from two important teachers – Srīmad Rājchandra and an ex-ascetic known as Chitrabhanu. (The Kanji Panth shows many features of neo-orthodoxy and in India those who adopt a neo-orthodox outlook generally cite Rājchandra and Kanji Swami as their inspiration. In Leicester, however, there are few, if any, of these neo-Digambars). Srīmad Rājchandra (1868–1901) was a lay Jain from Saurashtra, renowned for his austerities. Despite his spirituality he refused to become an ascetic and was generally anti-ascetic in his stance, largely because of his rebuttal of sectarianism. Although not denying the inspiration of Mahāvīr's teachings in any way, he felt his own insights (typified by the 142 stanzas known as 'Atma Siddhi' – self-realisation) were better suited to this present *duṣamā yuga* (unhappy age). He also made his own canon of Jain scriptures of those which he considered to be best suited to the needs of the modern laity. This stress on adapting Jainism to modern times (or rather, finding in Jain writings and teaching that which is best suited to modern times) is the keynote of neo-orthodoxy and is found in the teachings and writings of Chitrabhanu also. Chitrabhanu started his career as a Śvetāmbar ascetic (Munishrī Chandraprabhasagarji) but left his order after many years and married one of his disciples (note that all three of the neo-orthodox leader figures mentioned have rejected asceticism in their own ways). He now divides his time between India and the United States, where he has established a Jain Meditation Centre. His teachings are more eclectic than those of Rājchandra and perhaps closer to those of Rājneesh (who was himself born a Jain) although his 'movement' does not in any way approach the cult status of the Rājneesh organisation. In 1980, Chitrabhanu came to Leicester and was warmly approved by all I spoke to (he is less well thought of in India where his personal affairs, particularly his marriage and renunciation of ascetic status, are the cause of much opprobrium).

In its rejection of traditionalism and orthodoxy, neo-orthodoxy rejects sectarian divisions and *jāt* divisions (as well as making the 'scientific' adherence to Jainism an achieved, not ascriptive, status). As the constitution of the Samāj was drawn up by some of the fervent neo-orthodox Jains it can be said that the Samāj and the centre are 'officially' neo-orthodox. In the table, I briefly summarise some of the more important differences between the tendencies, and the relationship between them.

As mentioned earlier, orthodoxy was not a belief pertinent to Leicester (because of the absence of ascetics) but some practices were followed which were indicative of orthodox behaviour – for example, some women would recite a *mantra* asking for forgiveness[11] when they lit the gas fire or stove, a *mantra* which in India would negate the violence caused by the death of insects which might be residing in the firewood or cow-dung cakes – but these were few and pertain only to specific individual behaviour.

Thus in Leicester we can identify two fully operational tendencies –

[11] I use the phrase 'asking for forgiveness' to avoid an awkward circumlocution. The orthodox viewpoint holds that it is the act of making these confessions that frees the soul of *karma* caused by the *hiṃsā* and not that a higher being is being asked to intervene in one's destiny.

*Characteristics of belief categories in Leicester*

| Orthodoxy | Heterodoxy | Neo-orthodoxy |
|---|---|---|
| ascetic paramount | pro-ascetic | anti-ascetic |
| emphasis on ritual | emphasis on faith | emphasis on rationality |
| exclusive belief structure | inclusive belief structure | selectively exclusive belief structure |
| aim of religion is to achieve *mokṣa* | aim of religion is to please God | aim of religion is to secure individual/societal peace |

heterodoxy and neo-orthodoxy. Certain individuals (the president, most of the rest of the committee, and several other members of the Samāj) were committed wholeheartedly to neo-orthodoxy and had a degree of religious fervour not found in most of the Srimalis. Heterodoxy – by its nature a form of compromise and opportunism – had no fervent apologists and was in any case not always recognised by its followers: what I would describe as heterodox behaviour – belief in a creator God, or performance of Hindu ceremonies on death anniversaries – would be taken by the actor to be true and correct behaviour and not contradictory to the tenets of Jainism in any way. Neo-orthodoxy on the other hand was largely self-cognisant and its adherents perceived both the narrow-mindedness of orthodoxy and the laxness or eclecticism of heterodoxy. However, in order to discuss the structure of the contemporary Jain Samāj and to analyse its dynamics within the context of the cultural strategies adopted by other Asian groups in the city, it is necessary to impose the categories of belief – the tendencies – on to the Leicester Jain population in some way.

For the purposes of directness and clarity I discussed heterodoxy as a set of features distinct from those features which make up the other two categories. It is obvious however that one of the features of heterodoxy – the syncretism (termed 'inclusive belief structure' in the table) – enables it to encompass features of the other two tendencies. That is, when an individual who usually adopts a heterodox viewpoint espouses one of the other tendencies temporarily, he is able to do so because of his heterodoxy. For example, in the said-meditation of *pratikramaṇa*, meticulous attention to performing the right motions of hands and limbs, although the actor might be ignorant of their significance, could be termed orthodox behaviour. The use of an electric torch to read the text by – an *ahiṃsā*-less form of illumination to the modern mind, despite the ascetic injunction against electricity – could be termed neo-orthodox behaviour. Thus the diagram depicting the tendencies (above, p. 246) can be redrawn:

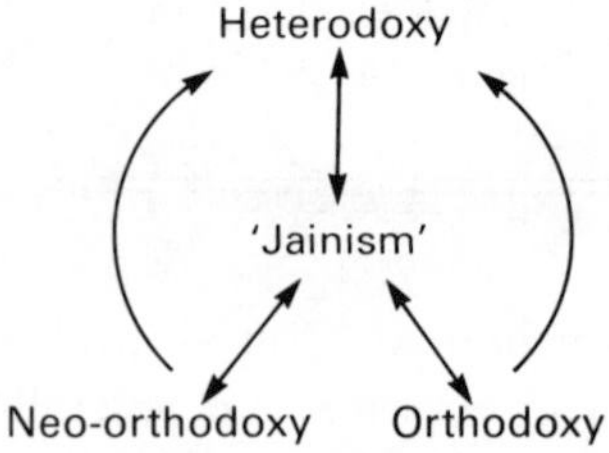


As mentioned above, neo-orthodoxy, while expressed occasionally by many Jains, is adhered to almost exclusively by some, by virtue of the fact that some of its features are predicated upon a rejection of the other positions. Once an individual identifies and accepts these features, the paradox of returning to one of the other viewpoints becomes apparent and the individual becomes committed to the neo-orthodox viewpoint (hence the 'conversion' experiences mentioned above). Discussing the nature of ideology, E. Gellner has pointed out its cognitive sovereignty (1979: 122). That is, ideologies are able to explain all aspects of the material and social world to the believer. Adding to this, we might say that the recognition of paradox marks the beginning of ideology (that is, belief which can be instrumentalised), by bounding it and defining it in opposition to that which it is not. In this example the move is away from 'tendency' to a corporate group. Yet the move is one way, there can be no recognition of paradox from the heterodox viewpoint and therefore no transition from amorphic belief structure to ideology. Thus it would not be accurate to say that in Leicester there are two opposed groups of Srimali Jains. It would be true to say, however, that there is a small group which has marked itself off from the rest and which perceives its existence in terms of opposition to the rest. This group consists mainly of the committee (mostly wealthy professionals) and their supporters (mostly the retired businessmen I refer to as 'elders'). Moreover, it would be true to say that there are oppositions and tensions within the community which are articulated as though between two distinct groups.

However, while an actor from the heterodox tendency would see his opposition as opposition towards another member of his own (that is, the only) group, an actor from the neo-orthodox group would see his opposition as opposition towards a member of another group. This is essentially because the heterodox think in terms of caste (*jāt*) while the neo-orthodox think in terms of religion. Informants from the heterodox group (that is, 'the rest') occasionally confided to me that they were unhappy about the direction the Samāj was taking, that they saw large sums of money being spent to no apparent purpose. The basis of their unease lay in their 'communal' outlook. The Jain Samāj, in their eyes, was synonymous with the Srimali community and thus the advancement of the Samāj should have been translated into benefits for the community – to reinforce the difference between them and other communities, especially the Halari Visā Oswals with whom they shared a religious identity. Yet the Srimali leadership did not seem aware of its communal obligations. On the other hand, neo-orthodox individuals occasionally criticised 'the rest' to me, claiming that they had no interest in the real issues of religion, but were concerned only with their mundane social matters. The Samāj, however, held together, neither side able or willing to voice its dissatisfaction openly, as its mutual reliance was too great.

## *Conclusions*

The academic study of Jainism often presents the religion as a cohesive and unified body of doctrine, the only schism considered worthy of note being that between Digambara and Śvetāmbara. Similarly, those who follow the religion are generally considered to be united in belief and to constitute a 'community' in the general sense of the term. My own research has shown that the laity (both in Gujarat and overseas) is divided in many ways and furthermore, as demonstrated above, that the religion itself is open to various interpretations which may legitimate different courses of action. Should we then abandon any notion of a 'Jain community'? I think not, simply for the reason that a notion of community is perceived by the actors themselves.

While various social factors (*jāt*, residence, occupation and so forth) can serve to link small groups or micro-communities of Jains, the religion itself (or perceptions of the religion) can act as a tie for all Jains. In this way, Jainism serves as a resource pool, a set of elements, from which an identity can be constructed.

The fracturing of the 'doxa', or basic belief core of ideology, into heterodoxy (the challenge) and orthodoxy (the reification) has been dealt with by Pierre Bourdieu (1979: 159–71) who states that such a process marks the beginning of class relations. Religious ideology differs from the total ideology that Bourdieu discusses, because in it the doxa is already broken: all 'great' or 'world' religions are characterised by their quality of self-awareness (see Eisenstadt 1984). Because of this notion of self-awareness (brought about through the realisation that there is a greater and better social order possible, whether on earth or in heaven) there is no 'universe of the undiscussed/undisputed' (Bourdieu 1979: 168). Instead, there is a religious system which offers the potential for various interpretations, each of which holds the promise of salvation.

In Leicester I identified two of these interpretations: the heterodox strategy which sought to consolidate a meaningful secular (*jāt*) identity using Jainism as religious justification, and the neo-orthodox strategy which sought to throw Jainism open as a religious identity for all. Yet in using Jainism in this way, the Srimali Jains of Leicester, like all other Jains in India and abroad, have constructed a community. They literally share a common culture, belief and practice, not because all Jains hold all elements of the religion as personally meaningful – no system, religious or otherwise, can be totally and completely internalised by every individual – but because the system can be fragmented into (possibly overlapping) bundles of features, each of which is seen by the holders as representing the whole.

Similarly, there is a consciousness of identity as Jains. This may not be, perhaps cannot be, dominant in all situations. Like ethnicity, religious identity is situational and may vary in intensity from one individual to the next. Nevertheless, the fact that it is named, that it demands certain behaviour in certain situations, that it can be called upon as a rallying-point (by the ascetics in India and by lay leaders overseas) and most importantly that it is perceived by the actors to be an internally coherent system, serves to reify the notion of community that is attendant upon such an identity. 'Community' is not an a priori quality of a group of Jains, or of all Jains: it is something that they, from the conceptual category of 'Jainism', create for themselves.

# 17

# The foundations of community among southern Digambar Jains: an essay on rhetoric and experience

Michael Carrithers

The Digambars of the Deccan constitute one of the largest populations of Jains in India. They are concentrated in Kolhapur and Sangli districts of southern Maharashtra and in Belgaum district of northern Karnataka. The 1971 census gives a total Jain population in these three contiguous districts of 262,856, marginally higher than the Jain population of greater Bombay. Moreover V. Sangave, using that data, has shown that outside the urban areas of Bombay and Ahmedabad these three districts have by far the highest density of Jains in India (Sangave 1980: 37). When I refer to 'Jains' in this chapter they will be southern Digambars unless specifically noted.

I will write chiefly of the period from Independence up until 1985, when I finished fifteen months of fieldwork in the region.[1] In other words, the present tense which I use really refers to a specific historical period, the recent, post-Independence past.

When Jains wish to refer to themselves they often speak of *jain samāj*. Sometimes the English translation would be 'Jain society', or even 'Jain people', as when some characteristic, say wealth or farming expertise, is being attributed to Jains. In that sense *samāj*, like English 'society', can be relatively colourless and uncomplicated.

But *samāj* is more often used in an evaluative, persuasive sense, and in those contexts it means something closer to the English 'community', with all the confusing ambiguity, colour, and emotional force which that term can carry with it.[2] In this chapter I will try to unravel

[1] Fieldwork was conducted with a grant from the Economic and Social Research Council of the U.K. This chapter was revised during a Research Readership leave awarded by the British Academy.

[2] Indeed though the word is now quite natural in Marathi, I believe that it is in fact a relatively recent coinage out of Sanskrit – there meaning 'assembly' – to translate the English 'community'.

some of what Jains today mean when they speak of Jain *samāj* in this more loaded way. And in particular I will concentrate on the connection between the influential and important secular senses which have been given to Jain *samāj*, and the older and, on the face of it, more essential religious sense.

I have found this an extraordinarily difficult problem. One difficulty is that the language of 'community' often expresses people's desires and aspirations rather than the reality of their situation. *Samāj*, in other words, is not always a descriptive term; it can be used rather in a rhetorical, prescriptive way, to persuade or encourage. So *samāj* can refer to an ideal rather than real situation, and in this perspective the problem is to see where rhetoric ends and sober evaluation should begin. The difficulty is exacerbated by the fact that *samāj* in Marathi and 'community' in English are also used in social scientific discourse in India as technical terms. Indeed both these senses, the rhetorical and the social scientific, lie side by side in the writing of V. A. Sangave, whose book *Jaina Community: a Social Survey* (1980), embodies the ideals of both positivistic value-free sociology and committed and conscientious social reform.

Under these circumstances it seems best to treat the word *samāj* in an interpretive way, as a Marathi word which has no clear or easy equivalent in English, and whose meaning must therefore be illuminated by revealing its varying usage in a specific social setting.

I should stress from the outset that the rhetorical use of the word has special consequences for how it must be understood. Since rhetorical language embodies ideals which are pressed on an audience or readership, such language is part of a social process, the process of realising – or failing to realise – those ideals in practice. Consequently the judgement of the success or failure of the rhetoric of *samāj* is crucial to understanding the rhetoric itself. Sometimes talk of *samāj* seems peculiarly powerless and peripheral to the reality of Jains' social life, but sometimes it seems directly relevant, cogent, and effective. Sometimes the talk evokes unrealisable dreams, but at other times practical possibilities. Occasionally it sounds like the anonymous public language of any Indian group, but often it strikes an unmistakably Jain note.

Let me began by rehearsing at some length – but without a great deal of illustration – the larger, complex argument which might make sense of *samāj*.

The most frequent use of the word, and the most active thinking about Jains as a collectivity, has taken place in a specific setting, the formal discourse of lay Jain leaders in the late nineteenth and twentieth centuries. Both their vocabulary and their attitudes are very much in the mould of other reformers who preceded them, such as the Arya Samajists among Hindus, Brahman social reformers in Poona, earlier Jain reformers in Bombay and the North. In this respect the southern Digambars have only followed on as part of that much larger movement which mingled the political and social ambitions of the new, and newly educated, class which was to be so important in making modern India. In any narrative of that wider current the southern Digambars would only be a small and local eddy, and some of what I write here might easily apply to other communities as well. But in any case the language and practices created out of that wider world now seem wholly natural among the Digambars, and their local expression of reform and Protestantisation has been markedly tenacious and in some ways idiosyncratic.

Most but not all of the local Digambar leaders have been members of the professional classes: early in this century they were lawyers and civil servants, and later they included lecturers, doctors, and cooperative leaders when those categories came into being. They were and are a self-selecting group and their activity is voluntary and unremunerated, except in the coin of social regard among Jains. Their discourse has always concerned specific policies and attitudes which they wish to urge on their constituency, who for the most part are far less well educated.

The policy recommended may sometimes be expressly political, but more often Jains are exhorted to some social or educational undertaking. In the early part of the century reformers campaigned against child marriage and for widow remarriage, for example; later they recommended an enlightened attitude to intercaste marriage, at least among Jains; and right throughout this century they have campaigned for education. Lay leaders have pursued some religious policies as well, such as the publication of religious tracts.

There are many more or less local platforms on which such leaders might speak: a temple managing committee, the board of a Jain school, an *ad hoc* committee for some Jain charitable cause, and so forth. A lay leader in one Jain setting will almost inevitably be active in some other setting as well. But the most important leaders share one platform, that of a secular regional voluntary organisation, the Daksin Bharat Jain Sabha, the South Indian Jain Association (hereafter the Sabha), which was founded in 1899. They have also written in the pages of the Sabha's newspaper, *Pragati āṇi Jinavijaya* (hereafter *Pragati*), which began in 1902. There is no other region-wide lay institution such as the Sabha, and no Jain publication so widely distributed in the region as *Pragati*. Religious leaders, naked ascetics and others, have been greatly influenced by the laymen of the Sabha. Moreover the Sabha has enjoyed remarkable longevity in comparison to other, similar voluntary organisations in India: its newspaper, for example, is one of the oldest continually published community periodicals in Maharashtra (Divekar 1981: 55–72). The Sabha has shown relatively steady growth since its beginning, and at present boasts 4,000 members, each of whom receives a copy of the newspaper weekly. Though the meetings and publications of the Sabha are by no means the only public platforms for discourse among Jains about *samāj*, the Sabha has effectively set the tone for such talk, and remains the most widely recognised and authoritative source of such ideas.

Sabha leaders, like the leaders of other communities, have used the word *samāj* in a bewildering variety of ways, but one recurring theme has been their assumption that *samāj* refers to a uniform, bounded population with common interests, who are in effect all those returned on the census as Jains. This is a fragile and rather too optimistic basis for rhetoric, since the Jain population is very diverse. Many who responded as Jains on the census have little to do with Jain religious institutions or beliefs. By far the majority are farmers, but some are merchants, and the last century has seen the rise of the professionals themselves. There are five distinct Jain castes who practise caste endogamy. Some Jains speak only Marathi, some only Kannada, while many are bilingual. Some are rich, but many are poor; some are well educated but most are not. Some vote for Congress, others for opposition parties. Such distinctions make for real distinctions in interests: for the most part Jains act politically as members of a party, economically according to their position in the economy, religiously as individuals exercising individual choice, and so forth. Apart from exceptional occasions I will discuss later, the divisions of the Indian political economy in this century have cut across the population of Jains.

Three uses of *samāj* are particularly relevant for our understanding of Sabha rhetoric. The first of these is *samāj* as an improving community, concerned with advancement of all kinds but especially educational advancement. This improving notion of *samāj* has been prominent in Sabha rhetoric from the beginning. It has been used to convince Jains to create educational institutions for themselves or to take advantage of existing institutions. Partly because of these efforts, and partly because individual Jains have independently understood the use of education, this sense of *samāj* has come to have some purchase in social life. It has come to correspond, in other words, to some real interests and real practices among Jains. The improving community possesses a material infrastructure, the bricks and mortar of the hostels owned by the Sabha, one or more located in each chief city of the region. These hostels represent almost all of the Sabha's considerable fixed capital, and yearly about 1,000 students take advantage of their accommodation to attend urban colleges.

But the many rural Jain schools and colleages of the region which have sprung up since Independence might also be laid indirectly to the Sabha's account, since they have been supported or founded by Sabha members, and the Sabha played a vital part in encouraging the habit of education among Jains in the region. All people who are Jains by birth are eligible to use these institutions, and a great many do so. The improving community is, to that extent at least, a realistic definition of *samāj*.

A second sense of *samāj*, one of Jains as a purely political community, has also been present in Sabha rhetoric. This sense has far less purchase in social life, as was vividly proven at the first general election campaign after Independence, fought in the closing months of 1951.[3] A number of Sabha members, among them the then editor of *Pragati*, resolved in a public meeting that Jains should support Congress, and urge their common interests through Jain Congress candidates. Though the Sabha took no official stand, this policy was strongly urged through *Pragati*.

But in the event this attempt to mobilise Jains and give them a distinct voice within the ruling party failed. Of ten Jain candidates proposed to Congress, only three were put forward at the election.

[3] I draw all of this from the issues of *Pragati* for the relevant dates.

Other Jains ran as independents or for the Socialist party. The result was that though Congress won, it won without any specific debt to Jains. The sense of Jain *samāj* as a commonality of political interests remained purely ideal and ineffectual. Jains did not then, and do not now, have a routinely common political interest. The institutions of politics are the political parties and especially Congress, and the political sense of 'Jain community' is only of a distinct category of voters: a category sometimes to be wooed, mostly by non-Jain politicians, but not one organised as a pressure group.

In discussing these first two senses of *samāj* I have proposed roughly three criteria, what is the image of *samāj* envisioned by lay leaders? Does that image correspond to a distinguishable population with real interests in common? Does there exist an institutional infrastructure to empower that image in action and sentiment?

These questions are particularly difficult to answer as regards the third sense of *samāj*, Jains as a religious community.

What image of the religious *samāj* do leaders envision? By and large, the policies urged by leaders in the Sabha are secular; and by and large the conceptions of *samāj* which they project are also secular. Yet from the beginning the Sabha has also mentioned among its purposes those which are *dharmik*, religious, though directly religious activities have been relatively little stressed in the Sabha's history. They have mostly mostly been limited to the publication of religious tracts or religious advice in the pages of *Pragati*. Much of the discourse about *samāj* has in fact ignored, or merely taken for granted, the institutions of Jainism proper – the temples, priests, ascetics, and other figures. Sabha leaders, in espousing the improving community, have sometimes even actively opposed the influence of those primeval institutions.

But lay leaders of the Sabha do sometimes call on a specifically religious sense of *samāj*, and when they do so they have had a strongly idealised notion in mind. They have meant Jains as the bearers, not of the ritual practices, but of the ideals of Jainism, such as *ahiṃsā*, compassion, truthfulness, and liberality in giving.

This conception illustrates splendidly the distinction between the ideals of rhetoric and cold reality. For while Jains certainly espouse these ideals, they are as a group no better – and no worse – at exemplifying their religious ideals than anyone else. They find it difficult to live up to what is after all a very demanding set of principles. Moreover, their putative common religious identity cannot easily or perspicuously be understood in any numerical sense, as actual attributes of a populace of individuals. There is too much heterogeneity in attitude, commitment and practice among Jains, and the abstractions of basic principles do not convert easily into concrete interests or reasons for acting. If we looked to such measures, we might arrive at the uncertain and shifting image of Jain attitudes so clearly set out in Marcus Banks' chapter.

But when we ask after the institutional infrastructure of this conception of *samāj*, the case is different. For there does exist a primeval institutional matrix within which Jains most surely experience themselves as Jains and as bearers of the ideals, if only fitfully and only at some point in their lives. This matrix is formed of the temples, priests, ascetics, teachers and participating laity – and of their ceremonial practices. This complex has had, for more than a millennium, the capacity to reproduce itself – and in so reproducing to give a secure core of Jains a sense of themselves as *srāvaka*s, 'listeners' to the teaching of Jainism. They may not be ideal or perfect Jains, they may not be frequently active, but they are available to the sentiments evoked by the rhetoric of Jain leaders. Such sentiments have provided the base in experience which underlies to one degree or another all the senses of the word *samāj*.

But this connection between religious sentiments and secular rhetoric is in fact far from obvious or direct. In the rest of this chapter I want, first, to present and anatomise a fragment of Sabha discourse about *samāj* and then to sketch the institutional matrix of Jain experience.

## *Discourse*

Let me now examine a representative document on *samāj*, the inaugural speech of a new president of the Sabha at its annual general meeting in 1985. The speech was delivered exactly as it appears in a printed pamphlet which I collected at the meeting. Though I could have chosen many other documents, this one fairly evokes the range of Sabha rhetoric as it now appears.

The speaker, Mr S. T. Patne of Kolhapur, was a markedly prosperous businessman in his seventies who had also been active in a very wide variety of civic, educational and religious causes. The presidency of the Sabha has for the most part been conceived as an honorary position, though the president can take an active role. The honour has often been given to Jains of great eminence outside the region, such as Digambar magnates in Bombay, partly in the hope of gaining some wider influence or help with some ambitious project. The incumbent is nominated by the executive committee of the Sabha. As I understand it, Mr Patne was elected rather because he was a local figure who exemplified local conventions and who was guaranteed to take a traditional, unadventurous line.

His conservatism was particularly attractive to the electors in the light of recent events. (I have written of these at some length in Carrithers 1988.) Between 1983 and the delivery of the speech on 19 January 1985, a bitter confrontation had arisen between Digambar Jains of the region and the majority and politically dominant Marathas, concerning a Jain pilgrimage site, Bahubali hill. The Bahubali Affair began with a parochial argument between the Digambars and the small but influential immigrant Svetambar community over access to temples on the hill. But with extraordinary cunning a Svetambar leader engaged Maratha politicians in the struggle, and, once they joined in, matters escalated out of anyone's control. The Svetambar antagonists were pushed to the back of the stage, and the affair became a face-to-face confrontation between Marathas and Digambars not only on the hill itself, but throughout the region. Maharashtra State ministers, and even Central Government and Mrs Gandhi herself, eventually became embroiled. It was a very serious and potentially bloody encounter that was by no means solved by the time of Mr Patne's speech, even though the Chief Minister of Maharashtra, a Maratha, attended the Sabha meeting as a pacifying gesture.

The Bahubali Affair engendered arguments within the Digambar fold as well. Some, such as the recently removed editor of *Pragati* or the previous president, were marked by their failure to solve, and indeed their willingness to inflame, the dispute. In this setting Mr Patne's attitude was irenic rather than inflammatory, and his speech was conventional rather than innovative, statesmanlike rather than narrowly topical. He alluded to the affair only once, obliquely. He otherwise expressed uncontested sentiments which Sabha members hold in common, and in so doing touched the notions of *samāj* which are common currency among Jain leaders.

Let me précis the beginning of his speech. Comments are interposed in square brackets.

After the customary welcoming remarks, Mr Patne observes that the meeting is taking place in Sangli, on the grounds of one of the several colleges of the Latthe Education Society [a markedly prosperous and effective charitable institution originally sponsored by Sabha members after Independence and frequently praised in the Sabha newspaper], and indeed in the central meeting-hall of that Society. He remarks that a number of the Sabha's meetings have taken place in Sangli, but that now, through the Latthe Education Society, great expansion has taken place. This is cause for great satisfaction in the educational development of Jains.

Following professions of modesty, Mr Patne notes that the Jain *samāj* [here meaning all Jains everywhere] and that of India as a whole form one constituency. He then considers how, in the nineteenth and early twentieth centuries reforming movements arose: for Independence, for education, for religious and social reform. Among Digambars A. B. Latthe [advocate, sometime chief minister of Kolhapur State and later member of the Bombay Legislative Council], founder of the Sabha, was prominent.

At the beginning of the twentieth century the level of education in the [Digambar Jain] *samāj* was low, 8 per cent of men and 1 per cent of women being able to read and write. For thirty years members of the Sabha campaigned arduously, often by touring from village to village, to raise this standard. This effort was to a large degree successful.

The period between 1930 and Independence marked a second period of the Sabha's history, when Sabha members and the Jain *samāj* awoke and joined in the Independence struggle. Many Jains gave up their own interests and joined with other *samāj*s in the common cause. When Independence was achieved members of the Jain *samāj*, such as Bhaurao Patil, had success in founding education societies and building schools and colleges.

Also after Independence Jain youth of the *samāj*, educated from the Sabha's hostels and elsewhere, began to work selflessly for the development of the country. Some worked in the cooperatives, others in education, industry, commerce, the professions, and government. They contributed greatly to the development of India. He mentions twenty-three such youths by name, now elder members of the Sabha. [Of those whose occupations I know, four are advocates, two doctors, three college or university teachers, seven prominent industrialists or businessmen, two prominent farmers and cooperative leaders, and three politicians.]

I remarked earlier that rhetoric is part of a social process of realising ideals in practice, and I think this patch of Mr Patne's speech can best be understood in just that sense. It is not, however, the fiery, demanding language which characterised a good deal of the Sabha's earlier exhortations to educational enterprise.[4] That earlier language was critical, sometimes shocking, calculated to motivate, and it stood at the beginning of one or another of the enterprises of Jain education. Mr Patne's, on the other hand, is late, valedictory, retrospectively self-congratulatory rhetoric, recollecting in tranquillity a project brought to a successful consummation. He reassures and compliments those listening in the large meeting-hall on the spacious grounds of the Latthe Education Society's premier college: if he persuades them of something, it is that they must continue the good work.

In constructing this congratulatory rhetoric Mr Patne uses the word *samāj* with some of the ambiguity which later in his speech will become crucial: he uses it indifferently to refer to Indian society as a whole, to Jains as a whole throughout India, to Digambars in particular, and to the collection of different *samāj*s – Marathas, Jains, Brahmans, Lingayats, etc. – which make up India.

This rhetorical slippage is particularly significant in two places. First, where he mentions the involvement of Jains in Congress during the Independence movement, he manages to suggest that since the activists were Jains, and members of the Sabha, the glory of their patriotism somehow rubs off on the Jain community as a whole. And second, in mentioning Bhaurao Patil, he implies a far greater role for Jains and the Sabha in education than they in fact had: for in the case of

[4] The earlier language, the language of the beginning of the process, is perhaps best exemplified in this translated excerpt from a *Pragati* editorial of 10 March 1952, shortly after the founding of the Latthe Education Society:

You've got money, you're ready to spend it. That's good, but isn't it a mistake to spend money without thinking? You've got milk in the house, but nobody feeds it to snakes! Today attitudes have remained on the side of doing prabhavana [glorification, conspicuous consumption] for the uplift of society [rather than religion] . . . [Don't spend on unnecessarily grand religious buildings and ceremonies for] though there might be some merit in expensive religious ceremonies, whoever thinks they want to get some merit should give to [one or another school or educational foundation] or the new Latthe Education Society . . . or start an independent charitable education society, and thus give the gift of knowledge [jnānadān]! . . . Today merit is education, politics is education!

Patil, the greatest part of his activity was not among Jains at all, and indeed he turned his back on the Sabha. These are conventional assumptions among Jains, and it is just this sort of pointed ambiguity which makes Jains' – or anyone's – talk about community so difficult to pin down.

But if Jains cannot take quite so much credit for Independence, nor the Sabha quite so much responsibility for educational improvement, Mr Patne's discourse nevertheless possesses a solid core of dispassionate observation. He owes at least some of the facts and the running commentary to V. Sangave's sociological writings, but he has also been a keen recorder of the larger scene himself.[5] It is a fair comment that Jains as a whole have more than kept pace with processes in the Indian political economy in the twentieth century. In this perspective we might say that Mr Patne is using not only the rhetoric of the Sabha's own successful project, but is also grafting the rhetoric of larger projects – Independence, social reform, educational development throughout southern Maharashtra – onto his own. After all, as a municipal councillor in Kolhapur, as a member of the Rotary Club, and as an executive officer of many civic institutions, he is well practised in such language.

Having presented the commonly accepted view of the Jain *samāj* as an improving community, Mr Patne begins the second third of his speech with more generally Indian sentiments. He remarks innocuously enough that many of the dreams of Pandit Nehru have remained unfulfilled. A new generation has grown up, he says, who expect the fruits of development to fall into their hands without effort. Cinema and novels are having a deleterious effect. For some years 'the moral station of *samāj* [society in general] has slid drastically'. Discord and self-indulgence have become rife. But then he says this (I quote his words directly):

In these circumstances a new problem has been placed before the followers of Jainism [*jainadharmācā anuyāyāpuḍhe*] who cherish [*japnāryā*] the eternal values such as truth, *ahiṃsā*, and non-possession [*aparigraha*]. For the past thousands of years the founders and teachers of Jaina *dharma* have set their

[5] See Sangave 1980. But Mr Patne has also been his own historian, sociologist and economist, having kept a running notebook for forty years, not only on daily prices in all the relevant markets for the agricultural commodities in which he deals, but also on political and social affairs which might touch those prices.

moral stamp on those of other faiths. Today as well by the example of [good] conduct this stamp must be set on other communities. This responsibility falls on followers of Jainism. In the future this responsibility will fall on the shoulders of Jain youth.

Mr Patne then goes on to exhort the youth in the hostels, as well as the members of a Jain youth movement, the Vir Seva Dal. They are to work tirelessly, selflessly, to exemplify the values of Jainism to others. They are to work for village self-improvement, moral uplift, and 'social awakening' (*samājajāgṛti*). If they do so, he says, '*samāj* and nation will grow strong'.

Let me first say something about the project rhetorically envisioned here. The mention of Nehru, of the moral decay of society and so forth suggests stale conventional moralising, but against the wider contemporary background it does have a certain freshness. Since about 1982 a small group of energetic younger Sabha members have turned their efforts to creating the Vir Seva Dal youth movement, whose branches perform voluntary works, such as building village roads. They have also been pursuing a campaign in the region under the slogan 'give up vice [smoking, drinking, meat-eating] and plant trees'. This campaign is aimed at society in general, but my impression is that it has met with huge indifference among non-Jains, and uncertain success among Jains.

There is also in the movement a flavour of frustrated political aspiration seeking an outlet, for Jains are after all only a small minority with very dim political prospects. Local groups of Jains who aggressively prosecuted the Jain cause during the Bahubali Affair sometimes did so under the Vir Seva Dal banner. One of the Vir Seva Dal's founders became involved only after his own political aspirations were frustrated by physical intimidation. And indeed the Vir Seva Dal has consciously taken some ideas from the militant Hindu chauvinist Rashtriya Svayamseva Sangh. But on the other hand it has also taken ideas from the less strident boy scouts and the anti-communal Rashtra Seva Dal as well, and many village chapters have done nothing more than the members might have done without it, such as help renew Jain temples. There have been youth movements among Jains earlier this century which disappeared without trace, and it is conceivable that the Vir Seva Dal may follow them. Or it may persist as a voluntary self-help organisation. What is certain is that no one but Jains would imagine that Indian society could at all accept reconstitution by Jains on a Jain basis.

Against this judgement of the project's unlikelihood, the liveliness and strength of Jains' notion of themselves is the more striking. Mr Patne's rhetoric enshrines not merely the pre-eminence of Jain values, but the unashamedly rivalrous superiority of Jains. They are fit to be the spiritual and moral tutors of all India. He characterises them as those who 'preserve' or 'chant' or 'meditate on' – *japṇe* – the values of truth, non-possession, and *ahiṃsā*.[6] It is true that Jains do in fact honour those values through their rich religious culture. Yet only the ambiguous slippage of rhetoric warrants the leap from the idealised reverence for values to the implication that those values are actually achieved. And moreover *japṇe* can also have an ironical sense, as merely to chant or give lip service, and that sense is at least consistent with Mr Patne's monitory tone. In this passage Mr Patne manages simultaneously to admonish Jains, and to congratulate them on their justly deserved and firmly established sense of superiority. A similar slippage occurs when Mr Patne speaks of Jain 'followers' in the present tense, but suggestively allows them to participate in the glory of the 'founders and teachers' of the 'past thousands of years'.

Devices of this sort appear routinely in such rhetoric. A sort of positive charge is attached to images of the *samāj* without the speaker or writer ever arguing for such a valuation. For an audience or readership without the experience and sentiments of Mr Patne's audience, such statements seem merely ambiguous, merely contradictory. But Jain listeners are able to supply a good deal of sense of their own to such utterances, to render them reasonable and forceful. These supplied notions of superiority are treated as axiomatic and fundamental, as unquestionable and obvious.

What is the source of these notions? The Sabha takes little or no responsibility for espousing Jainism as such. Indeed the Sabha often takes a sceptical and critical view of Jain institutions. Later in his speech, for example, Mr Patne criticises *muni*s, naked ascetics, for recommending expensive and pointless temple-building projects and rituals. His taste, and that of many of his educated peers, would be rather for the publication and dissemination of religious tracts. This is

[6] Actually the most literal translation of the term would be 'mutter or sub-vocalise in religious devotion or meditation'.

a kind of Jain Protestanism so like the late nineteenth- and twentieth-century Buddhist Protestantism of Sri Lanka, or of reformers in India such as the Arya Samaj. On such evidence alone we would infer that the educated elite is quite opposed to the traditional institutions of Jainism. And this impression might be strengthened by the largely secular and indistinguishably middle-class Indian attitudes of the Sabha. If the Jain response to Sabha rhetoric depended on the Sabha alone it could hardly have survived till today.

The only source of the Jain response must therefore lie with those so doubtfully regarded traditional institutions. And in that perspective the obviousness of Jain superiority must stem from more than just rhetoric. It must stem from experience, experience of the primeval institutions of Jainism. So let me now look more closely at the formation of the sentiments underlying Mr Patne's modernising language.

## *The institutional foundations*

My argument concerning the fundamental sentiments of Jainism is a functional one: the institutions of Jainism are organised so as to preserve themselves and therefore to reproduce Jainism as a set of attitudes, notions, practices, relationships, and physical settings. This means, first, that the institutions produce among Jains sentiments of loyalty, concern, and attachment to themselves. Such sentiments are experienced as natural and compelling: they form a standard which guides elders in forming the next generation, and which give Jains an enduring sense of worth. Second, the institutions produce among Jains a cognitive sense of Jain teaching, and of the uniqueness of that teaching, so that what is reproduced is distinctly Jain. I make this second point because many of the practices which form Jain sentiments are not markedly distinct from those in the surrounding society, and without someone to insist on the doctrinal and practical peculiarity of Jainism, Jains would blend with the surrounding society until they were indeed Jains in name alone. Third, this sense of loyalty and distinctiveness is inextricably mingled with the sense of rivalrous superiority on which Mr Patne called so easily.

Functional explanations are at present in disrepute because they have been thought to be based on faulty logic and on assumptions, such as a natural tendency for society to attain equilibrium, which are demonstrably false. These objections do hold for some functional arguments but not for others.[7] In the case of Jainism, the key to the functional effect of Jain institutions is just that Jains *intend* the reproduction of Jainism: they intentionally train themselves, and the younger generation, to be Jains, and they are specifically concerned to make Jainism flourish as a set of religious institutions. These intentions are embodied in the phrase *jaina dharma prabhāvana*, 'the glorification and encouragement of Jainism', a phrase applied to acts of religious giving by laymen, but also to missionising or sermonising by religious virtuosi. Jains may disagree over how to achieve *prabhāvana*, but on balance the sum of Jains' intentions, put into practice, have preserved Digambar Jainism for 1,500 years in southern India. Institutions have changed, but their animating will has persisted.

Let me begin with what might be called the local complex of Jain institutions, those which the allegedly untutored *muni*s sponsor so energetically. These subsist among local, face-to-face communities[8] of Jains resident in a village or city neighbourhood. Each such community possesses a common structure; the local Jain families as providers of material wealth to the temple and to ritual observances, the temple itself with its temple priests, and the cult of domestic and lay asceticism which is pursued in both home and temple.

In my experience every Jain village settlement or urban neighbourhood is dominated by one of the two largest Jain castes, Caturthas or Pancamas. These local castes (sub-castes in Adrian Mayer's terms[9])

[7] It is of course Radcliffe-Brown's functionalism which seemed the most objectionable because he assumed the objective of institutions to be the stability of society. J. Cohen has however resurrected functionalism to underpin a theory of change and transformation – that is, Marxist theories of capitalist history – and in so doing has provided us with the reasoned arguments to support functional explanation in other spheres as well. See J. Cohen, *Karl Marx's Theory of History* (London, reprinted with corrections 1984), chaps. 9 and 10. The key is that the logic of functionalism is sound if human agency and human intentions are included in the reckoning.

[8] This is a sense of the word 'community' which I have not so far mentioned. I take it to be unproblematic, even if the collectivity so designated is fuzzy at the edges. I have not often heard the word *samāj* used with this sense, and when I have its sense has been made unambiguous, as in *gavācā Jain samāj*, 'the village's Jain community', used of the Jains of a particular village.

[9] Or as Mayer (1960: 4) writes, a 'kindred of cooperation'. The exceptions to endogamy occur among well-educated city-dwellers. In an earlier generation marriage between Jain

are almost entirely endogamous and indeed tend to marry partners from the local community or nearby. Uncle-niece and cross-cousin marriage are common, and marriage is often repeated between families. Jains represent such a local community as kinsmen, and themselves as a close-knit group. In collecting family histories, for example, I found that, even when my informants could not easily trace a connection to some local person, they still insisted that a relationship existed. There is more mobility than these representations would recognise, but in any case most Jains have a deep feeling of relatedness to a known local group.

These local families collectively gather funds to build or maintain the village temple, hire the priest (*upādhye*) or priests to preside over domestic and temple ritual, and subsequently preserve the temples's fabric and support the priests' families. They collectively invite a *muni* – should one be near by – to stay in the village during the rainy season retreat (*cāturmās*). It is they, in short, who possess the material means to reproduce Jainism.

In practice the funding and management of a local temple lies in the hands of Jain men as heads of household, though women may contribute independently and may have a good deal of influence on expenditure, especially for religious purposes. Temples are now managed under legislation as charitable institutions, and in my experience it is men alone who gather for the annual general meeting of the temple society, and it is they who plan any other large-scale activity. It is also my experience, drawn chiefly from the urban temple I know best, that leadership in temple affairs is voluntary, falling to older men inclined to engage in religious activities, and who can wield persuasive influence as elders, kinsmen, and neighbours. Any serious undertaking, such as the renovation or expansion of an old temple or the building of new one, is so expensive that they must call on the community as whole to bear the cost.

The centre of local Jainism is the temple. A temple must necessarily possess one image room in which one properly consecrated image of a *tīrthankar* is kept, but it may also be elaborated: it may have multiple

castes occurred as part of Jain support for the non-Brahman movement. Recently very well-educated Jains, characteristically doctors who met future spouses while training, or Jain businessmen operating on an all-India scale, have taken to marrying those of other religions as well.

*tīrthankar* images, an anteroom, a hall beyond the anteroom, or it may have these as well as a second or even third storey with image rooms, anterooms, and halls on each storey. The temple may also have a *mānastambha*, a 'pillar of pride', set before the temple and bearing another properly consecrated image. On balance a local community can afford to undertake only one – or if very prosperous, two – such major building programmes in a generation. Recent prosperity has accelerated such building throughout the region. Written into the structure of the temple is the history of the local community, its relative wealth and its rhythms of temple renovation and expansion.

Attached to a temple are at least one family of *upadhye*s, priests. They form a caste whose men enjoy a monopoly of expertise in performing the rites of passage, such as marriage and initiation, for the local families. They perform daily *pūjā*s to the image, preside at the more elaborate *pūjā*s at festival periods or at the consecration of a new image, perform occasional rituals to consecrate a new house or to ward off illness, and administer vows. Traditionally – if not quite so frequently in these days of print and increased literacy – priests preached to the laity at the temple, using the rich legendary literature (*purāṇ*) of southern Jainism. They act as astrologers and diviners. Priests used to have *inām* lands granted by the village, but since those lands were alienated they have subsisted on other income, on fees and on their right to use and sell the sometimes very substantial offerings of foodstuffs made by worshippers.

Material wealth and religious technology are however merely adjuncts to the central feature of local Jainism's reproduction, the cult of domestic asceticism. Let me begin by discussing the chief bearers of the cult: women.

The sexual division which dominates Indian society appears also in the reproduction of Jainism. Whereas the sphere of men lies in the wider economy and society, the sphere of women is, in the Marathi phrase, *cūl āṇi mūl*, hearth and children. The only permissible extension to this is attendance at temple as worshippers – *cūl*, *mūl*, *āṇi mandir*. From an individual point of view it is not surprising that women should seize this opportunity beyond the confinement of the hearth. From a collective point of view, women's special concern with physical reproduction inevitably implies a special concern with cultural reproduction as well. Much the same point is illustrated very well by Josephine Reynell's chapter. Women bear and feed not merely young bodies, but young Jains.

The special connection between women and Jainism can be measured roughly by the observation that, among worshippers at the local temple where I conducted most research, more woman-days were spent than man-days. A *muni* once commended this female piety to me with the remark that it made the Kolhapur region a particularly fertile ground for Jain culture or civilization (*saṃskṛti*). A proper upbringing (*saṃskār*) is conducted by women in the home through inculcating such principles as vegetarianism, personal cleanliness, honesty, and self-control directly in her children.

Civilized Jain behaviour also involves participation in religious activities proper. Beyond simple attendance at temple, this means undertaking some ascetic vow, *vrata*. Vows are undertaken ceremonially at a Jain temple under the tutelage of a priest. The central act of almost all vows is a fast, which is frequently interpreted to mean taking no food or drink at all. The fasts take more or less elaborate forms, being repeated monthly or yearly, for a period of one or more years, for one day at a time up to a month at a time.

Almost every Digambar has some experience of fasting, especially at festival periods, and many take fasts which are repeated for ten or even sixteen years. Some fasting may begin in late childhood or adolescence, and my understanding is that less fasting is expected of boys than of girls. Some fasts, such as the *Purnimā* or full-moon fast taken by young brides, are so widely practised that they are practically compulsory. Many fasts are undertaken collectively at the temple, as during the rains retreat period. This lends a public dimension to the practice, making it visible to other members of the Jain community.[10] But even in those cases fasting is domestic just insofar as it is undertaken mostly by women, and the example of such women is felt most strongly at home, rather than in public. As one Jain asked me rhetorically: what would you feel if your mother cooked and served your meal, while she herself takes nothing, not even water?

The domestic culture of fasting is ornately patterned, and a great deal of ritual detail must be mastered. Each fast is accompanied by a story, and most of the stories are drawn from the southern Digambar

[10] Southern Digambars do not for the most part have processions in the street to announce the completion of a particularly arduous fast, as do Gujarati Svetambars in Kolhapur.

*purāṇa* literature.[11] It is difficult to convey in this short space the sheer richness, the elaboration of gesture, ceremony, goods, and stories which surround the act of fasting, or the lasting effect of such intimately witnessed self-denial.

This cult of asceticism might in itself be enough to account for Jains' enduring sense of worth, but the point must be reinforced by two observations. First, asceticism is everywhere highly valued in India and Indian women in general engage in fasting in some form. But the ideology of fasting differs, as do many of the practices, and Jains are convinced that theirs is by far the more strenuous asceticism. Jains make this comparison especially with Brahmans, but with other castes as well. So there is always an implicit comparison between themselves and others that is available to Jains through their experience of domestic asceticism.

Second, there is an assemblage of practices which are common to both the domestic and the religious dimensions of Jain life which come under the heading of 'practising purity', *sohāḷa pāḷṇe*. A woman must bathe, for example, whether she is going to the temple or cooking a meal. She must avoid contact with people of other castes, and if she is touched by such a person on the way to temple, she must return home and bathe again before entering the temple. These same restrictions apply to cooking as well. The key acts of domesticity, like those of worship, are marked by the same everyday observances.

Women I spoke to did not differentiate between domestic and religious observances, and when I asked my research assistant[12] to outline all the occasions on which these and similar rules are relevant, he too mixed religious and domestic occasions indifferently. These rules are, in other words, indistinguishably part of the same notion of *saṃskār*, proper upbringing, blending religious and domestic together, making the experience of purity in the home and purity at the temple equivalent. And from this it follows, with the same associative logic of sentiments, that whatever value is lent to Jainism in the temple can be lent to Jains' domestic life.

[11] The sources so far as I can determine are the *Ādipurāṇa*, the *Padmapurāṇa*, and the *Harivaṃsapurāṇa*. These were ordinarily mediated to the laity by temple priests, *upādhyes*, who memorised or kept handwritten vernacular translations of the relevant stories and the schedule of observances for each fast. Now there are texts available in print which describe such practices.

[12] Professor Sheetal Upadhye.

Now these rules are also more or less those which mark high castes throughout the region and India as a whole. And if the comparison of Jains with others is available through comparing asceticism, the contrast is all the more vivid, all the more unconsciously implicit, through comparing purity. Jains expressed the opinion that such practices of purity distinguish them as Jains, but in fact the very same practices and attitudes distinguish them also as a high caste. As Mukund Lath's chapter shows, Jain savants have continually sought to draw a distinction between caste practices and Jain practices, a point echoed by many Sabha leaders today. But because the practices are equivalent at a deep level of imagery and experience, these attempts have had no lasting effect. For most Jains today and in the past, the experience of caste reinforced by the circumambient society, and the experience of Jainism reinforced in temple and ritual, blend into one. The superiority experienced through caste becomes sentimentally attached to Jainism as well.

Furthermore, this experienced superiority in Jainism creates the sentiments, implicit in Mr Patne's rhetoric, which are as necessary to the projects and rhetoric of Sabha leaders as they are to the longevity of Jainism. Jains traditionally lend lavish support to temples and religious figures, and the same generosity can be tapped by the Sabha. Many Jain men, for example, regard giving to the Sabha as equivalent in merit to giving to the local temple.

In fact it might seem that such strong sentiments, bred in the soil of local Jainism, are not only necessary but also sufficient to the lush growth of both Jainism and the Sabha. But this is not the case. The very feature which reinforces Jainism, its happy consonance with surrounding practice, is also in the long run a source of formidable difficulty. In general form and many details local Jainism is very like the circumambient Hinduism; Jains themselves very frequently participate indifferently in Hindu and Jain practices; and at many periods, such as the end of the nineteenth century,[13] it seemed likely that Jainism would disappear into the Hindu mainstream, as so many religions, such as Buddhism, had done before. Had that happened the picture would be one of a caste cluster[14] which had retained its forceful

[13] At that time 'Jains considered that their religious duties . . . were completed simply by going to temple [once a year] to get a new sacred thread' (Sangave 1976: 15).

[14] The phrase is used by Irawati Karve (1961).

sentiment and its sense of worth, which could for a time still be called Jain, but which had one by one lost the distinct practices and attitudes which actually differentiate Jains from others.

I witnessed many episodes which suggest that these same processes of erosion occur today, but let me recount a piece of hearsay which, even if not accurate in all details, nevertheless captures the nature of the problem. The events happened while I was in the field, and concern a small local group of Kasars, traditionally Jain traders in brassware, well to the north of Kolhapur. A Jain *muni* had passed nearby on foot on his way to the North, and in the ensuing enthusiasm they began building a temple. When the temple was nearing completion, however, a dispute broke out: some still wished to instal an image of a Jain *tīrthankar*, but others now insisted that it should be dedicated to the Hindu god Dattatreya.

What this suggests is that local communities and local Jainism have the power to produce strong motivations, but do not in themselves possess the means to guide those motivations in the long run. In the narrow historical perspective to which I have limited myself, Independence to the present, this difficulty does not seem very great. A longer view suggests that it is in fact a problem, and that the formation of specifically Jain sentiment depends on other factors as well: the *muni*s, naked ascetics, and *bhaṭṭārak*s, caste gurus. These are not local, but regional or even all-India figures. They wield the authority and learning to guide local communities in specifically Jain practices. They owe their very identity to what is unique in Jainism.

Of the two the *muni*s are accorded the greatest respect, as men who have fulfilled the principles of Jainism to such an extent that they have renounced clothing and home, and live a peripatetic life which may take them on foot to the farthest corners of the subcontinent. Their broad view of Jainism is in fact a consequence of their peripatetic life, for apart from the season of retreat (*cāturmās*) they must by rule travel from place to place, from local community to local community. Their loyalty is vested in no one local community. Their authority derives from allegiance, not to the local cult of temple and priest, but to the more universalistic principles of Jainism which they exemplify. It is true, as Mr Patne alleged, that some *muni*s today are relatively uneducated and encourage expenditure on features of local Jainism such as temples and rituals. But the sheer nakedness of any *muni*, and

12 A procession of laymen forms naturally behind the naked *muni* Vidyanandaji Maharaj as he goes on his way. The Jain flag flies in the background. Bahubali, near Kolhapur in Maharashtra.

the striking singularity of the rituals that surround him, can only create a strong sense of Jainism's quite separate tenets and ideals.

Since Independence two issues have stirred Jains as a whole in the region, and in both cases *muni*s were largely the focus of Jain feelings. Shortly after Independence the Bombay Temple Entry Bill was applied against Jain wishes to Jain temples, and a Jain *muni*, the great Santisagar, became the rallying-point for Jains all over the state. Recently two *muni*s, Samantabhadra and Vidyanandaji, stood up for Digambars in the Bahubali Affair. *Muni*s are capable of mobilising Jain opinion on such extraordinary occasions in a way that no one else could achieve. In that respect they must be counted as a potent force in the long-term reproduction of Jainism.

Yet *muni*s do not possess, as a feature of the religious landscape, the inevitability of the temples and priests. There are now very few of

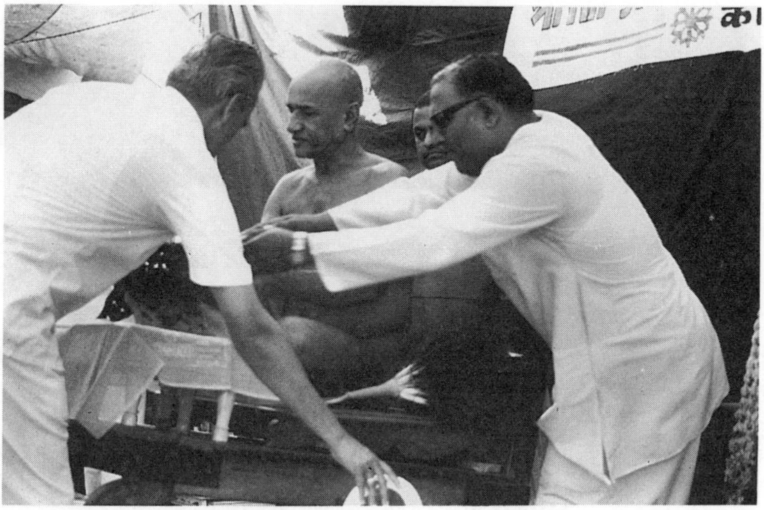

13 Wealthy and pious Digambar Jain laymen fuss around the naked *muni* Vidyanandaji Maharaj before a large public meeting in Kolhapur, Maharashtra.

them, and I suspect that has always been the case. Most of the *muni*s now active are pupils of Santisagar, who died in 1956 and in a long lifetime revived the institution of *muni*s from near extinction almost single handedly. *Muni*s are self-chosen, and there has been no reliable way to ensure that the institution has longevity. The Kolhapur region has been particularly fertile in producing *muni*s in this century, who have been responsible for much of the vitality with which Jainism in the region seems imbued. But in a much longer perspective the *muni*s seem volatile, subsisting in the will of individuals with an ascetic bent and not in routine cultural reproduction.

Routine reproduction seems to have lain with *bhaṭṭārak*s. *Bhaṭṭārak* means, roughly, 'teacher'. There are several spread through South India, but only two in the Kolhapur region, Laksmisen and Jinasen. The name devolves on whoever holds the present incumbency of the seat. Each *bhaṭṭārak* disposes of a large temple-cum-dwelling-cum-monastery, a *maṭh*, in Kolhapur, as well as others spread around the region. Each presides over one Jain caste, Laksmisen over Pancamas and Jinasen over Caturthas. At present their role has fallen into desuetude, and though they appear at many religious occasions they seem absolutely necessary mainly at the

14 The *muni* Vidyanandaji Maharaj addressing a large public meeting in Kolhapur. The tent and loudspeaker system have been rented through donations from prosperous Jain laymen.

consecration of a new temple, where they act as a sort of honorary president.

When *bhaṭṭārak*s still had something of their full function, at the end of the last century, they held very large landed estates. They had some right to adjudicate disputes over religious property, to grant such property, and to decide disputes over caste matters for their respective castes.

In these respects they represented Jains as a collectivity in the pre-modern political economy. Their legal powers and land grants were given, or certified, by the local king, and they represented Jain interests to that power. The legitimacy of Jains as an established part of the polity was recognised through them. Such at any rate was the position of the Hindu caste gurus described by Conlon (1977), and there is every reason to believe that the same was the case here. A notable feature of both the caste gurus and the *bhaṭṭārak*s was that they toured frequently among their constituency, dispensing advice and collecting donations. *Bhaṭṭārak*s still do so today.

*Bhaṭṭārak*s also bore responsibility for the reproduction of Jain learning. They held some authority over priests, and the present

Jinasen told me that his predecessors actually certified priests and kept a register of those serving Caturtha villages. *Bhaṭṭārak*s held and still hold large collections of manuscripts, not only the ritual texts which they share with priests but also doctrinal and philosophical texts, and their very title assumes them to be learned. This function has now been partly usurped by print, scholarly publication, and lay associations such as the Sabha, but traditionally it must have been *bhaṭṭārak*s, more than the naked peripatetic *muni*s, who reliably transmitted Jain dogma. If the local and domestic institutions preserved the spirit of devotion to Jainism, then the *bhaṭṭārak*s preserved access to those 'founders and teachers' of long ago whom Mr Patne evoked with such feeling.

So the *muni*s act as charismatic, and the *bhaṭṭārak*s as routine, leaders. As leaders they require the resources and devotion of their followers, which Jains have over the centuries provided lavishly. And in return, the leaders have provided the guidance which has conserved a distinctly Jain spirit among the distractions of an opulent and variegated religious environment.

## *Conclusion*

Though I did hear the word *samāj* in everyday use, its natural home is really in the relatively formal settings of Sabha discourse, speeches and newspaper articles. It has become a rich, polysemous, and evocative keyword, even though it probably originated as a modern coinage from Sanskrit reflecting the administrative Indian English word 'community'. The word is not often used when a specifically religious sense of Jains as a collectivity is meant. Indeed in his speech Mr Patne used different terms when he intended that meaning.

Yet, as I have tried to show, the word could not have such force if it did not rely, however indirectly, on Jains' experience of themselves as such a religious collectivity. Or to put it another way, in speaking of *samāj* Sabha leaders are suggesting an 'imagined community', to use Benedict Anderson's term,[15] but they depend on an experienced face-to-face community of temple-goers to supply force to the imagination.

[15] Anderson 1983. Anderson stresses that newsprint and literacy have helped create nationalism, but in India at least they have also helped to create a corresponding communalism.

As I have described them, the Sabha seems still young and tentative, still proposing projects which may or may not be successful, while the far older institutions of Jainism proper seem firm, enduring, and predictably effective. This is perhaps a fair reflection, for while Jainism as such can be judged an historical success on a scale of millennia, the Sabha is so far a creature of its time and place, late colonial and early post-colonial India. In any case the rhetoric of the Sabha owes an unacknowledged debt to the sentimental force of these older institutions.

But we should bear in mind that Jainism, too, is an affair of rhetoric and projects. The project is individual human perfection, and the rhetoric, the optative injunction to cultivate perfection, is written throughout the homiletic and ritual life of Jains. Just as Sabha leaders will their projects, so Jains will that perfection, as they will the longevity of Jainism itself.

# Conclusion

Michael Carrithers and Caroline Humphrey

The discussions of a Jain 'community' in this book have not always been in agreement. Yet we feel that the idea is useful. It can be seen to be operational on at least two levels, that of the notional or ideal community (Carrithers, Banks), a theory held by Jains themselves, and that of actual communities, several of which are described in this volume. Even in the latter sense 'community' points to a reality which is complex, multivalent, subject to many historical contingencies, and often virtually in abeyance. Nevertheless, there are distinct sections of Indian society, made up of Jains, which cannot be adequately defined in terms of other prevalent concepts, such as 'caste', 'sect', 'class' or 'political group'. If such groups can best be described as communities, even though not all of the criteria outlined in the position paper (chapter 1) may be present at any given time, the essential element is the matter of social reproduction. The Jains, with their history stretching over millennia, give us an example of this process – one for which this book has only been able to hint at the complex agencies involved.

The chapters submitted by contributors provided us with defining criteria of community additional to those in the position paper. One of these in the synchronic dimension is the intensity of interaction occurring within the given social group (Cottam Ellis). When considered, this leads to the question of the dominant identity within a choice of identities. Do people who are Jains have most to do with other Jains, and if so, does this have the effect that they consider their dominant identity to be Jain? One important point to emerge from these chapters is that the women's point of view here may be different from that of men. Several papers (Reynell, Carrithers and Banks), suggest that women find public identity through specifically Jain institutions (*pūjā* at the temple, ritual fasting, confessions, etc.), whereas men may find it elsewhere, for example in business or caste associations which are shared with non-Jains. It is significant that Cottam Ellis and Singhi, both of whom emphasised the male point of view, are the two contributors who concluded that the Jains they studied do not form a community (in the sense of taking a dominant identity from being Jains).

It is clear, however, that everyday interaction is not the whole story. The historical or longer chronological perspective shows a reality of community which is not necessarily shown in daily life. An example is the mass pilgrimages held to celebrate sacred anniversaries. Virtually all Jains take part in these at some point in their lives. Some people spend a remarkable amount of time trundling in buses or trains, or even walking as a penance or to acquire merit, to distant holy sites. At these places there can be an immense convergence or assembly of Jains. The celebrations in February 1981 at Sravana Belagola in Karnataka, itself normally a tiny and sleepy town, of the 1,000th anniversary of the consecration of the statue of Bahubali are a case in point. Tens of thousands of Jains attended from all over India. This elaborate ritual, the *mahāmastakābhiṣeka*, has been performed every fifteen years or so in recent times.

Another crucial feature to emerge from many of the chapters (e.g. Humphrey, Sangave, Banks) is the importance of conflict and sectarian differences between Jains as markers of community. Paradoxical as this might seem at first sight, it was generally concluded that such conflict can and does only take place within the framework of accepted values. It is the shared values which define what is the focus of competition, whether this be pilgrimage sites (see Carrithers 1988), temples or even 'magical' images of the Tīrthaṅkar (Humphrey, chapter 13, this volume). Thus, although the fissiparous tendencies of the Jains on sectarian matters has often been noted, the corresponding fact that sub-sects are engaged with one another, and define their stance primarily as against other Jain groups, has been neglected. The importance of this can be seen from the following two cases. Sangave shows in his paper that early in this century Digambar 'Dasā' Jains, debarred for reasons of caste from participating in common worship, reacted to a court decision against them *not* by setting up their own sub-sect, but by joining the Śvetāmbars. In the 1930s there occurred a similar case in reverse: Kanji Swami, a Sthānakvāsī Śvetāmbar monk, resolved his differences with his sect by leaving it with his followers and joining the Digambars. This is now a significant movement among Digambar Jains in the North and has survived and gained strength after Kanji Swami's demise. We point to these examples as a socio-religious phenomenon which deserves future investigation. It is not known, for example, what happened to Sangave's Dasā folk when they 'converted'. Śvetāmbars and Digambars normally do not intermarry. Are the new Dasā Digambars accepted as marriage partners by their religious *confrères*?

Let us leave the subject of 'community' and turn now to Jain society in general. One significant feature to emerge is the importance of women. This was not immediately apparent because in scripture and iconography women are given particular and secondary roles, and the doctrinal assessment of women's moral 'worth' is lower than that of men: among Digambars, for example, women must be reborn as men before they can achieve enlightenment. In highly public and open ceremonies such as pilgrimages or *pratiṣṭhā* rites women are normally invisible or allotted a clearly inferior place. In ascetic organisation monks take precedence over nuns. But, as Reynell's pioneering research has shown, women are crucial in the actual preservation and reproduction of Jain practices and values (Reynell in this volume, and Reynell 1985a). This is recognised informally by Jains in the idea that it is on women's religious devotion the men's economic success depends. Something analogous is true of Hindus, for example women taking *vrata*s for their husbands. But the difference is that while both Jains and Hindus take such vows for instrumental purposes, in the Jain case such vows and fasts always have a *mokṣa* orientation as well. This is given public recognition, as when after some spectacularly arduous fast a woman is carried, weak but triumphant, through the streets of her native town to general rejoicing. Furthermore, as the greatest number of Jain ascetics are women, it is common, indeed the rule, for men to find themselves being given religious instruction by women. We do not know, however, whether the high religious standing Jain women have in practice can be related to a high status accorded them more generally in social and economic life (Sangave 1980). There is an intriguing hint in Jones' paper that this may be so: the biggest moneylender of all in his community was in fact a Jain widow. Further comparative research is necessary on this subject.

The differences brought out in these chapters between Jains in the south and north of India seem to correspond to differences between the rural and the urban. In the north complexity of organisation and the tendency to sectarian fission seem to arise in the intense competitive urban environment. The competitive idiom is carried even into intracaste and intrasect relations, as in the public auctioning of ritual roles so clearly described in Singhi's chapter. In the South, although such competitiveness is not absent, the Jains appear rather as a solidary elite in the rural-based political economy. The *bhaṭṭārak*s, as it were 'abbots' of Jain religious property, are still very much part of the scene, and their power, though now much diminished, stems from involvement with peasant states. In the South, Jain castes are just castes, endogamous, but not further divided by sectarian differences. In other words, Jain castes here behave very much like Hindu castes; and this was the case especially before the twentieth-century reform movements. Now there is some intermarriage and much interdining, but all indigenous Jains are Digambaras and there have been no new sectarian splits. There are fewer ascetics amongst Digambara than Śvetāmbara Jains, and few, if any, doctrinal arguments between them – indeed, ascetics here are not particularly active in doctrinal/philosophical matters.

In the North, on the other hand, leaders in the urban environment, both lay and ascetic, compete with other leaders. A characteristic pattern is for lay leaders to back differences on the doctrinal level between *ācārya*s. Because of the long history of schism and the development of schools and traditions, *ācārya*s themselves are more numerous and more learned than in the South. Some Jain sub-sects are exclusive, while others are proselytising. There has been a tendency for sectarian differences to spread outwards from the cities into the countryside, for example, as new temples are built, but the rural environment is not really conducive to the maintenance of such distinctions in the long term. As Singhi's chapter shows, temples originally founded on a sectarian basis may, in a small town, actually come to function as common places of worship for the whole community.

In the South, the Jain lay population is basically sedentary, made up of farmers or small traders. Here, it is the religious leaders, the *bhaṭṭārak*s and the *muni*s who are peripatetic, visiting local groups by turn. In the North, the laity is also well travelled, has a relatively higher level of education, and a wider perspective. This may well be related to their more extensive business organisations and contacts. The 'Marwaris', although of course not all of them are Jains, are the classic example. Jains in the North recognise a broad sacred geography of all-India dimensions. Pilgrimage to holy sites dispersed over the country could be seen as a reflection of the interests in wide commercial travel – or, as Jains might prefer to put it, vice versa. Certainly the relation between the two is historically complex (Agrawal 1980). We would not argue that sectarian conflict over sacred sites is a direct expression of commercial competition, but the two have emerged over the centuries in a single environment, that of intense urban-based mercantile expansion. This is a subject on which further research is required. In the North, the higher levels of education and differentiation among Jains has led to a greater overt self-awareness than in the South. Evidence of this is the publication of numerous lists of Jain businessmen, directories, and Who's Whos, some of them on a sectarian basis and others not.

Jainism as a religion propounds the true path, the presumption of a superior way of life. Who is purest? Who is oldest? In the North these questions fuelled fissiparous tendencies, whereas in the South they determined Jain relations to the surrounding society. In the South Jain castes have related to low Hindu castes in the villages simply as high castes. But in the North, despite the internal differences, an identifiable Jain culture helped create the religious style of the merchant community as a whole. With the emergence of Gandhism, itself inspired by Jain ideals to a certain extent, this style was reinforced and given further legitimation. Both business and Gandhian styles derive from a wider Indian ideology which places value on asceticism and symbols of purity (Hay 1979). Carrithers argues that even in premodern South India this orientation towards purity gave Jains a functional role in the wider society which enabled them to maintain an identity in the long term.

In the North, the Jain style and the presumption of superiority, where it reaches outwards to confront other groups, defines itself against both lower-caste Hindu and tribal groups. Occasionally, as we see from Singhi, Hindus and tribals have combined in overt opposition to traders, 'Banias', in this case Jains. The Jains' economic success is popularly attributed to the magical power of their *sādhus* and sacred statues, which thereby attain a paradoxical value for their poorer neighbours. The deepest relation, of economic dependency and yet opposed cultures, is between Jains and tribal peoples such as the Bhils (Jones, Humphrey). This is dramatised in complex rituals in which both Jains and tribals participate.

Consciousness of Jain superiority is also inherent in the Jain use of royal/military symbolism (Dundas; Carrithers 1988). This has been elaborated over the centuries in the use by Jains of Pan-Indian languages and idioms to create a deliberately distinct ideology. Lath's chapter gives an important example of this technique. There are Jain versions of central Indian literature, such as the Ramayana, which change the nature and goals of the action, and go as far as inverting the moral import of the main characters (Jaini). There is a special Jain style in the *kathā* (story) literature. This is not simply a matter of historically distant texts, but stories which are widely and lovingly read, particularly by women (Reynell 1985a), who relate them to the younger generation.

This characteristic of Jain practice, the tendency to use the form and yet maintain a different meaning for important elements of Indian culture, is shown again in Jaini's chapter on popular religion. Jains worshipped Hindu *yakṣa*s (guardian deities) such as Āmbikā and Padmāvati, but the Jain religious leaders continued through the centuries to preach on their correct significance as protectors and attendants of the Tirthankars. Now it may well be that the Jain laity was not always correct or dutiful, and sometimes regarded the *yakṣa*s as intercessors, but they could hardly have been unaware of the doctrinal position. Indeed, Jaini notes that the semi-legitimisation of *yakṣa* worship within the faith might have forstalled the influence of Vaishnava and Śaiva *bhakti* movements among the Jain laity. The present-day popularity of worship of images of the Tīrthaṅkaras, noted by both Jaini and Humphrey, is not unambiguously a corrupt form. The *pūjā* to the Tīrthaṅkara is not something which the ascetics do, but for the laity it has a 'correct' motivation, the symbolic representation of the steps to liberation, and this sense is preserved even by people who do not always practise it (Humphrey 1984).

Similarly, Jains participate in caste without accepting the Brahmanical ideological framework of caste (Lath). So Jains will intermarry with Hindus of the same caste, and Jain women virtually always take up their husbands' domestic religious ritual, perhaps together with some Jain devotions. But intermarriage between Śvetāmbars and Digambars is extremely rare, perhaps because in this case domestic religious observances fall under the umbrella of the purity oriented religion directed by the *muni*s' religious ideology. Even the simplest rituals are different in detail in the two sects. These 'details' have wide symbolic import. Evidently doctrinal distinctions within Jain religion are more deeply felt than the Jain–Hindu interface. Rituals in the latter context simply fall 'outside religion', and it is with the same attitude that Jains view caste, which is simply not felt to be a religious matter (Lath, Singhi).

Of all Indian religions Jainism is most similar to Theravada Buddhism. Both hold the *śramaṇa* or wandering ascetic to be the essential exemplar of the true path of renunciation, an idea which coexists with and dominates various forms of lay religiosity (Jaini). How do we explain the different fates in history and society of these two faiths? The conference could not, of course, do justice to this vast subject, but did touch upon some significant points of difference.

The Jains, unlike the Theravadins, resisted the rise of popular cults based on the worship of relics, offerings to the dead, and the expectation of a future Teacher. Despite the strong social and emotional pressure that the medieval *bhakti* movements must have exerted, no cult of Śiva or Vishnu ever developed within Jainism, while forms of these cults are important in popular Buddhism in Sri Lanka (Jaini).

Whereas Buddhism retained its ties to political ideology in Sri Lanka and South-East Asia, Jainism lost such links with the rise of Vīraśaivism in the south of India and the arrival of Muslim power in the North. Thus, although Jainism retains a royal idiom (Dundas), it lost its ties to (or functional place within) an effective political ideology. In medieval South India there were Jain kings or at least kings willing to act as Jains, and Jains developed an ideology of kingship (Dundas, Jaini). When Jains lost actual power as a religiously defined group, unlike the Brahmans, they retained the royal idiom in Jain contexts, but could only participate in political reality on other terms, that is, as members of a highly educated and wealthy middle class. In the North, they also retained the royal idiom in internal ritual contexts, but were able to adapt to Muslim public styles.

Also, as Carrithers has remarked, insofar as Jains always fitted into a pan-Indian style of status through purity, which they themselves had helped to create, they managed to retain a reasonably high position in the political economy as a whole.

We conclude by stressing the fact that Jain society is pervaded by Jain teaching. There are, to our knowledge, no sizeable and coherent groups of Jain origin which are purely secular in their orientation. Of course some people are more devout than others, and some more influenced by Western secular life styles than others, but even the most worldly tend to be highly aware of Jain values. This derives, we could perhaps say, from two deep and continuing sources: the strict teachings and instructions of the appointed leaders, ascetics and pandits, on the one hand, and the informal but devout upbringing by Jain women on the other. No one who has sat for hours in one of those vast gatherings of Jain laymen and, especially, women in a preaching-hall could ignore the devotion which the laity accord the religious teacher. This is a latter-day re-creation of the circle gathered at the feet of the Tīrthaṅkar and this is why we have called this book *The Assembly of Listeners*.

# Glossary and pronunciation

## PRONUNCIATION

These are the minimal rules which will allow approximately correct pronunciation.

Vowels are short or long. Long vowels are indicated by the mark ¯.

G is hard, as in *got*
C is pronounced as English *ch*
M is nasalized, resembling English *ng*
S is as in English
Ś sounds like English *sy*, and
Ṣ sounds like English *sh*.

Consonants with an *h* after them are aspirated, that is, given an extra breathy character, as in pi*th*ead.

Ṭ and ḍ are retroflex, pronounced by placing the tip of the tongue on the ridge behind the upper front teeth.

V is rendered part-way between an English V and an English W.

## GLOSSARY

*ācārya* Literally 'teacher'. It is usually used by Jains of all sects to designate a particularly high-ranking teacher, and the status may have been certified by ceremonial means

*Agrawal* = *Aggarwal* A caste of Jains and Hindus

*ahiṃsā* Literally 'non-harming'. The basic principle of Jainism which enjoins avoidance of acts deleterious to any living being

*ambil* (*ayambil*) A type of fast permitting a particular food to be eaten once a day. No oil, ghee, sugar, salt, or curd is permitted, nor dry or green fruits

*aṇuvrata* The five 'basic' or 'lesser' vows, applicable to laymen. They take the form of abstaining from harmful or evil conduct. These are *ahiṃsā* (non-harming), *satya* (abstention from lying), *asteya* (not stealing), *brahmacarya* (celibacy or proper sexual conduct), and *aparigraha* (abstention) from covetousness or attachment to material things)

*aparigraha* Abstention from attachment to material things. One of the five *aṇuvrata*s

*āratī* (*ārtī*) Waving a lighted lamp before a revered object as part of an act of worship

*ātman* Soul or self, equivalent to the term *jiva*

*bhagwan* Literally 'lord'. Often used for 'God' to refer to a Tirthankar

*bhakti* Devotion. May mean 'devotion' in a simple sense, but is usually tinged by its meaning as 'devotion to God', or to a guru, in the great Hindu theistic devotional sects of India

*bhaṭṭārak* Literally 'teacher'. Traditionally these figure as caste guru to a caste, and represented that Jain caste to the royal power. They also kept libraries and had responsibility for overseeing important ceremonies, and it is only these later responsibilities that have remained in their original form today

*Bisa* (*bisā*; *visā*) Literally 'twenty', the higher status section of several Jain castes

*boli* Bidding in an auction for right to perform part of a ritual

*caturmās* (*caturmas*) Literally the 'four-month', the period of the rainy season retreat when ascetics give up wandering

*chatri* A small shrine devoted to some famous teacher, often containing a footprint icon

*dāna* (*dān*; *dan*) Almsgiving, especially to ascetics or spiritually accomplished persons

*Dasa* (*dasā*) Literally 'ten', the lower status section of several Jain castes

*Dasahra* (*Dasera*) A Hindu festival

*deva* (*dev*) Literally 'God', but often used as an honorific for the *tīrthaṅkar*s or other exalted figures

*dharma* Religion, holy law, duty

*dharmaśāstra* The Brahmanical science of right conduct and/or a text or texts pertaining thereto

*dharmaśāla* (*dharmasala*) A hostel for pilgrims to a holy place

*diwan* Minister, official

*Digambar* (Digambar) Literally 'sky-clad', naked or without clothes. The name refers to that sect of Jains whose ascetics go naked

*dīkṣā* (*diksha*) Initiation into ascetic status

*Dīwālī* (*Dipavali*) A Hindu festival

*gaccha* (*gacch*) A sub-sect, tracing pupillary descent from a single ascetic founder

*gotra* Lineage group
*hāt* Bazaar
*hundī* An instrument of credit used in traditional banking
*jāti* (*jāt*) Literally 'kind'; the word can refer simply to caste, or to some other apparently natural division among people, animals, or things, e.g. the Brahman *jāti*, the Christian *jāti*
*jātra* (*yatra*) Pilgrimage
*jñāna* (*gyān*) Knowledge, especially spiritual knowledge
*mahajan* Merchant
*Mahāvīra* (*Mahāvīr*) The founder of Jainism in this age of the universe
*malik* The owner or controller of property such as a shop, or an institution
*mānastambha* A pillar, (lit. pillar of pride) erected before a Digambar Jain temple. Four Tirthankars sit at the top metaphorically preaching to the assembly of listeners
*mantra* An efficacious verbal formula, holy word
*maṭh* (*maṭha*) The residence of a *bhaṭṭārak*, q.v.
*mela* A periodic gathering, fair, and/or pilgrimage.
*mokṣa* Liberation, release, the object of Jain asceticism
*muni* Literally 'silent one' or 'sage', an honorific applied to Jain ascetics
*mūrti* Idol, image to be worshipped
*mūrtipūjak* (*Murti Puja*) 'Worshipping images', the designation of the sect of Svetambar Jains who worship images of *tīrthankar*s (q.v.) in temples
*namaskāra* (*Namaskār*) = *Nokār mantra* A greeting. Also the designation of the *mantra* or holy words used in ceremonial salutation to the great persons of the Jain scriptures
*nirvāṇa* A synonym for liberation, release, *mokṣa*
*Oswal* A west Indian Jain caste of Swetambars
*paccakhāna* (= *pratyakhyāna*) Renunciation of foods or pleasures for a certain period
*pañcakalyān* The elaborate ceremony of installing a new image in a Jain temple
*pāpa* (*pāp*) Sin or evil
*paramparā* Lineage or line of pupillary succession
*parda* Purdah, seclusion of Women
*Pārśvanātha* (*Pārśvanāth*) The *tīrthankar* before Māhavīr
*paryūṣaṇa* (*Pājjūṣan; Parushan; Paryusan*) A yearly period of 8 or 10 days of collective religious observance, fasting, worship, and sermons during the rainy season
*prabhāvana* 'Encouragement' or 'glorification' of Jainism. Refers to any pious act, but especially to public acts and to acts of generous giving
*pradakṣina* Circumambulation of sacred site or image

*pratikramaṇa* (*pratikraman*) The ritual hoping for forgiveness from those one has harmed and renouncing past sins

*pratimā* The eleven stages of gradually increasing asceticism for laymen

*pratiṣṭhā* The 'establishment' of a new image for worship, that is, the elaborate ceremony of consecration (*pañcakalyān*)

*pūjā* Worship, usually before an image

*puṇya* Spiritual merit, achieved by doing good and especially by supporting religious persons and institutions

*purāṇa* (*puran*) The 'ancients', that is, the Jain texts which have the form of legendary history and hagiography

*Rāmāyaṇa* A Hindu epic

*Rāmlīla* Hindu festival

*rathayātra* A religious procession through a village or city which uses a ceremonial chariot, a *ratha*

Ṛṣabhdev (Ṛṣabhadera, Ṛṣabha, Adinath) The first *tīrthaṅkar*

*Sabhā* 'Association', short for the Dakṣin Bhārat Jain Sabhā, the South Indian Jain Association

*sādhu*, *sādhvi* Male, female ascetics

*samāj* The word used in many Indian languages to mean 'community', as in 'the Jain community'

*samavasaraṇa* The sacred assembly of all living beings who hear the divine sound emanated by a *tīrthaṅkar* on his achieving liberation.

*sāmāyika* (*samayik*) Short period of meditation and renunciation, practised especially by the laity

*saṅgha* (*saṅgha*, *sangha*) The order of ascetics and their lay followers. This term is also used for a pilgrimage

*savkar* (*sahukar*) Trader

*śāsana devatā* (*śāsan devatā*) A divinity supporting the teaching of Jainism

*sati* Ritual of self-immolation by widow of Hindu

*siddhi* Miraculous power

*śramaṇa* Literally 'striver', the appelation of that wide and varied group of ascetics from whom Mahāvīr originally stemmed

*śrāvaka* Literally 'listener', one who attends to a *tīrthaṅkar*, an adherent of Jainism. A layperson

*śrāvakācāra* The large body of Jain literature which prescribes forms of behaviour and asceticism to the laity

*Sthānakavāsi* Literally 'dwellers in halls'. The name of a Swetambar Jain sect which does not have temples

*Śvetāmbara* (*Swetambar*; *Svetambar*) Adherents of the sect of Jainism whose ascetics are 'clad in white', *śvetāmbara*

*tapas* (*tapa*; *tapasya*) Literally 'heat'. Austerity, usually in the form of fasting

*Tārapanthī* Reformist sect of Svetambars

*tīrthaṅkara* (*tīrthaṅkar*) A 'ford-maker', i.e. one of the twenty-four founders who, in present and past ages, founded or refounded the Jain teaching

*tithi* A date in the lunar calendar, often used to refer to a holy date

*tyaga* (*tyag*) Abandoning or renouncing something

*upādhye* One of the ceremonial priests who attend at temples and life-cycle rituals among southern Digambars

*upāsaka* A lay person attendant upon an ascetic

*upāśraya* (*upāśray*; *upasara*) A building provided by the laity for the ascetics to live in. Also used for preaching by ascetics and for fasting by laity

*vaiṣṇava* (*Vaishnava*; *Vaishnav*) Pertaining to, or an adherent of, the Hindu sect of Vaishnavism

*Vaisnava varṇa* One of the four hierarchical categories into which caste society is divided

Vardhamāna A name of Mahāvīr

*yakṣa* (*yaksha*) One of the deities attendant upon Jainism

*yati* Cleric with socio-economic functions in Śvetāmbara sect

*yātra* (*jātra*) Ritual procession and pilgrimage

*yoga* Ascetic discipline

# Select bibliography


Adams, D. A. 1980. Recent performance of rural financial markets. In *Borrowers and Lenders: Rural Financial Markets and Institutions in Developing Countries*, ed. J. Howell. London: Overseas Development Institute.

Agrawal, B. C. 1980. *Cultural Contours of Religion and Economics in a Hindu Universe*. New Delhi: National.

Aho, J. A. 1981. *Religious Mythology and the Art of War: Comparative Religious Symbolisms of Military Violence*. London.

Alavi, H. 1971. Kinship in West Punjab villages. *Contributions to Indian Sociology* NS, 6, 1–26.

Anderson, B. 1983. *Imagined Communities*. London: New Left Books.

Bailey, F. G. 1964. Capital, saving and credit in Highland Orissa. In *Capital, Saving and Credit in Peasant Societies* ed. R. Firth and B. A. Yamey. London: George Allen and Unwin.

Bailey, G. 1983. *The Mythology of Brahma*. Delhi.

Bakker, Hans 1982. The rise of Ayodhya as a place of pilgrimage. *Indo-Iranian Journal* 24.

Banks, M. 1985. On the Shrawacs or Jains: processes of division and cohesion among two Jain communities in India and England. Unpublished Ph.D. thesis: Cambridge University.

Forthcoming. Competing to get, competing to give: Gujarati Jains in Britain. In *Black and Ethnic Leaderships in Britain: The Cultural Dimensions of Political Action*, ed. Muhammad Anwar and Pnina Werbner. London: Routledge.

Bayly, C. A. 1973. The organisation of merchants in Benares, 1780–1830. Paper delivered at the postgraduate seminar, History Department, SOAS, University of London.

1975. The urban merchant family in North India during the nineteenth century. Kaplan Memorial Lecture, University of Pennsylvania.

1980. The small town and Islamic gentry in North India: the case of Kara. In *The City in South Asia*, K. Balhatchet and J. Harrison. London: Curzon Press.

1983. *Rulers, Townsmen and Bazaars: North Indian Society in the Age of British Expansion, 1770–1870*. Cambridge: Cambridge University Press.

1985. The pre-history of 'communalism': religious conflict in India 1700–1860. *Modern Asian Studies* 19.

Beck, B. 1973. *Peasant Society in Konku: a Study of Right and Left Subcastes in South India*. Vancouver: University of British Columbia Press.

Bell, C. and Newby, H. 1971. *Community Studies: an Introduction to the Sociology of the Local Community*. London: George Allen and Unwin.

Blunt, E. A. H. 1931. *The Caste System of Northern India with Special Reference to the United Provinces of Agra and Oudh*. London: Oxford University Press.

Bollée, W. B. 1977. A note on evil and its conquest from Indra to Buddha. In Lancaster (ed.) 1977.

1981. The Indo-European sodalities in ancient India. *Zeitschrift der Deutschen Morgenländischen Gesellschaft* 131, pp. 172–91.

Bonacich, E. 1973. Theory of middleman minorities. *American Sociological Review* 38, no. 5, 583–94.

Bottomley, A. 1964. The structure of interest rates in underdeveloped rural areas. *Journal of Farm Economics*, 46, no. 2, 313–22.

Bourdieu, P. 1979. *Outline of a Theory of Practice*. Cambridge: Cambridge University Press.

Braudel, F. 1979. *The Wheels of Commerce*. London: Collins.

Bruhn, K. 1983. Repetition in Jaina narrative literature. *Indologica Taurensia* 11.

Burghart, R. Renunciation in the religious traditions of South Asia. *Man* 18.

Caillat, C. 1975. Expressions de la quête spirituelle dans le Dohapahuda (anthologie Jaina en apabhramsa) et dans quelques textes brahmaniques. *Indologica Taurinesia* 3, 125–38.

Caplan, L. 1972. The multiplication of social ties: the strategy of credit transactions in East Nepal. *Economic Development and Cultural Change* 20, no. 4, 691–702.

Carrithers, M. 1988. Passions of nation and community in the Bahubali Affair. *Modern Asian Studies* 28, 281–310.

Carstairs, M. 1957. *The Twice-Born*. London: Hogarth Press.

Census of India 1981. *District Census Handbook Dungarpur*, series 18, Rajasthan, parts XIII A and B.

Cohen, A. 1969. *Custom and Politics in Urban Africa*. London: Routledge and Kegan Paul.

Cohen, J. 1984, *Karl Marx's Theory of History*. London: Routledge and Kegan Paul.

Conlon, F. 1977. *A Caste in a Changing World*. Berkely: University of California Press.

Coren, A. R. 1967. Tradition, values and inter-role conflict in Indian family businesses. Unpublished Ph:D. thesis. Cambridge, Mass.: Harvard Business School.

Cottam C. 1980. City, town and village: the continuum reconsidered. In *The City in South Asia*, ed K. Balhatchet and J. Harrison. London and Dublin: Curzon Press.

1983. The merchant castes of a small town in Rajasthan: a study of business organisation and ideology. Unpublished Ph.D. thesis, University of London.

Darling, M. L. 1947. *The Punjab Peasant in Prosperity and Debt*, 4th edn. London: Oxford University Press.

Dasgupta, B. 1977. *Village Society and Labour Use*. Delhi: Oxford University Press.

Desai, S. S. M. 1979. *Rural Banking in India*. Bombay: Himalaya Publishing House.

Divekar, V. D. 1981. *Survey of Material in Marathi on the Economic and Social History of India*. Pune: Bharata Itihasa Samshodaka Mandal.

Doshi, S. 1981. *Homage to Shravana Belgola*. Bombay.

Doshi, S. L. 1971. *Processes of Tribal Unification and Integration*. Delhi: Concept.

*Bhils: Between Societal Self-awareness and Cultural Synthesis*. New Delhi: Sterling Publishers.

Dumont, L. 1972. *Homo Hierarchicus: the Caste System and its Implications*. London: Paladin.

Dundas, P. 1985. Food and freedom: the Jaina sectarian debate on the nature of the kevalin. *Religion* 15, 163–88.

Eisenstadt, S. N. 1984. Dissent, heterodoxy and civilisational dynamics: some analytical and comparative indications. In *Orthodoxy, Heterodoxy and Dissent in India*, ed. S. N. Eisenstadt, R. Kahave and D. Shulman. Berlin: Mouton.

Erdman, H. I. 1975. *Political Attitudes of Indian Industry: a Case Study of the Baroda Business Elite*. London: Athlone Press.

Eschmann, A., Kulke, H., and Tripathi, G. D. (eds.). 1978. *The Cult of Jagannath and the Regional Tradition of Orissa*. Delhi: Manohar.

Fox, R. G. 1967. Family, caste and commerce in a North Indian market town. *Economic Development and Cultural Change* 15, 270–314.

1969. *From Zamindar to Ballot Box: a Community Change in a North Indian Market Town*. Ithaca and New York: Cornell University Press.

1971. *Kin, Clan, Raja and Rule: State-Hinterland Relations in Pre-industrial India*. Berkeley and Los Angeles: University of California Press.

Frankenberg, R. 1971. *Communities in Britain: Social Life in Town and Country*. Harmondsworth: Penguin Books.

Gardner, P. 1982. Ascribed austerity: a tribal path to purity. *Man* 17.

Gellner, D. 1982. Max Weber, capitalism and the religion of India. *Sociology* 16, no. 2, 1527–42.

Gellner, E. 1979. Notes towards a theory of ideology. In *Spectacles and Predicaments*, ed. E. Gellner. Cambridge: Cambridge University Press.

Gombrich, R. F. 1971. *Precept and Practice: Traditional Buddhism in the Rural Highlands of Ceylon*. Oxford: Oxford University Press.

Granoff, P. 1984. Holy warriors: a preliminary study of some saints and kings in the classical Indian tradition. *Journal of Indian Philosophy* 12, 291–303.

Gupta, B. R. 1976. *The Aggarwals: a Socio-Economic Study*. New Delhi: S. Chand Co. (Pvt) Ltd.

Gupta, C. S. 1966. *Census of India 1961*. Vol. XIV, part VII-B. Rajasthan: Fairs and Festivals.

Gupta, K. A. 1976. *Politics of a Small Town*. New Delhi: Impex India.

Habib, I. 1964. Usury in Medieval India. *Comparative Studies in Society and History*, 6, no. 4, 393–419.

Handiqui, K. K. 1949. *Yasastilaka and Indian Culture*. Sholapur: Jaina Samskrti Samrakshaka Sangha.

Harris, M. 1983. Times are good for the pawnbroker. *New Society*, 64, no. 1075, 459–61.

Harriss, B. 1980. Money and commodities, monopology and competition. In *Borrowers and Lenders: Rural Financial Markets and Institutions in Developing Countries*. London: Overseas Development Institute.

Hay, S. 1979. Jaina goals and disciplines in Gandhi's pursuit of Swaraj. In *Rule, Protest, Identity: Aspects of Modern South Asia*, ed. P. Robb and D. Taylor. London: Curzon.

Hazlehurst, L. W. 1966. *Entrepreneurship and the Merchant Castes in a Punjabi City*. NC: Duke University Press.

1968. Caste and merchant communities. In *Structure and Change in Indian Society*, ed. M. Sinher and B. S. Cohen. Chicago: Aldine Press.

Horner, I. B. 1951. *Book of the Discipline*. Vol. IV, London.

Humphrey, C. 1984. Some aspects of the Jain Puja: the idea of 'god' and the symbolism of offerings. *Cambridge Anthropology* 9, 1–19.

Jacobi, H. 1884. *Jaina Sutras* 1. Oxford: Sacred Books of the East XXII.

Jain, C. R. 1919. *The Key of Knowledge*. Arrah: Central Jaina Publishing House.

Jain, H. C. 1972. *Ancient Towns and Cities of Rajasthan: a Study in Culture and Civilisation*. Delhi: Motilal Banarsidas.

Jain, J. 1975. *Religion and Culture of the Jains*. Delhi: Bharatiya Jnanpith.

Jain, K. C. 1963. *Jainism in Rajasthan*. Sholapur.

Jain, L. C. 1929. *Indigenous Banking in India*. London: Macmillan.

Jaini, P. S. 1979. *The Jaina Path of Purification*. Berkeley: University of California Press.

1981. Bahubali in Prakrit literature. In Kalghatgi (ed.).

Jindel, R. 1976. *Culture of a Sacred Town: a Sociological Study of Nathdwara*. Bombay: Popular Prakashan.

Kalghatgi, T. G. (ed.). 1981. *Gommateshvara Commemoration Volume (A.D. 981–1981)*. Sravana Belgola.

Karve, I. 1953. *Kinship Organisation in India*. Poona: Deccan College Monographs, series 11.

1961. *Hindu Society: an Interpretation*. Pune: Deccan College.

Klatt, J. 1882. Extracts from the historical records of the Jainas. *Indian Antiquary* 11.

Klimburg-Salter, D. E. (ed.). 1982. *The Silk Route and the Diamond Path*. Los Angeles. UCLA Arts Council.

Kling, B. B. 1966. Indian and British businessmen in Calcutta, 1820–1860. Paper delivered at the American Historical Association, December 1966.

Kothari, K. 1982. The shrine: an expression of social needs. In *Gods of the Byways*. Oxford: Museum of Modern Art.

Kulke, H. 1978. Royal temple policy and the structure of mediaeval Hindu kingdoms. In Eschmann, Vulke and Tripathe (eds.).

Laidlaw, J. 1985. Profit, salvation and profitable saints. *Cambridge Anthropology* 9.

Lamb, H. 1955. The Indian business communities and the evolution of an industrialist class. In *Pacific Affairs*, 28, 101–16.

1959. The Indian merchant. In *Traditional India: Structure and Change*, ed. M. Singer. Philadelphia: American Folklore Society.

Lancaster, L. (ed.). 1977. *Prajnaparamita and Related Systems: Studies in Honour of*

*Edward Conze*. Berkeley: University of California Press.

Leach, E. R. 1977. *Political Systems of Highland Burma: a Study of Kachin Social Structure*. London: Athlone Press.

MacCurdy, D. W. 1980. Savings on loans in a peasant society. In *Conformity and Conflict*, ed. J. D. Spradley and D. W. MacCurdy. Toronto: Little, Brown and Co.

MacIver, R. M. and Page, C. H. 1961. *Society: an Introductory Analysis*. London: Macmillan.

Malvania, D. 1977. The story of Bharata and Bahubali. *Sambodhi* 6, 1–11.

Malvania, D. and N. Shah (eds.). 1981. *Studies in Indian Philosophy* (L.D. Series 84). Ahmedabad: L.D. Institute of Indology.

Mandelbaum, D. G. 1970. *Society in India*, 2 vols. Los Angeles and Berkeley: University of California Press.

Marriott, M. 1959. Interactional and attributional theories of caste ranking. *Man in India*, 39, no. 2, 92–107.

Mathur, U. B. 1976. *Census of India 1971*. Rajasthan, Part II–C(1), Social and Cultural Tables.

Mayer, A. C. 1960. *Caste and Kinship in Central India: a Village and its Region*. Los Angeles and Berkeley: University of California Press.

1978. Public service and private gain in Dewas. Paper given at Departmental Seminar, Department of Anthropology and Sociology, SOAS, London University.

Meillassoux, C. 1973. Are there castes in India? *Economy and Society*, 2, no. 1, 89–111.

Michaelson, M. 1983. Caste, kinship and marriage: a study of two Gujarati trading castes in England. Unpublished Ph.D. thesis, University of London.

Michie, B. H. 1978. Baniyas in the Indian economy: a case of stagnant entrepreneurship. *Journal of Asian Studies*, 37, no. 4, 637–52.

Miller, C. J. 1979. *Faith Healers in the Himalayas*. Kathmandu: Tribhuvan University.

Millman, H. A. 1954. The Marwaris: a study of a group of trading castes. Unpublished M.A. thesis, University of California.

Mines, M. 1972. *Muslim Merchants: the Economic Behaviour of an Indian Muslim Community*. Delhi: Sri Ram Centre.

Misra, R. N. 1981. *Yaksha Cult and Iconography*. New Delhi: Munshiram Manoharlal.

Morris, H. S. 1968. *The Indians in Uganda*. London: Weidenfeld and Nicholson.

Naik, T. B. 1956. *The Bhils: a Study*. Delhi: Bharatiya Adimjati Sevak Sangh.

Nand, N. 1966. Distribution and spatial arrangement of rural population in East Rajasthan. *Geographical Review* (June), 205–19.

Nelson, N. 1980. *Why has Development Neglected Rural Women? A Review of the South Asian Literature*. Oxford: Pergamon Press.

Nevaskar, B. 1971. *Capitalists without Capitalism: the Jains of India and the Quakers of the West*. Westport, Conn.: Greenwood Publishing.

O'Flaherty, W. D. 1976. *The Origins of Evil in Hindu Mythology*. Berkeley: University of California Press.

Pande, G. C. 1978. *The Sramana Tradition*. Ahmedabad: L. D. Series (no. 66).

Parry, J. 1979. *Caste and Kinship in Kangra*. London: Routledge and Kegan Paul.

Pettigrew, J. 1975. *Robber Noblemen: a Study of the Political System of the Sikh Jats*. London: Routledge and Kegan Paul.

Plant, R. 1974. *Community and Ideology. An Essay in Applied Social Philosophy*. London and Boston: Routledge and Kegan Paul.

Pocock, D. 1976. *Mind, Body and Wealth*. Oxford: Basil Blackwell.

Prabhakar, M. 1972. *Cultural Heritage of Rajasthan*. Jaipur: Panchsheel Prakashan.

Rahman, A. 1979. Usury, capital and credit relations in Bangladesh agriculture: some implications for capital formation and capitalist growth. *Bangladesh Development Studies*, 7, no. 2, 1–45.

Rajasthan District Gazetteers 1970. *Town Handbooks*, NS. Rajasthan, India: Government of Rajasthan in collaboration with the Central Gazetters Unit of the Government of India.

Reynell, J. 1985a. Honour, nurture and festivity: aspects of female religiosity amongst Jain women in Jaipur. Unpublished Ph.D. thesis: Cambridge University.

1985b. Renunciation and ostentation. *Cambridge Anthropology* 9, 20–33.

Rhys Davids, T. W. and C. A. F. 1921. *Dialogues of the Buddha* 33. London: Sacred Books of the Buddhists.

Richards, J. F. (ed.) 1981. *Kingship and Authority in South Asia*. Madison: University of Wisconsin Press.

Roy, A. K. 1978. *History of the Jaipur City*. New Delhi: Manohar Publications.

1984. *A History of the Jainas*. Delhi: Gitanjali Publishing House.

Sangave, V. A. 1976. *Daksin Bharat Jain Sabheca Itihas*. Sangli: Daksin Bharat Jain Sabha.

1980. *Jaina Community, a Social Survey*. Bombay: Popular Prakashan.

Shah, A. M. 1978. Horizontal dimension of caste in Gujarat. Paper given at Departmental Seminar, Department of Anthropology and Sociology, SOAS, London University.

Shah, A. M. and Shroff, R. G. 1959. The Vahivanca Barots of Gujarat: a caste in genealogists and mythographers. In *Traditional India: Structure and Change*, ed. M. Singer. Philadelphia: American Folklore Society.

Shah, S. 1979. Who are the Jains? *New Community* 7, 3698–75.

Sharma, D. (ed.). 1966. *Rajasthan Through the Ages (1)*. Bikaner: Rajasthan State Archives.

Sharma, G. N. 1968. *Social Life in Medieval Rajasthan*. Lakshmi: Navain Agarwal Publishers, Agra.

Sharma, S. R. 1940. *Jainism and Karnataka Culture*. Dharwar.

Shulman, D. L. 1989. *Tamil Temple Myths: Sacrifice and Divine Marriage in the South Indian Saiva Tradition*. Princeton: Princeton University Press.

Sivakumar, S. S. 1978. Aspects of agrarian economy in Tamil Nadu: a study of two villages. Part III: structure of assets and indebtedness. *Economic and Political Weekly*, 13, no. 20, 846–51.

Staal, F. 1982. The Himalayas and the fall of religion. In Klimburg-Salter (ed.).

Stein, Burton. 1980. *Peasant State and Society in Medieval South India*. Delhi.

1981. All the kings' mana: perspectives on kingship in medieval South India. In Richards (ed.).

Stevenson, S. 1915. *The Heart of Jainism*. London: Oxford University Press.

Stokes, E. 1978. *The Peasant and the Raj. Studies in Agrarian Society and Peasant Rebellion in Colonial India*. Cambridge South Asian Studies no. 23. Cambridge: Cambridge University Press.

Strandberg, E. 1981. Some remarks on the role of the lay followers in the Jaina community. In Malvania and Shah (eds.).

Strong, J. A. 1977. Gandhakuti: the perfumed chamber of the Buddha. *History of Religions* 16, 390–406.

Strong, J. S. 1983. *The Legend of King Asoka: a Study and Translation of the Asokavadana*. Princeton: Princeton University Press.

Sundaram, K. V. 1977. *Urban and Regional Planning in India*. New Delhi: Vikas Publishing House.

Sundaram, K. and Pandit, V. 1984. Informal credit markets, black money and monetary policy – some analytical and empirical issues. *Economic and Political Weekly*, 19, no. 16, 675–82.

T'ien, J. 1953. *The Chinese of Sarawak: a Study of Social Structure*. London School of Economics, Monographs on Social Anthropology, no. 12.

Timberg, T. A. 1971. A North Indian firm seen through its business records, 1860–1914. *Indian Economic and Social History Review*, 8, 264–83.

1973. Three types of Marwari firms. *Indian Economic and Social History Review*, 10, 1–36.

1978. *The Marwaris: from Traders to Industrialists*. Delhi: Vikas.

Timberg, T. A. and Aiyar, C. V. 1984. Informal credit markets in India. *Economic Development and Cultural Change*, 33, no. 1, 43–59.

Tod, J. 1829. *Annals and Antiquities of Rajasthan*.

Trivedi, R. K. 1965. *Census of India 1961*. Vol. V, part VII-B. Gujarat: Fairs and Festivals.

Wanmali, S. 1975. Rural service centres in India: present identification and acceptance of extension. *Area* 17, no. 3, 167–70.

Ward, B. E. 1960. Cash or credit crops? An examination of some implications of peasant commercial production with special reference to the multiplicity of traders and middlemen. *Economic Development and Cultural Change* 8, vol. 2, 148–63.

Weber, M. 1962. *The City*. Trs. and ed. by D. Martindale and G. Neuwirth. New York: Collier.

Wharton, C. R. 1962. Marketing, merchandising and moneylending: a note on middlemen monopsony in Malaya. *Malayan Economic Review*, 7, no. 2, 24–44.

Williams, R. 1963. *Jaina Yoga: a Survey of the Mediaeval Śrāvakācāras*. London: Oxford University Press.

Wilmington, M. W. 1983. Aspects of moneylending in Northern Sudan. In *Rural Financial Markets in Developing Countries. Their Use and Abuse*, ed. Von Pischke, D. W. Adams and G. Donald. Economic and Development Institute of the World Bank. Baltimore and London. Johns Hopkins University Press.

# Index